Academic & Professional Skills

Samantha Roberts
Coventry University

Pearson Education Limited
Edinburgh Gate
Harlow
Essex CM20 2JE

And associated companies throughout the world

Visit us on the *World Wide Web* at:
www.pearsoned.co.uk

This Custom Book Edition © 2011 Published
by Pearson Education Limited

ISBN–13: 978-1-780-16721-3

ARP impression 98

Printed in Great Britain by Ashford Colour Press Ltd.

Contents

Learning, skills and employment

In deciding to study, you have taken a major investment decision – to invest in yourself. This chapter looks at the market in which you will be operating as a graduate, and at what you can do to maximise the return on your investment by developing 'transferable skills'. These are the skills that will help you do well both as a student and as a manager.

Learning outcomes

By the end of this chapter you should:

- understand what is meant by 'transferable skills'
- be starting to plan how you can develop these skills during your studies
- appreciate the ways in which organisations have changed in recent years
- understand the implications of these changes for graduate employment
- appreciate what 'graduate recruitment' means to employers and what they seek when recruiting
- be beginning to consider what you might want from a job.

If you are at the start of your university studies, it can be enlightening to work out just how much investment you are making in yourself: in the time you are committing, the income you are forgoing and the fees you are paying. Presumably you are hoping that this will lead to an enjoyable and well paid career. The bad news is that this is by no means certain. I know some graduates currently facing their thirtieth birthdays in jobs that frustrate and bore them, and pay very little. Although the UK graduate employment situation improved dramatically from a low point in 1983, and was still improving at the time of writing, the job market may have changed significantly by the time you graduate. The good news is that if you start *now* to manage your learning, to think about the sort of job you want, and to develop the skills you need to be attractive as an employee, you can greatly increase your chances of a profitable and fulfilling career. The even better news is that most of the skills that employers value will help you get a better class of degree.

So, although looking at employment skills may seem slightly bizarre at this stage, when your career may seem impossibly far in the future, it makes a lot of sense. This chapter looks at the employment context to clarify *what* you need to learn, suggests ways of starting to develop your learning skills, starts you on the process of thinking about the sort of career you would like, and shows you how you can start to *use* this book to become a successful learner.

As you may already be discovering, learning at university (like learning at work) is likely to be very different from learning at school: the main responsibility will be yours, and you will be learning a much wider range of skills. You need to be able to *manage* your own learning: planning and time management skills are essential for this. You will need to learn with others: team working and communication skills will be important. You will need to locate and use a wide range of information sources: this will require knowledge management skills. But above all you need to understand what learning *means* at this level, why it is so important and how to do it well.

WHAT EMPLOYERS LOOK FOR IN GRADUATES

It is never too soon to consider what you want from your working life, and what employers think they want when recruiting graduates. The job market is highly competitive, and you can greatly increase your chances of a successful career if you start thinking *now*. If this sounds impossible, don't worry. This chapter will give you a clearer idea of what is important to you, and help you clarify your employment goals. The final part of the book will complete the process.

The introduction to Part 1 alerted you to the fact that you will need to *respond* at intervals, rather than merely sit back and read. The process starts *now*: you need to capture your starting position. Then you can return to it at intervals, develop your thoughts further, note how they are changing and check that you have not inadvertently ignored something important.

ACTIVITY 1.1

If you have access to anyone who employs graduates, ask them what they seek in recruits. Look in the recruitments sections of a few newspapers, or visit the websites of companies you might like to work for, and build a list of the qualities mentioned as essential or desirable in interesting graduate vacancies.

_____

_____

_____

Were you more impressed by the similarities between employers, or the differences? Employers are far from agreed on what being a graduate can bring to a job. Variation is not surprising, since recruiters will be seeking to fill widely disparate jobs: there are likely to be as many different views of what constitutes the 'ideal graduate recruit' as there are of the 'ideal husband or wife'. Employers may be looking for people to interact with customers, to solve technical problems, to work with pre-existing teams of various kinds, to 'fit in' and be effective as quickly as possible, or to act as a force for change.

Organisations may be huge or tiny, bureaucratic or flexible and innovative. What they seek from recruits depends on where they sit on these different dimensions. As a graduate this variability may be an asset. Someone, somewhere, is going to see your set of skills as just what they want. Your task while a student is to ensure that the skill set you develop is attractive to the sort of employer for whom you really want to work. This means deciding on the sort of job you want, the sort of organisation you want to work for, identifying those skills, and then making sure that you develop them.

You may also have been struck by similarities in requirements. My own recent and somewhat random trawl of the papers yielded adverts for:

- 'graduates who are ambitious, motivated, good communicators and able to work to deadlines'
- 'a rigorous approach to work matched by highly developed communication and interpersonal skills'
- 'a strategic thinker ... an excellent communicator with strong networking and negotiating skills'
- 'strong leadership skills, excellent communication and organisation skills, an ability to resolve complex problems and personal resilience and stamina'
- 'competency in a range of business planning issues, excellent writing skills and experience of giving effective presentations'.

Note the similarities. Every advert I found sought good communication skills, and many mentioned other interpersonal skills, planning skills and motivation. The Association of Graduate Recruiters (AGR) survey of summer 2006 suggested that team working, oral communication, flexibility and adaptability, customer focus and problem solving were the qualities most frequently sought by graduate recruiters. You will probably find similar requirements commonly referred to in your own investigations. It is these widely relevant, transferable skills that you need to develop, and which this book seeks to address.

KEY SKILLS AND APPLICATIONS FOR LEARNING AND EMPLOYMENT

Higher education's Quality Assurance Agency (QAA) has specified a set of core skills which it feels all graduates should have, and be able to apply at European and international levels. It has developed a set of benchmark standards for these. You can obtain the full set of benchmarking standards from the QAA website at **www.qaa.ac.uk**. They include:

- Cognitive skills – critical thinking, analysis and synthesis. You need, for example, to be able to identify assumptions, evaluate statements in terms of evidence, check the logic of an argument, define terms and make appropriate generalisations.

- Problem-solving and decision-making skills – quantitative and qualitative. You need to be able to identify, formulate and solve business problems, and generate and evaluate options, applying ideas and knowledge to a range of situations.

- Research and investigative skills – and use to resolve business and management issues, both individually then as part of a team. You need to be able to identify relevant business data and research sources and research methodologies, and for your research to inform your learning.

- Information and communications technology skills – you need to be able to use a range of business applications in any job.

- Numeracy and quantitative skills – data analysis, interpretation and extrapolation. You need to be able to use models of business problems and to draw conclusions from the information you obtain.

- Communication skills – oral and written, using a range of media. You need, for example, to be able to write business reports.

- Interpersonal skills – talking and listening, presentation, persuasion and negotiation. You need to be able to interact effectively with a range of people, including colleagues and customers.

- Team-working skills – leadership, team building, influencing. You need to be able to manage or contribute to team projects.

- Personal management skills – time planning, motivation, initiative – the need for these skills is obvious.

- Learning skills – reflective, adaptive and collaborative. You need to be motivated to learn and able to do so effectively in a range of contexts.

- Self-awareness – sensitivity and openness to others who are different from you. You need to be alert to how others will react to situations – the significance of 'emotional intelligence' is now becoming recognised.

ACTIVITY 1.2

For each of the above categories, think about your current skill level (use any available evidence, including feedback from friends, teachers, past employers and your own feelings). Give yourself a rating on a scale of 1 to 10, where 1 is very low, 10 as high as you can imagine needing. File your responses for future reference, as you will need them for subsequent work. (An electronic proforma is available to make this easy.)

The relevance of these sets of skills to work is fairly obvious – but will be highlighted whenever the skills are addressed in the book. What may be less immediately apparent is the extent to which these 'employment skills' will help you to learn more effectively at university, and to get better marks. Communication is obviously crucial to working with others, for example in group projects. Good communication skills will help you to present information face to face, and to write better assignments. Self-management skills are valuable for improving your own learning and performance and performing your own part of a group's task. Addressing problems involves using information. You can see not only that the skills are relevant in both contexts – they are highly *transferable* – but that they are closely interrelated. Finding a simple classification of something as complex as higher-level human skills is difficult.

There have been many other attempts at providing lists of sets of skills. For example, Harvey *et al.* (1997), drawing on information from a wide range of graduate employers, suggested the importance of looking at skills involved in:

- fitting in – blending into a team and becoming effective quickly
- persuading – whether within the team or in relation to the wider organisation or customers beyond it
- developing ideas – analysing situations rather than merely responding to them, often best done in a team
- transforming – which adds to all the above the ability to apply intellectual skills and leadership skills in order to steer change.

You may find this shorter list helps you think slightly differently about the skills you have and need to develop. Although it covers much of the same ground, the emphasis is slightly different. Finally, you might like to look at the results of a study carried out in the USA (Luthans *et al.*, 1988) into what a wide range of managers actually did. They found that managerial activities could be categorised into the following four sets:

- communication – paperwork and exchanging information

→ Ch 2
- 'traditional management' – planning, decision making and controlling (more on this in the next chapter)
- networking – interacting with outsiders, socialising and politicking
- human resource management – motivating, disciplining, managing conflict, staffing and training.

ACTIVITY 1.3

Look back at your assessment of your own strengths and weaknesses in the light of what you have subsequently read. Amend your earlier list if improvements suggest themselves at this point. Add in any areas where you now feel that your study, as well as your employability, might benefit from development.

As you will now realise, the many activities scattered throughout the book will often be cumulative, and you need a file (paper or electronic) in which to store your responses to these for easy subsequent reference. You will probably find it useful to file your answers and notes by chapter to start with. Once you have accumulated enough material, there will be suggestions as to how you can organise your notes into a more structured *personal development file or ePortfolio.*

→ Ch 3

CAREERS WITHIN TODAY'S ORGANISATIONS

Earlier I suggested that careers are becoming far more fluid: this means that at regular intervals you will need to think about what you want from work. This will allow you to decide which jobs are most likely to meet your needs, and then to concentrate on the most relevant skills for development.

ACTIVITY 1.4

Log your initial thoughts about working life, both good and bad. Don't agonise about your answer. Just write down the first thing that comes into your head. Aim to write down between 10 and 20 words in response to the following prompts:

The things I am afraid a job might be:

_____

_____

Characteristics of my ideal job would be:

_____

_____

If possible, discuss your answers with four or five other people, to see where their views differ from yours and where they are similar. How many of you are afraid a job will be boring? How many of you want it to offer variety or the chance to meet interesting people? Do you want the chance to learn more, or to travel, or to help other people? Is status important? Were the responses from those who had already had jobs different from those who had not? If the discussion made you aware of things that are important to you but which you had omitted from your list, then construct a revised version and file this as well.

Career – a series of jobs seen in retrospect?

If your 'fears' included boredom, predictability, lack of freedom (the sort of thing that I was worried about most as a student), you were possibly thinking of the traditional 'graduate career' within a large, many-layered organisation, where good behaviour and following the rules would lead to steady progression. Large employers do still recruit graduates, but massive organisational restructuring in recent years has reduced the volume – though at the same time many of these jobs are if anything more interesting.

The 'career' as an organised succession of increasingly senior jobs has probably always been less common in reality than people believed. I can still remember being struck in 1971 by the 'definition' of career as 'a series of jobs seen in retrospect' by Ruth Lancashire, then one of the main researchers in the area, speaking at a conference on careers. Charles Handy (1989) describes how, when starting his first job in the 1950s, he was given an outline of his future career. This was to culminate in a job as chief executive of a particular company in a particular country. He left long before he was in sight of this pinnacle, but already both the projected company and the country had ceased to exist.

Certainly my own subsequent 'career' could not have been planned and seemed at the time to have been driven primarily by external forces. Yet the different jobs I have done have prepared me remarkably well for my present role, one which is more rewarding than any job I could have dreamed of as a student. And careers are becoming ever more 'unplanned' because of the ways in which organisations are changing.

Competitive pressures have driven major restructuring. Organisations have sought to cut costs and increase the speed with which they can respond to competitors and to changes in markets. Developments in information and communications technology have meant that many of the things which managers traditionally did – to do with filtering and funnelling and transmitting information – no longer need so much human intervention.

Organisations are changing

Most large organisations responded to competitive pressures by taking a hard look at their hierarchies and 'delayering', cutting out whole layers of middle management, just the sort of jobs which many graduates have filled in the past. While this decimation of management in itself cut employment costs, many organisations 'downsized' or 'rightsized' (euphemisms in this area abound) more generally, reducing the number of employees at other levels too. They also identified their 'core' business and concentrated on this, looking at ways of contracting out more peripheral activities such as cleaning, catering, warehousing, IT and even graduate recruitment.

The aim was to avoid using full-time permanent staff for non-core work. Such staff are expensive, and it may be slow and expensive to reduce staffing when business is poor. Increasingly, organisations have 'outsourced' non-core activities to specialist suppliers. Flexibility in staffing was also increased by using part-time employees or those on short-term contracts. Also, many large, specialist departments at 'head office' have been reduced by devolving a lot of their responsibilities to line managers.

Cartoon by Neill Cameron, www.planetdumbass.co.uk

IMPLICATIONS FOR GRADUATE EMPLOYMENT

Graduate recruitment prospects at the time of writing are extremely favourable, and the organisational changes outlined above make it clear why the 'thinking' skills developed by means of a degree are so important. The AGR Graduate Recruitment Survey (2006) (www.agr.org.uk) of some of the UK's leading employers showed that the current upward trend is continuing, with more vacancies than at any time since 1995. (Note that in this survey large private sector organisations in the vicinity of London are over-represented, but trends elsewhere may be similar.) Of course, it is impossible to predict what the situation will be by the time you graduate. If you want to track the situation you can find information each year from the Prospects website (www.prospects.ac.uk).

Note, however, that even in the highly favourable 2006 situation, the employers in the survey received an *average* of 28 applications for every vacancy (down from 37.6 in the 2003–04 recruitment year and 42.1 in 2002–03). The most attractive vacancies will receive many more applications than this. So use this book to develop your skills, and make yourself highly attractive to potential employers.

It is worth noting the expansion in opportunities for interesting employment in a wide range of organisations. Some are in smaller enterprises, others at levels which previously would not have attracted graduates, but which now offer precisely the challenges and satisfactions that would have been deemed lacking in the past.

If present trends continue, you can expect to work for a wider range of organisations than did your parents' generation and to change organisations, whether by free choice or necessity, every few years. If you want a higher-level job you may *need* to move: flatter organisations inevitably offer far fewer promotion opportunities than their multi-layered predecessors. So developing a 'career' will require positive action on your part and moves through several organisations.

Alternatively, you may change because you are seeking to develop additional skills or to broaden your experience. This is an important consideration: the wider your skills and experience, the greater your chances of obtaining a higher-level job, or of finding another role or job if your own falls victim to restructuring. It is vital in the current situation to take responsibility for your own development, always considering yourself through the eyes of potential employers. This will maximise your chances of continued satisfying employment, come what may.

Seeing yourself as a product

You will thus need to regard yourself as, in one sense, a *product*, one which you are continually developing with an eye to the *market* for this product, now and in the future. Those responsible for marketing a product find that SWOT analysis is a useful framework for thinking about their strategy. If you have not yet come across this, it is very easy to understand and use. SWOT is shorthand for thinking in terms of:

- Strengths – which you already have, and might build on.
- Weaknesses – which you have but could possibly reduce or otherwise work around.

■ Opportunities – which the market offers and you might be able to exploit better than other people.

■ Threats – again from outside, which you need to be aware of and take action against.

Figure 1.1 shows this framework diagrammatically. To carry out a SWOT analysis on yourself, fill in each of the boxes. Note that you need to be continually alert to likely developments in the employment market, aware of the types of skill and experience that are assuming importance and have a sound assessment of your own skills and experience. You also need to think about how you can *continually* develop these in ways that will open up future employment opportunities. Otherwise you may find you face an ever more restricted range of possible jobs.

Being highly employable means:
■ seeing yourself as a product
■ watching the market
■ developing yourself continuously
■ being prepared for change.

Such an approach means taking a much more active, and proactive, approach to your own 'career', seeing it as *your* responsibility rather than that of your employers. Seeking continuous learning and development will be a part of this. You will probably need to make absolutely sure you take advantage of all the training and job moves available in your company. If your employer does not encourage training, you may need to pursue a further qualification in your own time and at your own expense while working. The prospect of taking responsibility for your own development can be somewhat frightening. However, if 'boredom' and 'security' were listed as fears rather than as desiderata in the activity above, the excitement and risk associated with owning your own future should appeal to you.

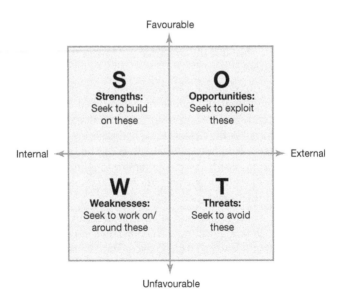

Fig 1.1 **Framework for a SWOT analysis**

The level of competition in the job market means that you need to start *now* to think about the skills that employers need and look for (not always the same thing) and about how to develop these and to *demonstrate* that you have developed them.

ACTIVITY 1.5

Use the SWOT framework, and the work you have already done during this chapter to organise your thinking about your own strengths and weaknesses as they might be seen by future employers. Supplement your research into current employer requirements by thinking about likely trends in the job market that may have altered the situation by the time you graduate. If possible, compare your analysis with those of two or three other people, and modify it if this comparison prompts new ideas. File the final version for future reference. Pay particular attention to your strengths – the developing area of strengths-based coaching suggests that building on your strengths is likely to be far more important in developing your potential for success than trying to bring areas of weakness up to the same level as your strengths You need to address any weaknesses that would stop you from being effective. But once you have achieved an acceptable level of competence in your weaker areas, your focus could usefully move to developing those areas where you are already strong.

What working feels like

If you have not yet had a job, the world of work may seem singularly opaque. Your 'hopes and fears' listed earlier may have been fairly one-dimensional in consequence. And the discussion of structural changes above may have been interesting but not hugely helpful in terms of giving you a clearer picture of what working will really be like. Indeed, given the variety of possible work experiences, it is hard to do this. But the importance of work to your whole future life cannot be overemphasised.

Hating your job is grim. It can even make you physically ill. A huge amount of absence from work is attributed to stress. An experienced and, until then, successful manager told me recently that he had been to see his doctor because he could no longer eat, sleep or think straight. Whenever he heard his manager's voice he felt physically sick. Indeed, when telling his doctor about all this he burst into tears. A stressful job with an over-controlling boss had reduced him to total misery and an inability to function.

→ Ch 2 (Some techniques for managing stress are suggested in Chapter 2, but the best way of managing it is to avoid such situations.)

In contrast, a challenging and worthwhile job can leave you exhilarated and longing to get back to work the next day. The difference between these two extremes is so important that it is worth making every effort to take the challenge posed by this book seriously and do everything you can *now* to ensure that your working experience is positive. This starts with exploring your own views about work, a process that you will need to repeat at intervals throughout the book, and indeed throughout your working life.

ACTIVITY 1.6

List as many words as you can that might be used to describe any of your own experience of work. Ask as many other people as you can to provide up to 10 words which describe their own experience of current, or previous, work.

_____

_____

You may have been surprised at the emotional level of some of the responses you get. Work forms a major part of most people's lives. For some, it is boring, so routine and dehumanising that it is highly stressful and each day becomes something to be endured with difficulty. For others, work is so exciting that they would far rather be working than doing anything else. For some, it is a source of self-esteem; for others, the treatment they receive totally destroys any self-esteem they may have had. Many marriage breakdowns are blamed on the stresses and demands of one partner's job (or both jobs). Some jobs have specific health or physical risks associated with them. More generally, sickness rates correlate to different sorts of work. Studies show that to be without a job at all is highly stressful, destructive of self-esteem and associated with ill health and relationship difficulties.

In evolutionary terms, the centrality of work is perhaps not surprising. Survival has almost always been dependent on wresting food and physical safety from a competitive, if not hostile, environment, normally as part of a social group. And reproductive success, as with other primates, will have depended on status within that group. Without work (whether hunting and gathering or farming or manufacture of some kind), the life expectancy of a person and of any dependants would have been short indeed. Indeed, family members would have been involved in work from a very early age. Survival without work is, in evolutionary terms, very recent.

If you feel it would be helpful to know more about what different types of work offer, there are a number of steps that you can usefully take. The first is to pursue any opportunities for work placements during your course (the learning opportunities offered by such placements are important in a number of different ways). The second is to extend the previous activity and to ask as many people as possible to describe their work experience to you in more detail. Try asking relatives, friends already in employment, fellow students who worked before the course started or who have already been on work placements. The third is to read about the experience of others, and suggested reading is given at the end of this chapter.

If you are asking people about their work experience, which may after all be extensive, it can help to have a framework of questions. If you are working in a group, discuss possible questions, and agree a common list. The following are merely suggestions to get you started:

- What most surprised you on starting work with your present employer?
- What are the most common difficulties you encounter at work?

- What are the most common frustrations?
- What has given you most satisfaction in the past week (or month or year)?
- If you could choose a new job, how would it be different from your present one?
- How would it resemble your present job?
- How much freedom do you have at work?
- How much impact do you feel you have on the way the organisation operates?
- What advice would you give to someone starting out in your organisation?
- What characteristics would the ideal employee have in your organisation?

The answers to such questions will reflect the person answering as much as the job they are doing. The same job could be very satisfactory to one person and hardly bearable to another. Nevertheless, if you can question a number of different people of graduate or equivalent ability about their experience, you should be better informed than before about the characteristics of jobs and possible reactions to them. This should help you become more aware of the nature of the type of job you would like yourself.

ACTIVITY 1.7

Devise a set of questions for asking about work experience, preferably with a group of others, and use this to question a range of people. If working in a group, discuss the results, comparing what those you asked seem to want from work with what *you* think you might want, and using what they say about their work experience to extend your own expectations and awareness. Add any additional 'wants' to your 'ideal job' file entry. You can find a starter questionnaire, based on the questions above, on the website.

STRUCTURE OF THE BOOK

Use the brief overview which follows to help you see how to make best use of the rest of the book. Try to get a feel for how you can use it to develop those skills which you will need, both to succeed as a student, and to be highly desirable to potential employers when you start to apply for jobs.

The first part of the book maps out 'the territory' of employment, management skills and learning. Once you are more familiar with this context, and the more general learning skills that you will need, you will be better able to use the second part of the book, which addresses the specific skills that you will need in order to do well academically: reading critically, and taking effective notes; writing – and arguing – clearly; working with numbers; using computers and the Internet; and doing well in assessment (including exams). You may already be more than expert in some of these areas. If so, it will be good time management to identify and concentrate on those where you are weaker. Although the main aim of this part is to help you do well in your course, most of the skills covered will be also be useful long after you have graduated.

The third part reverses this emphasis. It addresses communication and other aspects of working with other people, either one-to-one or as a member of a team. Although you will need these skills while a student and will have many opportunities to develop them, you have already seen that they are crucial to success at work.

The fourth part addresses skills of equal relevance to study and work: the 'trained mind' that graduates were traditionally deemed to possess. More specifically, it looks at the skills needed to react creatively and appropriately to complicated situations, to investigate them, gather and make sense of relevant information and decide on a way forward. Your course will be addressing problem-solving skills within a specific academic area, but much of the teaching may be implicit. This part of the book aims to make aspects of these skills more explicit and to increase your awareness of them. This should shift slightly your approach to study, so that you are better prepared to tackle problem situations at work.

In the last part, the different areas are brought together in looking at project management, both in general and in the context of any project that is part of your course. Finally, the 'project' of finding a good job is addressed. In this way the circle is completed and you will come back to the issues raised in this chapter, refining your work objectives and developing the skills needed for making a successful job application and doing well in interviews.

The structure of the book in terms of the skills covered can be charted as shown in Figure 1.2. Inevitably, there are many interconnections between the skills covered in different chapters. In particular, the end of the book is designed to draw on almost all that has gone before. You can see that when you are ready to organise your file you will face a considerable challenge. But by then you should have a clearer idea of the skills that are important to you for more effective study, as well as those which are likely to be important to your chosen prospective employers. This will make it easier to design a system well suited to your particular situation.

This chapter has looked mainly at the world of work, arguing that there is a substantial overlap in the skills needed for study and those for employment, and that given the competitive nature of employment you need to start *now* to think about what you want from a job, and what skills you will need to develop it. You will find as you work through the book that each skill addressed will have the added benefit of helping you gain higher grades. This will help you further in your search for a better job. The transferability of most of the skills covered has its roots in two factors. One, obviously, is that if you are studying a course designed to prepare you for employment, then you are likely to be asked to develop those skills that employers value. The second, and less obvious, factor is that the most successful managers are those who continually develop themselves. The ability to learn is vital in a world where organisational contexts are fluid and constantly presenting new challenges. Becoming an effective learner is thus crucial to both contexts. And it is effective learning, along with the equally important ability to display your learning ability, that this book primarily addresses, as the next two chapters make clear.

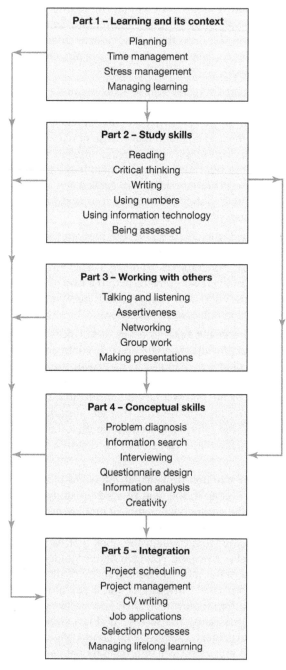

Fig 1.2 A skills framework for the purpose of this book

SUMMARY

This chapter has argued that:

- Studying for a degree represents a major investment: there are opportunity costs as well as direct financial costs.
- To get good grades, and become an attractive employee you need to take responsibility for your own learning.
- Graduate opportunities have improved in the past few years but the situation is still highly competitive. Organisational restructuring has broadened the range of interesting jobs available.
- You can expect to work in several different organisations during your lifetime: managing your own career is important.
- To make yourself attractive to prospective employers you need to develop and demonstrate the skills they seek.
- The transferable skills which this book seeks to develop are relevant to both study and employment.
- These skills are interpersonal as well as intellectual, and include the skill to learn from experience as well as reading, the ability to manage yourself, basic skills in numeracy, literacy and IT, interpersonal, group-working and communication skills, and skills in analysing and solving problems.

Further information

- Fineman, S. and Gabriel, Y. (1996) *Experiencing Organisations*, Sage. An easy-to-read set of stories told by students after their six-month work placements.
- Frost, P.J., Mitchell, V.F. and Nord, W.R. (eds) (1997) *Organisational Reality: Reports from the Firing Line*, 4th edn, Addison Wesley Longman.
- **www.agr.org.uk** – the Association of Graduate Recruiters – for information from the perspective of the employer.
- **www.careers.reading.ac.uk/staff/FullReport.pdf** – this provides an interesting overview of the changes in graduate employment in the ten years to 2006/07.
- **www.prospects.ac.uk** – 'the UK's official graduate careers website' for a range of information on graduate employment.
- **www.qaa.ac.uk** – the Quality Assurance Agency – where you can find information on benchmarking and academic standards.

Assessment at university

How tests and examinations work

University assessment systems are complex and rather different from those used at school or college. This chapter clarifies the terminology involved and explains the rationale for different modes of assessment, while later chapters discuss how to tackle specific question types.

Key topics
- Forms of assessment
- Marking criteria and grading schemes
- Modules and progression
- Degree classifications and transcripts

Key terms
Aggregate mark   Class exam   Exam diet   External examiner   Finals
Formative assessment   Learning objective   Marking criteria
Oral exam   Peer assessment   Summative assessment   Transcript

Your university is an educational institution with a legal charter entitling it to award its own degrees. These degrees are granted on the basis of performance in exams and assessments, which may vary in character depending on subject and institution. As a result, each university has its own conventions regarding style of question, format of exams and marking criteria. No two universities are the same. It is essential that you take into account how the exam system operates in your own institution *before* you start revising.

Exam format

This should never come as a surprise to you as you should have checked up on it by looking at past papers and by confirming with lecturers that there have been no changes to the style of examination.

Exam papers and diets may be structured in different ways, according to discipline. The design may reflect the different aspects of learning that your tutors wish to assess (Ch 17 and Ch 19). For example, there may be a multiple-choice component that tests your surface knowledge across a wide range of topics, while an essay section may be included to test your deeper knowledge in fewer topics. Papers and questions may carry different weightings towards an aggregate mark.

Various levels of choice are given to reflect the nature of the field of study. In professional disciplines there may be a need to ensure you are knowledgeable in all areas, while in other subjects a certain amount of specialisation may be acceptable. Some exam papers are divided into sections, and you will be expected to answer one or more questions from the options within each of these. This format allows a limited amount of choice while ensuring that you have covered all major areas in your studies. You should take these aspects of exam paper design into account when arriving at a strategy for revision and exam-sitting (Ch 15).

● Forms of assessment

Each degree programme and every unit of teaching at university (usually called a 'module') will have a published set of aims and learning objectives or outcomes. Your performance in relation to these goals will be tested in various ways.

- **Formative assessments** are primarily designed to give you feedback on the quality of your answers. In some instances these are known as 'class exams'. They generally do not count towards your final module assessment, although sometimes a small proportion of marks will carry forward as an incentive to perform well.

- **Summative assessments** count directly towards a module or degree assessment. Many summative exams are held as formal invigilated tests where you work in isolation. These may be known as degree exams and, in the honours year, in some institutions, as 'finals'. These exams may comprise several sittings or papers, perhaps covering different aspects of the course, and often lasting for two or three hours each. The collective set of exams is sometimes known as an exam diet.

In some cases, in-course work will count towards degree exams (continuous assessment). This can take the form of essays, projects, and special exercises like problem-based learning. However, the majority of marks are usually devoted to formal invigilated exams where the possibility of collaboration, plagiarism and impersonation are limited, and you will be expected to perform alone under a certain amount of time pressure.

Problem-based learning (PBL)

This is a form of learning where you are asked to investigate a specific problem, usually related to a real-life professional situation, which may be open-ended in nature (that is, not necessarily having a 'right answer'). You may be part of a small team asked to consider the problem, research the underlying theory and practice that might lead to a response, and arrive at a practical solution. Assessment of the exercise will focus not only on the solution you arrive at, but also on the way in which you arrive at it, so here process is often at least as important as the product. There may be group- and peer-assessment elements that contribute to your grade.

● Marking criteria and grading schemes

Who marks your papers? How do they do it? Often students are unsure about this. The norm is for papers to be graded by the person who delivered the lectures, tutorials or practical classes. With large classes, alternative mechanisms may be employed:

- the marking may be spread out among several tutors;
- especially in multiple-choice papers, the marking may be automated;
- where teamwork is involved, peer assessment may take place.

Peer assessment

This is where the members of a study team are asked to assign a mark to each other's performance. This might take account, for example, of the effort put in, the conduct in the assigned team role(s), and contribution to the final outcome. Clear guidance is always given about how you should assign marks. One point of this method is to help students become more aware of how work is assessed by academic staff.

Each university will publish assessment scales, usually in handbooks and/or websites. Some operate to a familiar system of banded percentages, often related to honours degree classifications, while others adopt a different form of band 'descriptors'. Find out which system applies in your case and consult the general marking criteria used to assign work in each band. This will give you a better idea of the standard of work needed to produce a specific grade, and may help you to understand feedback.

To maintain standards and ensure fairness, several systems operate. For example:

- there may be an explicit marking scheme that allocates a proportion of the total to different aspects of your answer;
- double- or triple-marking may take place and if the grades awarded differ, then the answer may be scrutinised more closely, possibly by a external examiner;
- papers are usually marked anonymously, so the marker does not know whose answer they are grading;
- the external marker will confirm the overall standard and may inspect some papers, particularly those falling at the division between honours grades or on the pass/fail boundary;
- accreditation bodies in the professions may be involved in the examination process, and some answer papers may be marked by external assessors appointed by these bodies rather than by university staff.

 External examiners

These are appointed by the university to ensure standards are maintained and that the assessment is fair. They are usually noted academics in the field, with wide experience of examining. They review the exam question papers in advance and will generally look closely at a representative selection of written papers and project work. For finals, they may interview students in an oral, to ensure that spoken responses meet the standard of the written answers, and to arrive at a judgement on borderline cases.

● Modules and progression

Modular systems of study at university have been developed for several reasons:

- they allow greater flexibility in subject choice;
- they can efficiently accommodate students studying different degree paths;
- they make it easier for students to transfer between courses and institutions;
- they break up studies into 'bite-sized' elements and allow exams to be spread out more evenly over the academic year.

The set of modules that make up a degree programme are usually selected to build on each other in a complementary way, and to allow you to develop skills that you can take forward to the next level of study. Therefore, you should avoid:

- dodging seemingly difficult or unattractive subjects;
- 'closing the book' on a subject once it has been assessed; or
- limiting your degree options.

Modules are usually assessed in a summative end-of-module exam, perhaps with a component from in-course assessment. In some subjects, borderline cases are given an extra oral exam. If you fail the end-of-module exam (and any oral), a resit may be possible. Resits usually take place towards the end of the summer vacation. The result is usually based solely on your performance in the resit exam.

At the end of each academic year, and after any resits, you will be required to fulfil certain progression criteria that allow you to pass on to the next level of study. These criteria are normally published in course handbooks. If you fail to satisfy the criteria, you may need to resit the whole year or even to leave the university. Sometimes you may be asked to 'carry' specific modules: that is, study them again in addition to the normal quota for your next year of study. Some institutions may place a condition on your re-entry, for example, achieving a certain level of marks or passing a prescribed number of modules in order to progress. This would normally be discussed with your adviser/director of studies.

Appeals against termination of studies

Students' studies may be terminated for one of several reasons, but most commonly failure to meet attendance or progression criteria. Occasionally, termination will be enforced due to disciplinary reasons, for example, in a case of plagiarism. Students will normally be offered a chance to appeal and will be expected to produce evidence of any extenuating circumstances, such as medical certificates, or notes from support service personnel. Such students may also wish to ask tutors to support their application where the tutor is aware of their personal situation.

● Degree classifications and transcripts

Students with superior entry qualifications or experience may join university at different levels. There are also a range of exit awards – certificates, diplomas and ordinary degrees. However, the majority of students now enter at level 1, and study for an honours degree. This encompasses three years of study in England, Wales and Northern Ireland, and four years in Scotland. Credit will normally be given for years of study carried out abroad or in work placement, according to specific schemes operated by your university. This includes participation in European Community schemes such as ERASMUS or LINGUA (see **http://europa.eu.int/index_en.htm**).

Sometimes entry into the final honours year is competitive, based on grades in earlier years. Some universities operate a junior honours year, which means being accepted into an honours stream at an earlier stage and with special module options.

Nearly all universities follow the same honours degrees grading system, which is, in descending order:

- first class (a 'first');
- upper second class (a two-one or 2:1);
- lower second class (a two-two or 2:2);
- third class (a 'third');
- unclassified.

(Certain universities do not differentiate the second class divisions.)

In some institutions, these classifications will take into account all grades you have obtained during your university career; sometimes only those in junior and senior honours years; and in the majority, only grades obtained in the finals. This makes the finals critical, especially as there are no resits for them.

Once your degree classification has been decided by the examination committee or board, and moderated by the external examiner, it will be passed for ratification to the university's senate or equivalent body for academic legislation. During this period you will technically be a graduand, until your degree is conferred at the graduation ceremony. At this time you will receive your degree certificate and be entitled to wear a specifically coloured hood for your gown that denotes your degree and institution.

Job prospects with different degrees

In a competitive job market, your chances of being considered for a position may depend on your degree classification, but employers also take into account other personal qualities and experience. Research positions that involve reading for a higher degree, such as an MSc or PhD, usually require a first or 2:1.

Employers will usually ask to see your diploma for confirmation of your degree and may contact the university to confirm your qualification and obtain a copy of your transcript. This document shows your performance in *all* assessments throughout your career at the university.

 Practical tips for understanding the assessment system

Ask senior students about the exam system. They may have useful tips and advice to pass on.

Find out where essential information is recorded. This could be in a combination of handbooks and web-based resources.

If you don't understand any aspect of the assessment system, ask course administrators or tutors. Knowing how the system works is important and can affect your performance.

Notify your institution of any disability

If you have a disability, you should make the institution aware of this. You may have special concessions in exams, for example, using the services of a scribe, being allowed extra time, or having exam question papers printed in large print for you. Appropriate entitlements take time to arrange and you must ensure that arrangements are in place well before the exam date. Contact your department and disability support service for guidance.

 And now . . .

2.1 Carry out the necessary research to ensure you know how your university's exam system works for your intended degree. You should find out about:

- course and degree programme aims;
- learning objectives or outcomes;
- the format of assessments and proportion of in-course and final exam elements;
- timing of exam diets;
- assessment or marking criteria;
- the grading scheme;
- weighting of exam components;
- progression criteria.

2.2 Find out about in-course assessments and how they will contribute to your module or degree grade. Your course handbooks will normally include this information. Marks for in-course work can often be influenced by the amount of work you put in, so they can be a good way of ensuring you create a strong platform to perform well in summative exams. Some courses include an element relating to attendance as part of the assessment.

2.3 Examine past exam papers in your subjects to investigate how they are constructed. This will allow you to see whether there are subdivisions, restrictions or other features that might influence your revision or exam strategies.

Exploiting feedback

How to understand and learn from what lecturers write on your work

When you receive back assessed work and exam scripts, these may be annotated by the marker or provided in a standard feedback sheet. It is essential that you learn from these comments if you want to improve. This chapter outlines some common annotations and describes how you should react to them.

Key topics

- Types of feedback
- Examples of feedback comments and what they mean

Key terms
Formative assessment   Summative assessment

There are two principal types of assessment at university: formative and summative. Formative assessments are those in which the grade received does not contribute to your end-of-module mark, or contributes relatively little, while giving you an indication of the standard of your work. It is often accompanied by a feedback sheet or comments written on the script. Summative assessments contribute directly to your final module mark and include things such as end-of-term/semester exams, project reports or essay submissions.

● Types of feedback

The simplest pointer from any type of assessment is the grade you receive; if good, you know that you have reached the expected standard; if poor, you know that you should try to improve.

If you feel unsure about the grading system or what standard is expected at each grading level, your course, school or faculty handbooks will probably include a description of marking or assessment criteria that explain this.

How well are you performing?

The answer, of course, depends on your goals and expectations, but also on your understanding of degree classifications and their significance. Even in early levels of study, it may be worth relating percentage marks or other forms of grades (descriptors) to the standard degree classes - first, upper second, lower second, third and unclassified. Certain career and advanced degree opportunities will only be open to those with higher-level qualifications, and you should try to gain an understanding of how this operates in your field of study and likely career destination. In this way you will know the targets you need to hit in order to achieve these goals.

Written feedback may be provided on your assessed work. This will often take the form of handwritten comments on your text, and a summary commenting on your work or justifying why it received the mark it did. Sometimes the feedback will be provided separately from your submission so that other markers are not influenced by it.

Some feedback may be oral and informal, for example, a demonstrator's comment given as you work in a practical, or an observation on your contribution during a tutorial. If you feel uncertain about why your work has received the grade it did, or why a particular comment was provided, you may be able to arrange a meeting with the person who assessed your work. Normally they will be happy to provide further oral explanations. However, do not attempt to haggle over your marks, other than to point out politely if part of your work does not appear to have been marked at all, or part marks appear to have been added up wrongly.

Always read your feedback

You will want to do your best, so make a point of reading feedback carefully. Regardless of your grade, all comments in your feedback should give you constructive direction for later efforts and are designed to help you to develop the structure and style of your work, as well as encourage you to develop a deeper understanding of the topic. Where students ignore points, especially those about presentation or structure, then they may find themselves heavily penalised in later submissions.

● Examples of feedback comments and what they mean

Different lecturers use different terms to express similar meanings, and because they mark quickly, their handwritten comments are sometimes untidy and may be difficult to interpret. This means that you may need help in deciphering their meaning. Table 10.1 illustrates feedback comments that are frequently made and explains how you should react to obtain better grades in future. If a particular comment or mark does not make sense to you after reading these tables, then you may wish to approach the marker for an explanation.

Practical tips for dealing with feedback

Be mentally prepared to learn from the views of your tutors. You may initially feel that feedback is unfair, harsh or that it misunderstands the approach you were trying to take to the question. A natural reaction might be to dismiss many of the comments. However, you should recognise that tutors probably have a much deeper understanding of the topic than you, and concede that if you want to do well in a subject then you need to gain a better understanding of what makes a good answer from the academic's point of view.

Always make sure you understand the feedback. Check with fellow students or with the lecturers involved if you cannot read the comment or do not understand why it has been made.

React constructively to *all* your feedback. Make a note of common or repeated errors, even in peripheral topics, so that you can avoid them in later assignments.

Get to know the standard proof-reading symbols and the abbreviations used by your tutors. Lecturers and tutors use a variety of words and symbols to suggest corrections and modifications. Most symbols will be standard ones used in editing (for example, ≡ placed under a letter means that it should be capitalised). If you find you cannot understand them, consult one of the standard texts for readers and compositors (for example, *Hart's Rules*, Ritter, 2005).

Table 10.1 **Common types of feedback annotation and how to act in response.** Comments in the margin may be accompanied by underlining of word(s), circling of phrases, sentences or paragraphs.

Types of comment and typical examples	Meaning and potential remedial action
Regarding content	
Relevance Relevance? Importance? Value of example? So?	An example or quotation may not be apt, or you may not have explained its relevance. Think about the logic of your narrative or argument and whether there is a mismatch as implied, or whether you could add further explanation; choose a more appropriate example or quote.
Detail Give more information Example? Too much detail/waffle/padding	You are expected to flesh out your answer with more detail or an example to illustrate your point; or, conversely, you may have provided too much information. It may be that your work lacks substance and you appear to have compensated by putting in too much description rather than analysis, for example.
Specific factual comment or comment on your approach You could have included . . . What about . . . ? Why didn't you . . . ?	Depends on context, but it should be obvious what is required to accommodate the comment.
Expressions of approval Good! Excellent! ✓ (may be repeated)	You got this right or chose a good example. Keep up the good work!
Expressions of disapproval Poor Weak No! ✗ (may be repeated)	Sometimes obvious, but may not be clear. The implication is that your example's logic could be improved.
Regarding structure	
Fault in logic or argument Logic! Non sequitur (does not follow)	Your argument or line of logic is faulty. This may require quite radical changes to your approach to the topic.
Failure to introduce topic clearly Where are you going with this? Unclear	What is your understanding of the task? What parameters will confine your response? How do you intend to tackle the subject?

Table 10.1 continued

Types of comment and typical examples	Meaning and potential remedial action
Failure to construct a logical discussion *Imbalanced discussion* *Weak on pros and cons*	When you have to compare and contrast in any way, then it is important that you give each element in your discussion equal coverage.
Failure to conclude essay clearly *So what?* *Conclusion*	You have to leave a 'take-home message' that sums up the most salient features of your writing and you should not include new material in this section. This is to demonstrate your ability to think critically and define the key aspects.
Heavy dependency on quotations *Watch out for over-quotation* *Too many quotations*	There is a real danger of plagiarism if you include too many direct quotations from text. However, in a subject like English literature or law, quotation may be a key characteristic of writing. In this case, quotation is permitted, provided that it is supported by critical comment.
Move text *Loops and arrows*	Suggestion for changing order of text, usually to enhance the flow or logic.
Regarding presentation	
Minor proofing errors *sp.* (spelling) ⋏ (insert material here) ⌐ (break paragraph here) ⁊ (delete this material)	A (minor) correction is required.
Citations *Reference (required)* *Reference or bibliography list omitted* *Ref!*	You have not supported evidence, argument or quotation with a reference to the original source. This is important in academic work and if you fail to do it, you may be considered guilty of plagiarism. If you omit a reference list, this will lose you marks as it implies a totally unsourced piece of writing.
Tidiness *Illegible!* *Can't read*	Your handwriting on the exam script may be difficult to decipher.
Failure to follow recommended format *Please follow departmental template for reports* *Order!*	If the department or school provides a template for the submission of reports, then you must follow it. If you don't, then you may lose marks.

GO And now . . .

10.1 **Check out your department, school or faculty's marking criteria.** As explained above, these may help you interpret feedback and understand how to reach the standard you want to achieve.

10.2 **Decide what to do about feedback comments you frequently receive.** For instance, do lecturers always comment about your spelling or grammar; or suggest you should use more examples; or ask for more citations to be included? You might consider consulting your university's academic skills unit whose learning specialists may be able to help you improve in the necessary areas.

10.3 **Learn to criticise drafts of your own work.** This is equivalent to giving feedback to yourself and is an essential academic skill. Annotate drafts of your own work - this is an important way to refine it and improve its quality.

Learning and reflective practice

Good grades come from knowing what and how to learn. In today's rapidly changing business world, a successful career depends upon continuing to learn throughout your working life. This chapter will help you to understand the learning process, recognise your own preferred learning style and develop your learning skills, particularly your ability to use reflection as a means of learning. You will then gain better grades, and be able to maximise the learning potential of any situation you meet at work.

Learning outcomes

By the end of this chapter you should:

- have a better idea of what 'learning' means
- appreciate the difference between knowledge, concepts, skills and competence
- understand what is meant by learning style and recognise your own preferred style
- have started to develop less preferred styles
- be starting to develop your reflective learning skills
- understand the role of feedback in the development of both practical and conceptual skills
- have explored the learning opportunities offered by your degree programme, identified any gaps and be starting to plan to fill these
- be developing a systematic approach to evidencing skills relevant to employment.

We all learn from the moment we are born, but are often not aware of the process. As you work through this chapter you will become more aware of how you learn, and will start to apply your developing self-management skills to improve your learning both on your course and outside it. Managers or leaders who know how they learn, and who go on learning, are far more effective than those who lack this awareness.

LEARNING THEORY

Children are voracious learners, eager to master walking and talking and a host of other skills. They learn which people are important to them, how not to upset them (and how to infuriate them too). They learn to play games, to read and to manage their pocket money. As a child, you were probably seldom aware that you were learning, despite the rate at which you were doing so. You know that the official objective of higher education is to foster learning. You will hear the phrase 'lifelong learning' on the lips of politicians and many others. But how often do people look in detail at what helps and hinders the process? Indeed, what exactly *is* learning?

ACTIVITY 3.1

Write a brief definition of learning as you understand it. Discuss this with some other people if possible. Unless you have all just done a course on 'learning' which included an approved definition, you may be surprised at the range of possible ways of understanding the term.

_____

_____

_____

Traditionally, learning was seen as acquiring knowledge. There are still countries where 'education', even at university level, consists of telling students things and then testing that they can repeat them. The underlying metaphor is of 'jug and mug', with the 'knowledge' being poured from the jug (lecturer) to the mug (you). Yet in many situations, academic knowledge is not enough. You may *know* that to ride a bicycle you sit on the saddle and use your feet to turn the pedals and your hands to steer via the handlebars. But this knowledge would not stop you falling off the first time you tried to ride. Being able to *do* things is also important. Beyond both, there is the ability to *understand* and interpret situations and respond effectively, even if the situation is different from any you have yet encountered.

It is this learning of *conceptual* skills that is most exciting. And for this, the passive mug metaphor is singularly inappropriate. Learning conceptual skills is necessarily an *active* and continuous process, not a one-off operation performed on a passive recipient. Some fifty years ago, Krishnamurti approached the idea of learning from a very different background and for a different purpose, but came to a similar conclusion. He wrote of a psychological learning which goes beyond the accumulation of knowledge or the acquisition of skills. For example, he says:

> Learning is one thing and acquiring knowledge is another. Learning is a continuous process, not a process of addition. Most of us gather knowledge as memory, as idea, store it up as experience ... we act from knowledge, technological knowledge, knowledge as experience, knowledge as tradition, knowledge that one has derived through one's particular idiosyncratic tendencies. ... In that process there is no learning. Learning is never accumulative, it is a constant movement. ... You learn as you are going along.

> (Krishnamurti, 1995, meditation for 12 January)

Refer to your definition of learning above. Did it include *skills* as well as *knowledge*? Was there any reference to understanding, or to a conceptual dimension? One workable definition of the sort of learning that this book addresses, though it has an accumulative dimension that could be seen to conflict with the view quoted above, is:

> *Learning is purposeful activity aimed at acquisition of skills, knowledge and ways of thinking that improve effectiveness in future situations.*

This begs many questions about what constitutes effectiveness and which situations are relevant, but it teases out a number of dimensions that it will be useful to explore. It covers the three aspects of knowledge, skills and thinking. It also highlights the need to *use* what is learned and implies that others will only know that you *have* learned by observing your more effective behaviour. (You might, subjectively, know that you have learned something because you are aware of increased understanding, but others will need you to translate this into something – words or action – that they can observe.)

ACTIVITY 3.2

Rewrite your definition taking the above ideas into account. There is no need to use exactly the words above. Try to find a way of defining learning that feels right to you, as a reflection of what you now think learning is. Then think of three recent instances when you have felt you learned something of significance and check that each would be learning according to your definition. Note your thoughts below:

_____

_____

_____

Competence and vocational qualifications

In the UK, and some other countries, it was increasingly realised from the early 1980s that the important issue at work is what you can *do*, rather than merely what you *know*. This led to a profound change in the approach to vocational and professional training and qualifications, and the construction of a set of National Vocational Qualifications (NVQs, or SVQs in Scotland). Each of these qualifications is based on a set of occupational standards deemed to constitute competent performance at various levels within the occupation or profession. Organisations frequently construct their own set of standards, or competence frameworks, and use them as the basis for their recruitment and employee development. Professional institutes may also base their assessment of candidates for membership on a set of standards.

Although there is still not a single agreed definition of competence in the abstract, a working one is:

> *Competence is an underlying characteristic of a person, a mix of motives, traits and skills, leading to effective or superior job performance.*

The British competence movement has tended to emphasise 'effective' performance, the USA preferring 'superior'. This definition begs even more questions than the definition of learning, but note the emphasis on skills and performance rather than merely knowledge. This links back to the 'improved effectiveness' that is part of the earlier definition of learning. The reference to motives also links with the previous

→ Ch 2   chapter. Although in many situations competence will depend on underlying knowledge and understanding, it is the resulting performance that is critical.

Assessment for competence-based qualifications is therefore based on evidence of performance relating to the different elements of competence deemed important for that qualification. Candidates are asked to assemble a portfolio demonstrating their competence against each element of the standards. Throughout the book, you will be asked to file the results of activities directed towards developing (and demonstrating) your skills. This will result in a portfolio you can draw upon if you decide to seek a competence-based qualification, or for evidence to impress potential employers. It will give you a greater understanding of how to assemble such a portfolio, and practice in assembling evidence. This is in addition to the main purpose of the activities, which is to help you to *develop* the competences involved and appreciate their potential for use in job applications.

There are many different sets of standards, each complex and detailed, and all will be updated at intervals. There is therefore little point in trying to spell out all the elements of any one. Most sets of standards will reflect a wide range of employer views and can therefore be a useful guide to the skills that you will need in a job. This is particularly true of the GNVQ (General National Vocational Qualification) key skills, which were designed to be 'portable' and relate to many different occupations. Because this shift towards 'competence' has been one of the most significant changes in approach to education, training, assessment and recruitment in recent years, it is worth understanding the basic principles.

The approach provides a useful complement to more traditional teaching methods. An appreciation of the way in which complex skills can be broken down into elements, and how they can be assessed using separate pieces of evidence, will help your learning in general. It will also increase your chances of producing 'exhibits' which could be used for this purpose should you so wish. The GNVQ key skill 'improve own learning and performance' (1996) will be used to develop this understanding.

What are you learning now?

What more do you need to learn than the 'facts' about your chosen subject? How are

→ Ch 1   you becoming potentially more *effective*? The first chapter suggested some things that the government and employers think you should be learning – key skills to do with communication, working with others, using numbers, using IT, problem solving and, of course, 'learning to learn' in the applied sense of improving your own learning and performance in any situation. If you have never thought about the wider learning that your student experience offers, it is worth taking time for a brief audit of this. By the end of the book you should have a clearer understanding of the range of possible transferable skills and be able to update and expand your audit. Do not therefore spend too long on the following exercise. Regard it as a rough first draft.

ACTIVITY 3.3

Think about the courses you are studying this year. What broad areas of specialist knowledge do they address? What skills specific to your subject will you also be developing? Which of the above key skills can you develop within your studies? (For example, you can practise communication skills in class discussions, in negotiating extensions to deadlines with your tutor and in writing assignments. You can practise team skills when working with others on this book, or on group projects.)

List the things that you think you are currently learning. Leave space beneath each to write other things, and file this for future use. If there are key skills which you are *not* learning, for example if you have managed to avoid touching a computer or if there is no group work, log these on a separate list. Log also anything which you think you are supposed to be learning but for some reason are not.

Some difficulty with this exercise is inevitable if you are not used to thinking of such a wide range of learning and have not reflected on your own learning before. Don't worry – it will have raised questions in your mind that you will be able to answer later and highlighted areas that you need to think more about.

Kolb's theory

Even for specialist knowledge, an employer would probably be interested in your ability to use, rather than merely recite, what you know. Application is crucial but is something many students find difficult. The skill of applying conceptual frameworks is hardest of all. Yet it is crucial to the sort of learning you need from your studies.

Employers expect graduates to be able to *understand* problematic situations in order to respond appropriately. When the context changes you cannot simply do what you successfully did before. To adapt to a new situation you need to understand what you were doing in the old one, and why it worked there.

Organisational life is complex, and conceptual frameworks, that is, mental models, help you to make sense of it. Some of these frameworks or sets of assumptions you will already be using, probably without being aware of them. Kolb recognised the importance of these 'theories' and of the role of conscious reflection in their development (Kolb *et al.*, 1984). He suggested a model of how ideas and experience are integrated, with learning a circular rather than a one-off process of making sense of things. You do something, reflect on your experience, try to conceptualise it and then test these concepts through more experience. Figure 3.1 shows a simplified version of this process.

Several points come out of this simple model. First, learning is shown as an *active* process. Action generates 'experience' of the results of action, which is food for reflection. This reflection involves trying to make sense of experience in the light of existing ideas and understanding. 'Theorising' involves changing your ideas in order to make better sense of the experience. You then do something to test your improved theories, applying them in another context and seeing whether experience of the

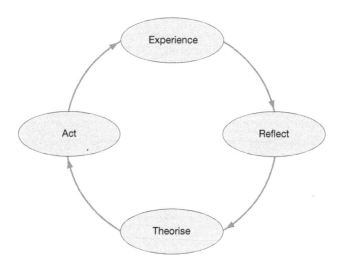

Fig 3.1 **Learning as a continuous process (adapted from Kolb)**

results of your action is as expected. By going round the loop again and again as you have new experiences, you can continue to develop your understanding.

If parts of the process are missing, learning will not take place. You could do something ineffectively for years if you never stop to think about how you might do it better. Experience without reflection will teach you nothing. A friend works for an appallingly bad manager. For decades the manager has never questioned the ways in which he operates. Indeed, he is completely unaware of the 'theories' or assumptions on which his behaviour is based. As far as he is concerned, the way he thinks is the only possible way: anyone who disagrees with him has to be stupid or perverse.

One belief is that a subordinate should account to his manager for every moment. Yet the job is one which requires thinking, networking and other 'invisible' activities for success. The 'control is all' assumption of this boss is making it impossible for my friend to perform. He and the rest of the team are currently actively seeking other jobs, purely because of this ineffective boss and his faulty assumptions.

Theory unlinked to past experience and untested in new contexts is equally unlikely to contribute to competence development. (In the 1980s most of those on MBA programmes were recent graduates. They tended to be avoided like the plague by most employers.) This is why work experience is a crucial part of an undergraduate business studies degree.

LEARNING STYLES

If learning is to be effective – and it is vital for your studies and for your subsequent career that it is – then feedback and reflection on experience are essential. You need to work to ensure that you get feedback on what you do, and on how you think, and to constantly reflect on your practice and the experience that results. But although this much is true for everyone, people vary in the way they learn, and it is essential to understand your own learning style. There are many different approaches to classifying learning styles. For example, Drucker (1999) suggested that some people learn best by listening, some by reading, some by writing and some by doing.

This may link with the suggestion (see, for example, Andreas and Faulkner's 1996 book on neuro-linguistic programming, or NLP) that people vary in their dominant sense. Some will talk in terms of 'I hear what you are saying', 'Tell me what . . .', 'That sounds as if . . .'. For these people, the auditory sense is strongest, and they will presumably learn by listening. Others say things like 'Show me . . .', 'I see what you mean . . .', or 'It looks as if . . .'. For them, vision is strongest, so they presumably would learn best by watching, or perhaps reading. Yet others will say 'It feels as if . . .', 'I can't quite grasp . . .', or 'You need to touch on . . .'. For them, the kinaesthetic sense is important, and presumably they would be the ones who would learn in a 'hands on', or 'doing' fashion.

ACTIVITY 3.4

Observe one or two friends talking for a while, noting whether they use 'seeing', 'hearing' or 'doing' words most. Once you have identified their dominant sense, ask them how they feel they learn best. If possible, then ask them to observe you and identify your own sense dominance. If not, observe yourself – it will be easier once you have sensitised yourself by watching them. Think about the implications of this for your own learning and note them in your file.

Honey and Mumford (1986) suggested that another way of classifying people is in terms of the stages in the Kolb cycle. Although all of the stages are necessary for learning, they suggest that people tend to be happier with some stages of the loop than others. They identified four different *learning styles* which reflect these preferences and developed an inventory to help people to identify their own. There are strengths and weaknesses associated with each style. You can get a 'quick and dirty' approximation of your own preferred style from the following. If you are really interested in your own style you should obtain the full inventory. (Your institution may have rights to use this.)

ACTIVITY 3.5

Think about each of the following statements. Check the one that is most characteristic of your own reaction to a learning situation.

1　I'm game to try it – let's get started.

2　I need some time to think about this.

3　What are the basic assumptions?

4　What's is the use of this?

Activists

If you chose statement 1 in Activity 3.5 you may tend towards activism. If so, you are probably open-minded and love new experiences, get bored easily, are highly sociable, love group decisions and bring welcome energy to a task. You are probably not very good at things which require consolidation, or indeed anything which requires sustained effort – even sitting through a lecture may be difficult. Producing a dissertation or other sustained piece of work will be extremely hard for you. You will scorn caution and tend to jump into things without enough thought. Other group members may feel you don't give them a chance in discussions and you may miss opportunities to learn from other people's experience.

Reflectors

If you chose statement 2 you may be a reflector, preferring to think about all possible angles before reaching a decision, taking a low profile in discussions, cautious and unwilling to leap to premature conclusions. You will thrive on dissertations, provided you do not spend far too long on planning, leaving no time for data collection and writing. You will be a great asset as an observer of others and provide useful feedback, but may not take opportunities to get feedback yourself.

Theorists

If you chose statement 3 you may be a theorist, approaching problems logically, step by step, analysing and synthesising, establishing basic assumptions, insisting on a rational approach. You probably hate uncertainty and will have trouble with the chapter on creativity, while loving complex problems which have a clear structure. You will hate having to work with problems where you do not have all the information you need, or where some of the factors can be assessed only subjectively. You may find it infuriating to work with people with a strongly activist style. You will love the more theoretical aspects of your courses, but when you come to apply them in a real situation you may be somewhat at a loss.

Pragmatists

If you chose statement 4 you will love new ideas *provided* you can put them into practice. You will hate open-ended discussion and love problems and the search for a better way of doing things. Theoretical aspects of your courses may leave you cold, but you will really enjoy any skills development as long as there is adequate feedback on performance. You will prefer learning from case study discussions to sitting through lectures and, if you are a part-time student, will benefit greatly from the chance to apply what you are learning to your job. You may tend to leap to practical solutions to problems without thinking about either the conceptual underpinning of what you are doing or whether a more creative approach might be possible.

Any simple classification of something as complex as learning will be an over-simplification. And the self-assessment questions above are crude. If you want a more accurate picture you need to work through the full inventory. But the strengths and weaknesses identified above suggest that if you have a strong tendency to one learning style then you need to be aware of its associated risks and plan ways of coping with these. Furthermore, it is worth seeing whether you can become a more effective learner by developing some of the strengths of your non-preferred styles. Your years as a student offer you an ideal opportunity to do this. The following exercise is designed to help. You will need to do the suggested activities over a period of time, in parallel with other work.

ACTIVITY 3.6

Decide which styles you need to develop. Choose at least six of the following activities and make an action plan for carrying them out. Monitor your progress at regular intervals. Describe your experience of each in your file. This could constitute a useful demonstration of your ability to learn.

To develop activism

- Do something completely out of character at least once a week (examples: talk to strangers, wear something outrageous, go to a new place).
- Force yourself to fragment your day, switching deliberately from one activity to another.
- Force yourself to take a more prominent role in discussions. Determine to say something in the first ten minutes. Volunteer to take the chair or make the next presentation.
- Practise thinking aloud. Next time you are thinking about a problem, bounce ideas off a friend, trying to get into the habit of speaking without thinking first.

To develop reflection

- In discussions, practise observing what other people are saying and doing and thinking about why (this will be useful in Chapter 10).
- Spend some time each evening reflecting on what you have done during the day and what you have learned from it. These notes could usefully be kept in your file.
- Aim to submit a perfect essay/assignment next time. Do several drafts, trying to get appearance and spelling, as well as content, as good as you possibly can.
- Select a topic you have covered in your course that really interests you. Try to find out as much as possible about it and write a short paper summarising this. (If you have the opportunity to speak about your findings, this will link to work on presentation in Chapter 11.)
- Before taking any decision, force yourself to draw up as wide as possible a list of pros and cons.

To become more of a theorist

- Spend at least 30 minutes a day reading something really difficult about one of your subjects, trying to analyse and evaluate the arguments involved.

- If you hit a problem, whether in your studies or elsewhere, try to identify all the causal factors involved, and work out how they were related and what might have averted the problem.
- Before taking any action, ensure that you are absolutely clear about what you are trying to achieve. Having clarified your objectives, see what you can do to increase your chances of success.
- Listen to what people are saying in discussions, trying to identify any dubious assumptions or faulty links in their arguments.
- Practise asking a series of probing questions, persisting until you get an answer that is clear and logical.

To become more of a pragmatist

- When you discuss a problem, make sure that, before stopping, you have agreed what needs to be done, and who will do it, in order to make things better.
- *Do* the practical exercises in this book!
- Ensure that you get feedback on the skills you are practising in the exercises.
- Tackle some practical problem (examples: mending clothes or appliances, choosing and booking a holiday, cooking a meal for friends).

You will find that working through this book will itself help you to develop all four styles to some extent, provided you do all the activities suggested.

THE ROLE OF REFLECTION IN LEARNING

The activities you have done in this chapter should have introduced you to a range of reflective activities, and started you on the road to developing a reflective learning style as part of a 'full circle' approach to learning. Reflection is now seen as crucial to professional development, and is receiving increasing emphasis in undergraduate studies in professionally relevant subjects. It is therefore worth looking in more detail at the role that reflection plays in learning. This will help you to use the process to full effect both for your own development and to meet course requirements for evidence of reflection as part of your assessment. This section therefore looks at how reflection 'works' to strengthen learning, and at why it is important to develop a lifelong habit of reflection. It also covers some of the main reflective tools.

Deep or surface learning?

Much of the argument for reflection rests upon the idea of 'levels' or 'depths' of learning. You might, for example, learn five key theories of motivation, their authors and the textbook diagrams in order to regurgitate them for an examination. This is one level of learning. But it is unlikely that you would then be able to go into a situation where staff seem to be demotivated, find out why and do something to improve the situation in the light of this analysis. Being able simply to reproduce material from the textbook seldom helps you sort out real-life problems. To do this you would require rather more understanding than is implied by mere reproduction, and a deeper level of learning.

Suppose that you get really excited about the idea of motivation and go on to do some more reading, comparing what different authors said and deciding the relative merits of the different theories you encountered, and their weaknesses, perhaps with a view to writing a new paper. Again, this level of learning is different from the simple ability to reproduce material. It is different, too, though in a slightly different way, from learning to apply ideas in a work situation.

Now imagine yourself to be the manager whose behaviour may be contributing to lack of motivation. You may think you are an excellent manager: you are firm with your team, you stand no nonsense. Then you learn that there are different styles of managing, and that the rather authoritarian way you have managed all your life may not be appropriate for your current team, which is made up of highly creative people tasked with finding new ways of doing things. It may be very difficult to come to terms with this, to set aside your long-held beliefs and assumptions and to start to think about people and their needs in a very different way. This is learning on a different level still.

In an educational context, Entwistle (1996) suggests that a *surface approach* is directed merely towards meeting course requirements, often when there is a feeling of being under pressure and/or worried about the work. Study is done without regard to its purpose, beyond that of passing the course. The material is approached as a series of unrelated 'bits'; there is an emphasis on routine memorisation, without making sense of the ideas presented.

A *deep learning approach* is driven by the desire to understand the ideas for yourself, and is associated with an active interest in the subject matter. Thus you try to relate each new idea you come across to your previous knowledge and to any relevant experience. You look for patterns and any underlying metaphors. You look carefully and critically at the author's evidence and logic. Material approached like this is far more likely to be remembered. And if ideas are related not just to other ideas but to relevant experience, they are far more likely to lead to improved practice. A deep learning approach is thus particularly important for any study of vocational relevance.

You might think that if you adopt a deep approach you will inevitably get better marks than by taking a surface approach. Usually you will. And you are more likely to be able to remember what you have learned after the course and be able to incorporate it into your practice as a manager. But it is possible to get so carried away by passion for a subject that you forget the course requirements altogether and actually do worse. It is therefore suggested that a third type of approach, the *strategic approach* is important. This is directed at doing as well as possible on a course, always alert to course requirements and the need to use time and effort to best effect in meeting them, balancing deep and surface learning in order to achieve this. Much of this book is devoted to enabling you to do just that.

Rather than making a simple 'surface–deep' distinction, Moon (1999, p. 128) suggests a series of levels of learning with increasing changes to the way you perceive and think

41

about the world. The division between surface and deep would occur around level 3. She indicates how your tutor or lecturer would detect this in your work. Note the presence of 'reflective' at the two deepest levels (4 and 5).

1 Noticing – represented as 'Memorised representation'.

2 Making sense – represented as 'Reproduction of ideas, ideas not well linked'.

3 Making meaning – represented as 'Meaningful, well integrated, ideas linked'.

4 Working with meaning – represented as 'Meaningful, reflective, well-structured'.

5 Transformative learning – represented as 'Meaningful, reflective, restructured by learner, idiosyncratic or creative'.

Although this book is trying to improve your ability to be an effective strategic learner, and to get really good grades, I firmly believe that it is deep learning which is of importance for your career after you graduate. The emphasis in many of the activities will therefore be to deepen your course learning towards the 'working with meaning' level. This is where you are really engaging with ideas and questioning – and perhaps improving – the mental models with which you make sense of the world. Moon describes this as 'a process of "cognitive house-keeping", thinking over things until they make a better meaning, or exploring or organising the understanding towards a particular purpose or in order that it can be represented in a particular manner'.

This form of learning is far more exciting than surface learning, and has a far more profound impact upon your ability to go on learning from the many experiences you will have throughout your life. Many professional organisations now require evidence of such ongoing reflective learning and practice as a condition for continued membership. If you already have a habit of 'reflective practice' you will need no convincing of its worth. But you may be relatively new to such learning, or yet to experience it. (There is a suggestion that the ability to learn in this way does not develop until around the age of 20.) If so, it is worth paying attention to developing the necessary skills.

The reflective process

You will remember that Kolb *et al.* (1984) suggested that for learning to take place experience needs to be followed by reflection, and then conceptualising, or theory building. Thus you move from action in the real world to a process of detached observation, taking place somewhere inside your head. Clearly this is not surface learning. But the nature of this process was relatively unspecified, and there are still differences of opinion as to how best to reflect. It is something many students struggle with. If you are finding the Kolb cycle a bit too abstract, you may prefer to use a simpler cycle. This was shown to me by one of the best management teachers I have ever met, Dr Reg Butterfield. It has three stages in the cycle: Wot? So Wot? Wot next? This is as 'simple' as can be, and with the misspellings and cartoon faces, totally memorable. At its centre is the essence of the whole process, the 'So wot?' 'So what' is the key question in almost any analysis, followed by the equally important issue of what, therefore, to do in the light of your analysis.

The basic elements for successful reflection include:

- time to reflect
- something to reflect upon
- medium for capturing reflection
- skills in reflection
- honesty
- feedback.

What follows is what seems to work for me and for many of my own students. It is offered for those of you who do not quite know where to start. If your own course has already given you tools, ignore what follows.

Successful reflection depends first and foremost on making time to reflect. Time management will be dealt with shortly, and once you are convinced of the value of reflection, making time for it will become a priority.

So what to reflect upon? Kolb suggests 'experience'. If you are studying while working you may have lots of experience to think about, but experiences gained during your studies are equally relevant to reflection. For example, you might be working on a group project. After a meeting you might ask yourself whether it went well, and if so why? Was there anything that might have gone better? How did you feel during the meeting? Was this how you expected to feel? Why? How did your own behaviour influence others in the group and contribute to the progress you made? Were there ways in which you might have been a more effective team member? What might you do differently next time?

You might reflect, individually or better still as a group, upon how well the team as a whole is progressing towards its objectives, and ask yourself whether there are ways in which this might be improved. Your reflections on your own and others' behaviour in the light of theory – perhaps motivation theory or what you have learned about effective group working – might also help you to realise the significance of parts of that theory that you had not appreciated before. It might make you aware of shortcomings in a particular theory in terms of its ability to cast light on your experience. You might reflect on the content of the project work in the light of theory you have been taught which is potentially relevant to the project itself, and whether you might make fuller use of that theory or seek other theories.

Some of your reflection might be prompted by reading or lectures. After the event you can usefully deepen your learning (and make it far more likely that you will remember the material) by thinking about how what you have read or heard relates to what you already know. Does it contradict other theories or support them? Does it suggest different interpretations of data on which they are based? Does it relate to your own experience, or to things you have read about business in the newspaper? What light does it shine upon things that you didn't fully understand before? Does it make you realise the importance of something that you had previously disregarded? Does it make you doubt something that you had previously assumed might be true?

Much of this more abstract reflection on the relation between different ideas and on the extent to which they are based on firm evidence relates to the *critical thinking* that you will see listed as a key learning outcome of most university-level study. This will be discussed further in the context of critical reading and writing answers to assignments which demonstrate critical thinking skills.

→ Ch 4, 5

Perhaps most important of all, since your primary objective during your course is to *learn*, is to reflect upon the learning process itself. For any experience, whether reading, lecture, other course work or work experience, ask yourself questions such as:

- How did that go?
- How did I feel about the experience?
- What did I learn from it? What did I fail to learn?
- How might I have learned more effectively?
- What will I do differently in future to help me learn better?

You can see from the above that reflection is about asking yourself (or yourselves if doing this in a group) a whole lot of different questions and thinking hard about the answers. It is about being prepared to think about how your own thinking is affecting your actions. It is about realising how your thinking is affecting what you are observing in a situation. You are more likely to be able to 'think about your own thinking' if you are working with one or more other people: this way you can find out that others see things differently from you, and then start exploring both the reasons for, and the implications of, these differences.

The role of feelings in reflection

You may have been surprised to see the 'How did I feel' question above, but exploring your feelings is an important part of reflection. Often, your feelings will highlight areas of concern that you have yet to put into words and signal profitable areas for reflection. Suppose, after a job interview, you ask yourself 'How did I feel?' and get the answer 'somewhat uncomfortable from the very beginning'. If you try to work out the source of this discomfort you may learn a lot. Ask yourself questions like: When did it start? Was it before I even walked into the room? Such reflection might show that you felt unprepared for the interview, with obvious implications for future action. Or perhaps you weren't sure about whether this was a company you wanted to work for – maybe you have concerns about the ethics of their product or way of working. This might affect your choice of companies to apply to in future. Perhaps you felt 'unworthy' of the job? If so, and assuming you were honest on your application and they decided to interview you, does this suggest that perhaps you undervalue yourself? Or did the discomfort start with a particular question that you were asked early on? If so, what was the question and why did it make you feel uncomfortable? I could continue, but you should see by now where exploring feelings can lead you.

Feelings can also be important when you are thinking about things you have read or which someone has said. They tend to be driven by your non-conscious, non-rational brain which has far more processing capacity than the conscious part. Discomfort here may mean that there is a mismatch that you have yet to access consciously. It may be that assumptions which form a central part of your way of looking at the world are being challenged. It is very easy, and feels comfortable, to dismiss such challenges as rubbish. Our very identity stems from the set of assumptions, values and beliefs about ourselves which act as a filter through which we see and interpret what happens to us. We tend to be very protective of our identities. It can be unsettling, even painful, to have them challenged. But it is through such challenges that 'cognitive housekeeping' – or even an extension to our cognitive house – is achieved.

One of my most profoundly disturbing experiences as a very young trainer in the civil service occurred during an interviewing course I ran for people working in the equivalent of 'Personnel'. I went through some of the relevant theory and guidelines for effective interviewing, and then had the course members role play interviews. Nothing very innovative. But a large number of the participants, mainly women in their middle years, who had been interviewing for decades, burst into tears. I had not said anything about their performance. But by reflecting on what they had done in the role plays in the light of the material we had covered, it had dawned on them that for years they had been really bad at interviewing. Part of their identity was 'expert interviewer', and they had been sure that 'their way' was the best, indeed the only way, of going about it.

There are three morals to this story. First, that the women needed to change their way of thinking not only about what they did but also about themselves, as a step on the way to doing it better. Second, it took honesty with themselves to bring about this change. In order to protect themselves they could have decided that the material I was teaching was wrong or that any feedback they received was useless. Honesty in answering reflective questions is an essential component in learning from reflecting. The third message is that such change can be seriously painful, and support may be needed. I was totally unprepared and unqualified to give such support, and failed those women quite badly. You are probably much younger than they were, but you still need to tread carefully when exploring your own assumptions, particularly about yourself, or when working as part of a group which is reflecting.

ACTIVITY 3.7

Think about something you have read or experienced, or perhaps received feedback on, which occasioned some discomfort. Think about your feelings in more depth and try to explore why you felt like that. Note any learning points from this exercise.

TOOLS FOR REFLECTION

You should by now be clear that the main item in your toolkit is a good list of questions. A number of such questions are given above. A slightly longer set is available online, but this is still far from comprehensive. You need to select those questions that work for you, in the contexts in which you are reflecting, adding any which are missing from the list and which you feel are important.

Reflection is essentially a dialogue based around these questions – and honest answers to them – so you need a medium within which this dialogue can take place. I have referred already to the need to create a personal development file as an aid to capturing, evidencing and managing your learning. You should by now have a number of responses to activities that are worthy of filing, so it is time to think about how best to organise this file.

Before doing so, it is worth exploring some of the terms that are used to refer to another important category of tools for reflection, namely different forms and formats that may be helpful. Key among these are learning logs, learning diaries, learning journals, development records, development plans, audio diaries and blogs.

Again, as this is a relatively new area, terms used do not yet have universally agreed definitions. However, some distinctions are worth noting. The first is between a simple record and writing with more reflective content. The second concerns the extent to which you move on from your reflection to planning further learning.

Simple recording

A learning log might be a simple record of what you learned and when. You could, for example, note key learning points from each lecture and each occasion when you did some course-related reading. A simple format would suffice: the following is but one example (adapted from Open University MBA resources for students in a distance learning context).

Event and date	Reason for doing	What I learned from this
2.11.2006 Read first part of course introduction	Required reading	Key management roles, current management challenges (ICTs, globalisation etc.), Kolb's learning cycle
14.11.2006 Attended first tutorial	Get better idea of course (and tutor) requirements	Need to make explicit reference to key concepts in assignments, need to submit on time, word-limit penalities, value of webgroups

Such a factual record can be useful both to sustain motivation and for quick reference after. Professional institutes may require a similarly basic record of continuing professional development. Thus the Chartered Institute of Personnel and Development (CIPD) requires members to keep a record of their development and suggests the following continuing professional development (CPD) recording format – though it allows any reasonable format to be used. (I've included an extract from my own record to show how this might reasonably be used.)

Key dates:	What did you do?	Why?	What did you learn from this?
May 05	Attended London seminar run by BIOSS on their consultancy model	Wanted to see whether this model would be appropriate for inclusion in new course 'The HR Professional'	How Jaques' ideas on levels have been developed into a full consultancy model – this would be a useful example of theory-driven consultancy

You will probably find it convenient to keep such core records online, both for ease of updating and because you may be required to use electronic means to submit your learning log for assessment or your CPD (continuing professional development) record for approval.

Learning journals – a reflective record

Learning logs and development records have their uses but are directed towards demonstrating that learning has taken place (or at least, towards claiming that it has). They do little to encourage reflection.

If you want to create a forum for the sort of dialogue – with yourself, or with others – that constitutes effective reflection, then slightly less structure may be helpful. Indeed, you may find it helpful to have almost no structure. This is where the idea of a learning journal comes in. Reflection is probably most effective if it happens soon after the event upon which you are reflecting, and in a way that is easiest for you to use. Many of my students use either their PDA (personal digital assistant) or a very small notebook which they keep with them at all times. Some make an audio recording – it is important that the medium is one that suits your way of thinking and which is convenient to carry around. You need to be able to note what it was that struck you, and any thoughts about 'wot and wot next' as soon as possible after the 'wot' happened to you, or you read about it in the business pages, or whatever. Thus in my own example above, on the train on the way home I noted in my little book (I'm a paper person):

This felt really weird – why? Think it was mainly time travel element. Last time I was in this room was 30 years ago – when I worked for the DE just around the corner and was doing my MPhil research on Jaques and his levels. Comforting that some ideas endure, though they seem to have developed it quite a lot. The 'flow' idea from Csikszentmihaly really resonates with my own experience of being over- and under-stretched. Someone mentioned this the other day as relevant to some other research. Wonder if/how it relates to coaching. Need to get his book and read more about it. If we want to demonstrate some HR consultancy underpinned by sound theory this would be a really good example to pursue. Need to contact BIOSS to see if they would be willing to provide a case study.

Part of the 'reflective conversation' needs to take place over a period of time, as your thoughts develop and also as you are able to distance yourself from the original event and your reactions to it. If you use a small notebook it is therefore useful to transcribe your jottings to a slightly more permanent location, whether paper-based, on your PC or online. If you have made an audio recording you might want to copy it on to your computer.

It is this rather more permanent record that is normally referred to as a learning journal. While a diary would normally have daily entries, the essence of journal keeping is to record things fairly often, and fairly soon after they happen, but not necessarily daily. Crucially, this record incorporates a strong element of reflection, and captures this in a way that is easy to come back to and add to. It is easy to come back to and modify an electronic record, and for this reason transcribing to your PC is strongly recommended. You can usefully print off your entries to date at any point when you want to peruse them in leisurely fashion in the bath or by a river.

If you prefer the tangibility and portability of a paper journal it is worth leaving alternate pages blank. You can then revisit entries and add further comment on how your thinking has developed or how this item relates to subsequent experience or reading.

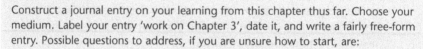
ACTIVITY 3.8

Construct a journal entry on your learning from this chapter thus far. Choose your medium. Label your entry 'work on Chapter 3', date it, and write a fairly free-form entry. Possible questions to address, if you are unsure how to start, are:

- What is the most interesting thing I have read in this chapter and why was it interesting?
- What are the three main things I have learned from it?
- What, if anything, that I previously thought was true now seems as if it may be wrong?
- What was new or surprising in the chapter?
- Was there anything missing that I expected to find? Can I find this some other way?
- What am I still unsure about?
- What did I dislike about this chapter and why?
- Was there anything that particularly interested me? Can I find out more about this?
- What do I intend doing differently as a result of reading this chapter?
- What do I need to do to make it more likely that I will carry out this intention?

The questions in Activity 3.8 suggest a journal based purely on words. However, reflection is likely to be far richer if you extend your recording to include diagrams such as mind maps or rich pictures (see Chapters 4 and 12). One of the key elements in reflection is looking at relationships between things, and diagrams are normally far better for this than are words. If you are doing comparisons between different ideas, say, you may also find it useful to use a table. The golden rule is to use what works for you and what works for the particular sort of thinking which the learning event requires.

→ Ch 4
→ Ch 12

Reflecting in a virtual learning environment

Many universities are creating virtual learning environments (VLEs) for students. These can have many purposes, and for some distance learning institutions they may be the place where most of the learning takes place. Face-to-face institutions may make more limited use of them, but one really useful function is to allow students to construct an 'ePortfolio'. This term is still used in a variety of ways, but it is useful to think of it in terms of an online space which is personal to you. In it you can have an area for constructing and storing your assignments, an area for storing resources you have gathered, study and/or development plans and your reflective writing, your CV and so on. Items in these various storage areas can be collated for different purposes. Thus you could easily extract a relevant part from your learning journal and insert it into an assignment and extract it again for a portfolio needed for accreditation by a professional institute. Furthermore, while parts of your ePortfolio may be private, other parts may be accessible by your tutor or, say, other students who are working with you on a project. This ease of access – both for you and for others – can be a great advantage. Another advantage is that back-up becomes the university's problem, not yours.

MANAGING YOUR LEARNING

→ Ch 2

Expanding the range of learning styles which you can use will improve your ability to learn. So too will an understanding of the ways in which you learn most easily. But you need also to *manage* your learning, using the self-management skills and the classic control model introduced in the previous chapter. It is this approach, with its emphasis on identifying learning needs, setting targets and monitoring progress, that is at the heart of the key skill of 'improving own learning and performance'. As was indicated earlier, the competence approach tries to break skills down into constituent parts. In this case, the skill can be seen as two elements:

- identify targets
- follow schedule to meet targets.

Targets need to be CSMART objectives (challenging, as well as the other criteria) which are fairly short term (achievable within three months) but which contribute to your achieving longer-term personal or career objectives. They should be based on an accurate assessment of strengths and weaknesses (and adequate evidence), should be agreed with your tutor, supervisor or other appropriate person, and regularly reviewed. These agreed targets need to be detailed as an action plan, with dates for achieving them shown. Dates for review of targets need to be included and any revisions as a result of review should be indicated, together with the reasons for change being needed.

Formats for planning

Figure 2.3 in Chapter 2 showed a simple planning chart which can be used to manage your studies as a whole. But your learning journal may throw up things which are more complex than the sort of 'learn X', or 'complete assignment Y' which such a chart easily accommodates. A slightly more complex format may thus be a useful supplement to an overall planning chart. Such a chart is trying to capture the further learning element of the 'wot next' in the Butterfield version of a learning cycle. You can simply extend your log or record to include a 'what next' column, and a column for target dates and for checking when action is complete. But a separate action plan, preferably driven by a combination of your course and your reflections from experience may work better for you.

Again a very simple format may serve. The following example uses a format derived from that suggested by the Chartered Institute of Personnel and Development for demonstrating continuing professional development (CPD) – a condition for remaining a member. (You will find that most professions now require members to show evidence of CPD.) It has four columns:

What do I want to learn?	What will I do to achieve this?	What resources and support will I need?	What will be my success criteria?
How to reflect more effectively	Experiment with the formats provided in this chapter to see what works for me. Discuss with tutor whether I could get some feedback	Notebook. Time. Input from others in my learning set. Feedback	To have actually kept journal for a month and submitted it for feedback To feel I'm learning more effectively To have used output from reflection to drive further learning via plan Feedback from tutor to say this approach is acceptable as evidence

A portfolio 'exhibit' to demonstrate that you are competent at managing your learning area would have to include not only your action plan (and annotations if you chose a brief format), but also a report which communicated your understanding of this whole process, for example detail on how strengths and weaknesses were identified, who agreed targets and why this person was appropriate. It would need to be clear that targets were indeed CSMART.

To show that you have *implemented* the plan according to schedule, using a combination of pure study and learning activities of different kinds and a range of learning materials, for example some computer-based, prioritising activities in order to make the best progress possible, you would need to report on how you did this. You would need to show that you did indeed meet your targets and that you used support from others effectively, though you were not totally reliant on such support, and that you applied feedback on your performance from supervisors, other students or colleagues, to help you learn. You would need also to show that you chose activities which were appropriate to the strengths and weaknesses you identified when setting your targets.

Showing that you had done all these things satisfactorily would probably be more complicated than showing that you could set targets and plan. Again, you would need to include a commentary describing and justifying all the aspects outlined above, for example your chosen priorities and learning activities, and the support you sought and obtained.

LEARNING OPPORTUNITIES AND HOW TO EXPLOIT THEM

By now you should realise that learning is a continuous process. This learning will include not only your ability to do something new (or improve your performance in an area), but also your way of thinking about what is happening, and making sense of it. Whether you think in terms of the control loop or the Kolb cycle, there is some process of sensing results of actions and modifying thinking and/or behaviour as a result: feedback is thus a crucial component. As almost any situation will offer the scope for such feedback, almost any experience offers the potential for learning. But there is an important first step. You need to want to learn, and this means accepting that you are not yet perfect and all-knowing! This may sound obvious in theory but can be quite → Ch 9 difficult in practice. Chapter 9 makes it clearer why. It is very comfortable to see yourself as competent and doing an excellent job. If things do go wrong it is easy to blame other people or outside factors. This is one of the ways of protecting your identity and feeling comfortable with it.

Should someone suggest that there might be room for improvement you see it as a slur on your competence and reject their point ('Yes, but . . .'). Just stop for a minute to check that you are not already saying that, whereas this point may relate to others, you would never act in this way yourself. It takes a reasonable degree of self-confidence to admit that we are not perfect. And many people are more insecure than they like to admit, even to themselves. People who are unsure of themselves will learn much less in steady-state situations: they will not dare to examine their own behaviour and seek feedback on how they can improve. Many of the books currently available on leadership stress the importance of self-awareness to effective leadership, and an honest self-appraisal as a route to this. (Justified) self-confidence is another key element in leadership.

If you are unsure of yourself you are likely both to avoid reflection and self-appraisal, and to avoid unfamiliar situations. Yet new situations and new challenges normally offer far greater learning opportunities than the steady state. Welcoming the new is an important aspect of creativity and of leadership. More prosaically, if you actively seek new situations, you are likely to progress faster in any job than the person who stays with the safe, familiar, 'official' role. This is because of the new skills, understanding and confidence that come from taking on the challenge. Of course you need to understand your strengths and weaknesses. You will lose respect if you push to be allowed to do something way beyond your capacities. Instead, offer to do small extra jobs when a superior is busy, or to cover for a → Ch 15 colleague who is sick. Take on a challenging, but realistic, project. Such things will be noticed by those who can influence your progress, as well as provide material for your CV.

If you have always 'played safe' you can usefully work at improving both your confidence and your motivation to learn. As a student you are in a relatively safe and supportive learning environment. You can take 'risks' very safely. So use the opportunity to experiment with non-preferred learning styles and to practise things you feel unsure about. If you are shy, force yourself to make contributions to group discussions and to make as many presentations as possible. If you hate IT, try to use as many of the bells and whistles on your computer as you can. Sign up for an optional course that you think you will find really difficult. Your confidence will be boosted by trying – and succeeding at – something you thought would be almost impossible. And your desire to learn will also grow.

Work experience

Explore the opportunities for gaining work experience as soon as possible if your experience is limited. Practising your transferable skills in a range of different contexts will help you develop them to a higher level. Potential employers will also be impressed. If your course offers the option of a placement year, start thinking about it *now*. If you are already committed to such a year, start thinking about the sort of placement that would offer the greatest learning opportunities. Think about how you can increase your chances of gaining such a position. If your course does not offer this kind of year, think instead about how to put your vacations to best use.

By the end of this book you should have a clearer idea of what skills areas are most relevant to you, and be much better at finding learning opportunities. But don't wait until then. Each chapter offers you the chance to reflect on your needs for learning and suggests approaches to meeting these needs. If you think about these and discuss them with other people, you should be able to take those actions you most need. Indeed, the activities you have already done should have started this process. And now that you have a clearer understanding of competence and of the learning process, you should be able to do this even better.

ACTIVITY 3.9

This is part of a major exercise which will produce one or more exhibits for a portfolio, provided that you gather evidence and write an explanatory commentary as outlined above. You need at this stage to think about learning which might be relevant to work. Since you need to show that you have used a variety of learning methods, choose something with a practical component, not purely academic learning. Subsequent chapters of this book offer a range of such areas. Your courses may well offer others, as may industrial placements or vacation work.

Select a relevant skill, assess your strengths and weaknesses using as wide a range of information as possible (past learning, exams, self-diagnostic tests, tutor feedback, and so on) and then plan your own development in this area, documenting everything carefully as you go along. If you want to work on an area where the opportunities will not be available for a while, then plan now when you will need to start work, log this prominently in your diary and make sure that you do start work, referring to this chapter as necessary, when the time comes.

ACTIVITY 3.10

Revisit the work you did in Activity 3.1 and the list of transferable skills outlined in Chapter 1. See whether you can add to your file note any learning opportunities that you missed – any situation where you can exercise a relevant skill, either practical or conceptual, and obtain feedback. (You should by now be more aware of possible opportunities.) Now think about whether there are things you are not learning but could be, if you sought the opportunity. The learning style exercises should have provided a starting point for thought.

Learning opportunities might come from adding a feedback and/or reflection dimension to things that you are currently doing, from taking a course that you had perhaps rejected as 'too difficult' or from taking advantage of opportunities outside your course during both term and vacations. Link this to the previous activity, to see whether you can progress your plans at all by taking a broader view of learning opportunities. You should be starting to get into a mindset of continually asking: 'What can I learn and how best can I learn it?'

ACTIVITY 3.11

Think about the past two weeks. What feedback did you receive on things you did? Did you consider it all carefully? Did you reflect on its implications? How might you have gained more feedback? What things did you not do that might have allowed you to learn? Did you take any decisions that would stop you from taking advantage of future potential learning opportunities?

If possible, discuss your thoughts with two or three other people and plan to do three things differently in the next two weeks to make learning more effective. Review progress and note down your reflections at the end of that period.

ORGANISING YOUR FILE

I have talked a lot now about the need to capture your reflections and your action planning in a file and you may be starting to feel that the activities directed at developing a file are just too time consuming. Relax – it doesn't take as long as you might think. And the potential benefits are enormous, even if you are not required to submit your file for assessment. Remember, you are trying to change some of the ways you think and some of the ways you do things so as to contribute substantially to your future success as a manager.

Any change takes time and energy until it is embedded in your normal way of working. In the previous chapter you needed considerable energy to improve your time management. Now you need to apply similar energy levels to developing the habits of reflective practice, of seeking learning opportunities and of using action planning and monitoring to ensure that learning is maximised.

Think back to what you learned about motivation, and apply this to motivating yourself.

- You need a clear goal, and one that will be rewarding to achieve. Remember: you are aiming to manage your learning in order to get a better degree than you otherwise would, and to prepare yourself for a really rewarding career.

- You need to believe that you *can* do it. Using proformas makes it very easy to get started and can be a great help in building your portfolio. If others can do it, so can you! Although the initial time may be a scarce resource, the process is designed to make your learning more effective in future, so should save time overall.

- You need to set yourself manageable milestones and to reward their attainment. Social rewards are powerful – you might like to work with someone on this.

(Providing such rewards is the business of a whole industry of life coaches, but working with a fellow student who is trying to do the same thing allows you to practise 'co-coaching', and give feedback and mutual support.)

You also need to continually reassess your strengths, weaknesses and development needs. It is particularly important to appreciate and value your strengths – from these come both your confidence and your 'competitive advantage' in a group or organisation. As you learn, you will probably become far more realistic in your assessments. To quote Drucker (1999) again:

> Most people think they know what they are good at. They are usually wrong. More often, people know what they are not good at – and even then more people are wrong than right. ... The only way to discover your strengths is through feedback analysis.

Drucker goes on to explain that this involves writing down expected outcomes of all key actions and decisions and revisiting them a year or so later, comparing what really happened with the expectation and learning from the discrepancies. This can be a powerful tool, and it is well worth adding a section to your file for this. It is another reason, too, for leaving space in your learning journal. But you could usefully revisit your SWOT at shorter intervals.

Once you are motivated to reflect and capture your reflections and learning, you can start to think about how you can usefully organise your file. Indeed, you may well be developing your thoughts already, and may be using an ePortfolio in a VLE (virtual learning environment) provided by your university to do so. Whatever the medium, it is important to have an 'at a glance' set of contents/index, so you know how to find things. If you are using paper, then sections will need to be clearly indicated. If you are working in an ePortfolio, it will be easy to link documents electronically. It might be useful to highlight items that you think are particularly good candidates for any official portfolios required for assessment for your qualification, or for a professional institute or a potential employer.

One section will need to capture your assessment (and reassessments) of your development needs. You will also need a planning section, with an overall plan and clear way of logging progress, and a set of specific action plans. You might also want to have a learning log section, where you plan each study session and note key learning points from that session. Your more reflective writing might be with this or a separate section. A section for filing odd resources on learning and self-management could be useful. And you may want to have a section devoted to managing group work. What suits you will depend on the structure of your course, any official file requirements and your preferred learning style. What is important is that you work out a file structure that works for you, and that you use it, and develop it, to maximise your learning.

SUMMARY

This chapter has argued the following:

▪ Learning, in the sense of developing knowledge, skills and ways of thinking that will make you more effective, is clearly crucial both while you are a student and when you start to work in a world that is highly competitive and rapidly changing.

- Learning is usefully seen as a continuous process dependent on feedback. Seeking situations in which such feedback can be obtained, and using it, will increase learning.

- Learning to understand complex situations (as is expected of graduates) involves trying to make sense of what happens, building new models reflecting this sense and testing them to see if experience confirms them.

- People tend to have preferred learning styles which emphasise one part of this cycle at the expense of others. Developing less preferred styles can make learning more effective.

- Reflection is a crucial element in learning, and a habit of reflective practice is essential for any professional.

- Reflection involves a dialogue, with yourself and/or others, in which you question your experiences and responses to them with a view to developing the way in which you think about them and your future practice.

- Learning will be most effective if it is managed, with learning needs identified and action plans drawn up for what needs to be done for the necessary learning to take place. These plans need to be implemented and progress reviewed, with target adjustment if need be.

- This needs to be supplemented by a constant alertness to the learning opportunities which are available, searching for new ones and willingness to take some risks in order to learn.

- Organising relevant materials (plans, reflections, etc.) into some form of personal development file or ePortfolio is essential.

Further information

- Andreas, S. and Faulkner, C. (1996) *NLP: The New Technology of Achievement*, Nicholas Brealey. This provides a range of exercises designed to increase your motivation and accelerate your learning.

- Honey, P. and Mumford, A. (1986) *The Manual of Learning Styles*, Peter Honey.

- Krishnamurti, J. (1995) *The Book of Life*, HarperCollins. This is a useful introduction to Krishnamurti's thinking, containing extracts from his writings during the period 1933–68. It addresses 'learning for life' in a very different way from the present book, but this different perspective can sometimes sharpen your awareness of existing assumptions and preconceptions.

- Moon, J.A. (1999), *Reflection in Learning and Professional Development*, RoutledgeFalmer.

- www.cipd.co.uk

Understanding the value of reflection

When we are asked to reflect on our developing skills, an event or a particular theory, we know it is difficult and generally feel 'what's the point?', even though we may know deep down that it is an essential skill. The pressure on managers to keep moving, to drive their plan forward and come up with new ideas is what we generally consider a manager should be doing. However, if we just *do* things without reflecting on the consequences then we are essentially a non-thinking and non-strategic learner and in later life a similar kind of manager.

By three methods we may learn wisdom: first, by reflection, which is noblest; second, by imitation, which is easiest; and third by experience, which is the bitterest.

Confucius – Chinese philosopher 551–479BC

In this chapter you will:

1. understand the value of reflection as a strategic tool;
2. know how to use several frameworks for reflection;
3. work through some of the models of reflection.

USING THIS CHAPTER

Estimate your current levels of confidence. Mark 1 (poor) and 5 (good) for the following.

I know why reflection is a strategic tool.	I know some of the frameworks for reflecting.	I can work through a structured framework of reflection.

Date: _____

1 Introduction

There is usually a big sigh when we are asked to reflect on something. Reflecting is not easy and it is more than just being in a reflective mood or daydreaming. In order to reflect on an event, you have to be able to describe the event as it occurred and state how things could have been done differently to create a better outcome. If the outcome is perfect, knowing why is equally important so that you are able to repeat the success. If you are reflecting on your skills, you need to describe how well you can do something now and what you need to do to improve. Reflection therefore enables you to verbalise (externalise) what has happened/how things are so you are able to capture the event or activity. It is an essential strategic tool.

Consider the following questions:

- What is it that turns experience into learning?
- What specifically enables you to gain the maximum benefit from the situations you find yourself in?
- How can you apply your experience in new contexts?

(Boud *et al.* 1985)

Boud *et al.* (1985) suggest that structured reflection is the key to learning from experience, and because reflection is difficult, we could do with some support.

2 What is reflection?

According to the *Encyclopaedia of Informal Education* (*InfED*), the American philosopher and educationalist John Dewey (1859–1952) is considered to be a significant figure in progressive education. How we think and reflect in the process of learning was key to his ideas. For Dewey, reflection was both active at the time an event is occurring, referred to as 'incidental reflection', and then later through making sense of that experience through 'systematic reflection', as without systematic reflection the learning can be lost. The poet T.S. Eliot wrote in *The Dry Salvages* (1944 and the third poem of the Four Quartets), 'We had the experience but missed the meaning', and this should be a pertinent reminder of the value of reflection.

The work of Dewey also influenced Donald Schön (1930–1997), another American philosopher. He is known for his work on the value of reflective practice in organisations and the term 'reflective practitioner'. Schön's position on reflection is not dissimilar to that of Dewey and Schön refers to *reflection-in-action* and *reflection-on-action*. *Reflection-in-action* refers to thinking and adjusting what we do 'on the hoof'. Being able to do this enables us to respond flexibly to a given situation and prevents us from sticking to rigid plans. *Reflection-on-action* refers to thinking about an event: what happened, how other people reacted, what the outcome was and the interrelationship between certain actions that affected the outcome. This is what we commonly think reflection is when we are asked to do it. For both Dewey and Schön, making sense of or making explicit what we have learned is the key value of reflection. Much of Schön's work concerned how society, organisations and individuals learn and develop.

How organisations learn became the research area of Peter Senge (1947–) and from him we have the concept of the 'learning organisation'. Learning organisations reflect the ability of individuals within that organisation to openly reflect on what has been learned and take that forward collectively to resolve issues and achieve common goals. Reflections from all individuals within the organisation are considered valuable. Senge refers to this work as the Fifth Discipline, and you may be asked to look at his work in your studies.

3 Why should we reflect?

Most of the time, we are thinking about things without being aware of it, or regarding it as 'reflection' at all. Your reflection at this point is IMPLICIT, it has value, but it is not captured or made explicit. Once you are asked to reflect or critically reflect on something, you start to make it EXPLICIT (i.e. you become conscious about what happened/is happening) and use it strategically. Take a look at Activity 1.

Hot Tip

Search on the internet using the search term 'conscious competence' and it will provide you with a series of informative sites that can help you realise why reflection is an essential strategic tool for a learner, whether as a student or an employee learner.

ACTIVITY 1 Why don't you like reflecting?

If you have already been asked to do some reflection or reflective writing, do you want to scream *WHY*? If you do, you are like many other people (not just students) who feel the same way. So, why are we generally so resistant to reflecting on our learning? One reason is because we have to confront something we may feel uncomfortable about and going back to look at it is not always pleasant. Also, we are not sure how to analyse what happened or what to do with the information we uncover. Look at the table below and tick the views that you have regarding reflection.

What I feel	Usually me	Why do you feel like this?
I find reflection difficult because I don't know what I am supposed to write.		
I find it a waste of time and it just takes too long.		
I can't see where I'm developing skills in my courses so how can I reflect on it?		
I don't know what to do with my PDP when I complete it		

Check the feedback section at the end of the chapter for more information.

This exercise is itself an example of reflection. You possibly had some difficulty getting started, but once you relaxed into it, I am sure you were able to tap into how you felt.

4 What skills do we need to reflect effectively?

Reflection is about you:

- understanding what happened or where you are now with an issue;
- being perceptive enough to 'see' what happened;
- recognising how you felt.

Being perceptive enough to 'read' what has happened and be in touch with your feelings about it will depend a lot on your emotional and social intelligence (see below).

Emotional intelligence

Daniel Goleman, author of the popular book *Emotional Intelligence* (1995), claims that intellectual IQ alone does not give us all the skills needed to be successful in everyday life. We need to develop self-awareness and recognise what others are feeling (empathy), know how to handle our emotions and to have self-discipline. This, Goleman claims, is emotional intelligence (EI). Group work projects, for example, if taken seriously, develop our interpersonal skills (emotional literacy). Similarly, the personal development planner is a tool that enables us to reflect on our progress and personal development. These aspects of your curriculum therefore have good reasons for being there.

According to the Emotional Intelligence network (www.6seconds.org), EI comprises, in essence, three areas: *know yourself, choose yourself, give yourself.*

Emotional intelligence categories	Questions	Application to your studies
Know yourself	▦ What makes you think and feel the way you do? ▦ What parts of your reactions are habitual or consciously thought through? ▦ What are you afraid of/anxious about?	Being honest with yourself enables you to reflect on your qualities and faults. You learn from your experiences. Reflect on this through your studies. This reflection should alert you to habitual actions such as how you behave in groups or how you are at public speaking. When you become aware of this you can then try to prevent yourself being a hostage to previously learned negative reactions.
Choose yourself	▦ How do you know what's right for you? ▦ If you were not afraid or anxious, what would you do? ▦ Can you increase your awareness of your actions?	Manage your feelings. If something starts to stress you, identify exactly what it is and objectively assess why this is a stressor for you. Can you manage it yourself or do you need help?
Give yourself	▦ Am I helping or hurting people? ▦ Am I working interdependently with others? ▦ Have I developed empathy? ▦ Do I work by a set of personal standards?	Be aware of your fellow students. When working together be alert to their needs as well as yours (be empathic).

Source: Adapted from the Emotional Intelligence Network (http://6seconds.org/index.php)

By developing your emotional intelligence, you have the grounding to develop your self-belief and self-confidence, which gives you the insight to see the value of reflection. You also become aware of your own behaviour and you may start to reflect how this impacts on the outcome of an event.

Social intelligence

In 2006 Daniel Goleman wrote another book, about social intelligence. For Goleman, emotional intelligence is concerned with how we handle ourselves and manage our emotions, while social intelligence is about having empathic skills, motivating and inspiring others and generally knowing how to work most effectively with others. We are all aware of people who give us a 'buzz' and make us feel good and those who just seem to drain us.

Social intelligence is about your:

- feelings of self-respect, self-worth;
- ability to use language effectively;
- understanding of social and organisational contexts;
- confidence in being honest (but not impolite!) which others will appreciate;
- empathic qualities, i.e. your ability to 'connect' with people.

In companies, staff appraisal can be carried out using the 360 procedure where everyone you deal with, above and below you, appraise you. As a student this doesn't happen, but your friends may give you feedback (and you them) as well as your tutors. Feedback is a good source for your reflection and you should use it positively.

NOTE If you search 'Daniel Goleman' on the Internet you will find many references to him as well as small videos of him talking about his ideas.

5 Are there frameworks to help me reflect?

There is no one technique for reflection, but very often if you have been asked to reflect you will be given a series of questions to answer. It is important to know the purpose of your reflection and have a structure on which you can focus. Is your reflection concerned with personal development or is it concerned with a particular learning event? Take a look at the lifecycle of the reflection process in Figure 10.1.

Your tutor will probably give you a structure to work from, but if you are left to devise your own then you will need to develop a framework that follows the reflection lifecycle in Figure 10.1. Below are some other frameworks that you could use to help you develop your own reflective cycle.

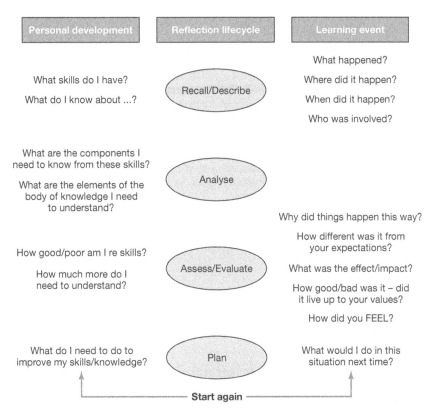

Figure 10.1 The reflection lifecycle

Gibbs (1988) Reflective Cycle

Description   *describe what happened*

Feelings   *describe what were you thinking/feeling*

Evaluation   *identify what was good/bad about the experience*

Analysis   *identify a sense/meaning you can make out of this*

Conclusion   *identify what you could have done differently*

Action   *what would you do differently next time?*

This is a fairly straightforward framework for reflection. Ideally you could use this model to reflect on group work or an oral presentation. If you keep each of your reflections from various group work projects, you can complete several cycles of this reflective framework. Why not start by taking one of your key skills, for example group work, and see how your 'Action' stage works (or not) with the next group project. If you are asked to write a reflective journal then this model would work well. You can repeat the cycle several times during a group project for example; this can be seen as *reflection-in-action*.

Rolfe *et al.* (2001) Reflexive Practice Framework

This framework uses three stages: WHAT?, SO WHAT? and NOW WHAT?

WHAT?	What was the purpose of this event? Describe the event and the people involved. What did I observe? What roles did others play? What was the most difficult/challenging part? What surprised me/was unexpected?
SO WHAT?	What did I learn about myself and those I worked with? What did I do that I thought was effective or not effective? Why was it effective? Could I have done anything differently? Have I improved my understanding of the event/situation? What are the general issues that I can take from this event/situation?
NOW WHAT?	What changes would I make if I repeated this experience? How do I take what I have learned forward – what do I need to do? Are there any areas where I feel it is difficult to make changes/move forward?

You can also apply this to a personal situation or an (critical) event like an oral presentation.

6 When will I need to use reflection on my course?

Reflection can occur in many ways during your studies, with some more formal (as described above) and others more informal and much shorter. One of the important characteristics of being a graduate will be this ability to be a reflective practitioner when you leave.

> *Critical reflection is taken to mean a deliberate process when the candidate takes time, within the course of their work, to focus on their performance and think carefully about the thinking that led to particular actions, what happened and what they are learning from the experience, in order to inform what they might do in the future (Qualifications Curriculum Authority, 2001, 8).*

Reflecting on your key skills

One generic area for reflecting on practice is via your personal development planning document and this is very often concerned with the current state of your knowledge and your developing key skills. If you have to do this, you will usually be given a structure for the document – see Activity 2.

ACTIVITY 2 Reflecting on your key skills

Take time to consider your key skills at this point in time. This table offers some suggestions, but feel free to use your own.

Key skill	Confidence level 1–5		■ Evidence of your competence ■ Plan progress
	Now	Aspire to be at end of the year	
Writing – I have the ability to write a variety of essays and reports clearly, accurately and coherently. I can write these documents with the correct structure and appropriate vocabulary.			*e.g. through tutor feedback*
Referencing material – I have the ability to correctly reference sources I use.			
Oral presentations – I have the ability to structure my talk so that it is focused and well organised. I use effective visual aids and engage with the audience through good eye contact.			
Working with others – I understand how groups work together and the issues involved in successful group work. I am developing my ability to work effectively in groups.			
IT – I have the ability to use standard office software effectively and software appropriate for my technical area.			
Application of number – I have the ability to carry out simple financial calculations, basic statistical techniques and use mathematics as needed for my course.			
Solving problems – I have the ability to solve more complex problems within my subject area.			
Improving your own performance – I have the ability to reflect on my progress and understand how to improve.			
Comment on skills you want to improve and why, and also on those skills you are happy with and say why.			

Commenting (a less emotionally loaded word than 'reflect') on your skills' development allows you to identify precisely where you need to improve and how to action that. How you *action* improvement is key to reflective practice.

Being able to work in a group and become a real team is also a key skill you need to develop and reflect on. See Activity 3.

ACTIVITY 3 Reflecting on your group working skills

Working in a team: reflective log

Setting up the team

Describe how you went through the stages of forming a team: eliciting strengths of individuals, forming ground rules, understanding the task and defining areas of responsibility. Could you identify team members with different roles? Check Chapter 5, 'Working in a real and diverse team'. What role did you play in the group?

Reflect

What would you do differently next time when forming a team? Reflect on how effectively the team worked together as a group. Reflect on how YOU could improve your role in a team.

Working to plan

Describe any working schedule/plan you may have developed for your project. How did you identify roles and tasks in order to complete your plan? Did you have structured meetings/agendas? Chair person? Minute-taker? Were there any problems getting the group together? How focused was the team? Did everyone take part? Were the actions from meetings clear? What do you feel about the outcome of your group project?

Reflect

What procedures did you have in place that worked or didn't work? What have you learned from the procedures you put in place? How would you change it next time (if necessary)? If your procedures were good, say why. Comment on how you would improve the team to make it function better as a real team. Also reflect on why the good points were good and how you can make sure you repeat this next time. How did YOU FEEL in the group?

Assessing the output of the group

Describe and **reflect** on your output from the group. Was the output to the standard required by the lecturer? Was the output at a lower standard than you wanted? How could you improve standards in a group next time? Did you feel YOUR output was far higher than expected and how did you feel about that?

Overall

What would you change next time in terms of your behaviour and group processes?

NOTE Remember, if you are being assessed on your reflection of group work or another learning event, you will get good marks for your ability to reflect and *not* whether you got something right or not. This kind of assessment is about you being honest and perceptive enough to see where the mistakes are and how you would deal with it in the future.

End-of-unit/module evaluation

Your tutor will probably give you a form to complete at the end of the course and there will be a space to offer your views on the delivery of the course. Take time to think about this in a truly reflective way and do not just enter comments based on your like/dislike of the tutor or the subject.

Giving feedback to your department/school in a more formal setting

Many institutions have something similar to a staff–student committee that enables student representatives for the year to put their views forward in a more formal setting. Once again, truly reflect on how your year is developing and give your comments to your representative. Try to consider all aspects of the issue you raised so that you are not moaning because things are not just how you like them.

Focus groups and surveys

Sometimes an issue may arise in your department/school and they want to find out your views. In order to do this they can (a) talk to you all as a group, (b) send out a questionnaire or (c) hold a focus group. A focus group is a sample of students from your department, who comment on the issue under discussion and give their views. Take this opportunity again to reflect on the improvements your department is trying to make.

Using feedback to reflect on your development

Feedback from your tutor – be that on your coursework, in class generally, or a one-to-one meeting – is an ideal opportunity for you to reflect on how you are developing. If you are not getting the feedback you need, why not make a note on your coursework to your tutor asking for a specific kind of feedback. This would really show your maturity.

Work-based learning and placements

This will be a more formal aspect of reflection. You will probably be given a learning agreement which will comprise a set of learning outcomes. You will be expected to show, with evidence, how your placement has achieved these learning outcomes. Your ability to reflect on the skills and knowledge you are developing at this time will be crucial.

7 On reflection

Reflection is essentially a strategic thinking tool that enables you to externalise an experience in order to learn from it. Being able to reflect is a skill that you need to learn and it doesn't always come easily. We need to become more observant during a critical learning event (here we are using 'critical' to mean important) in order to process what happened.

The exercises at the end of each chapter in this book are also a small reflective activity and the more you get used to doing these, the more comfortable you will be with reflection in general. Remember, this is a life skill you are developing and as a future business leader it is non-negotiable.

ACTIVITY 4 Upgrade your personal development planner

Grade your confidence on a scale of 1–5 where 1 = poor and 5 = good

My 'reflecting' skills	Confidence level 1–5	Plans to improve
I know why reflection is a strategic tool.		
I know some of the frameworks for reflecting.		
I can work through a structured reflective framework.		

Date: _____

Getting extra help

- Using the internet and searching on 'critical reflection', 'critical thinking', 'reflective practitioner' etc. will bring more information than you can deal with.
- If at all in doubt about any kind of reflection you have been asked to do, clarify what is needed immediately with your tutor.

Summary of this chapter

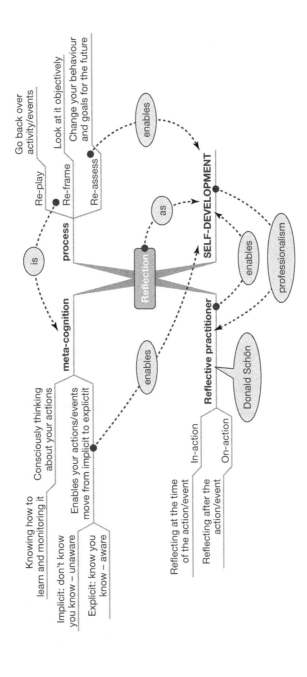

Feedback on activities

ACTIVITY 1: Why don't you like reflecting?

What I feel	Usually me	Think again
I find reflection difficult because I don't know what I am supposed to write.		Sometimes it is difficult when you first start to be objective about your own behaviour or the skills and knowledge you have. Work with a friend – you may want to exchange views about each other. Or, if you are reflecting on group work, do the following. Everyone places an envelope with their name on it and puts it on their chair. Members of the group write a comment ('you are good at', 'you could improve') on separate pieces of paper (anonymously) which are put it in that person's envelope. You then open your envelopes in private. This will give you something to consider for your reflection.
I find it a waste of time and it just takes too long.		OK, don't call it 'reflecting', sometimes the word can put you off. Make a list of some important key skills or things you need to know and note whether you can do them *well, OK or poorly* and work out how you can improve. If someone asked you in an interview if you were a good team player, how would you answer? If they asked what makes a good team player, what would you say?
I can't see where I'm developing skills in my courses so how can I reflect on it?		Each course/unit should have a description of what you'll be expected to do along with the assessment. Check the learning outcomes and the assessments (these should include a list of skills you're learning) and from this you can see what skills and knowledge you are developing.
I don't know what to do with my PDP when I complete it.		Your PDP should be part of every year in your degree. In some degrees it is built into the first year and then vaguely mentioned in years after that. Try to keep it up-to-date – this is for you and you can use it to adjust your CV and keep you prepared for those interviews, even for part-time work.

References

■ Boud, D., Keogh, R. and Walker, D. (eds) (1985) *Reflection: Turning Experience into Learning*. London, Kogan Page.

■ Eliot, T.S. (1944) 'The Dry Salvages' from the *Four Quartets*, available online at: www.tristan.icom43.net/quartets/ [last accessed September 2009].

■ Gibbs, G. (1988) This work is now out of print, but you can access it from http://distributedresearch.net/wiki/index.php/Gibbs_reflective_Cycle [last accessed September 2009].

■ Goleman, D. (1995) *Emotional Intelligence*. New York, Bantam Books.

■ Goleman, D. (2006) *Social Intelligence: The New Science of Human Relationships.* New York, Bantam Dell Publishing Group.

■ *InfED The Encyclopaedia of Informal Education*, www.infed.org/ [last accessed September 2009].

■ QCA (2001) Guidance on Key Skills Qualifications at Level 4, *Publication of the Qualifications and Curriculum Authority*. London [online] www.qca.org.uk/pdf. asp?/nq/ks/ks_guide.pdf [last accessed 12 December 2001]

■ Rolfe, G., Freshwater, D. and Jasper, M. (2001) *Critical Reflection for Nursing and the Helping Professions*. Basingstoke, Palgrave.

■ Schön, D. A. (1983) *Reflective Practitioner: How Professionals Think in Action*. New York, Basic Books.

■ Senge, P. (1990) *The Fifth Discipline: The Art and Practice of the Learning Organisation*. New York, Doubleday.

Succeeding in exams and assessments

Understanding the processes involved in revision and exam-sitting

This book aims to support students who want to succeed in university exams. Achieving this goal will be much easier if you start with a mental picture of the different processes involved in revision and exam-sitting and use this information to arrive at a strategy to guide your efforts.

Key topics

- Information gathering
- Information processing
- Information retrieval and delivery

Key terms

Autonomous learner   Displacement activity   Learning objectives
Learning outcomes   Learning styles   Marking criteria

If you wish to revise effectively, it is crucial that you know what you are trying to accomplish. One way of gaining this understanding is to divide the revision and exam-sitting process into components and look at what you need to achieve at each stage. The process is essentially about managing information – the facts and understanding gained during your course – and can be separated into three main elements:

- information gathering;
- information processing; and
- information retrieval and delivery.

If you do the right things in each of these phases you will greatly increase your chances of achieving excellent grades.

From Chapter 1 of *How to Succeed in Exams & Assessments*, 2/e. Kathleen McMillan and Jonathan Weyers. © Pearson Education Limited 2007, 2010 2011. All rights reserved.

● Information gathering

As a result of attending lectures, tutorials or practicals, and from carrying out additional background reading, you will have access to a large amount of information in the form of lecture notes, handouts, printouts (for example, PowerPoint presentations), tutorial or practical notes, textbooks, notes from textbooks and other sources, coursework you may have carried out, and online material. You will probably be able to consult two other vital resources: learning objectives (or learning outcomes) and past exam papers. You should not forget to consult any feedback that you received on coursework assignments as this may give you useful direction on areas of weakness or aspects that require more attention on your part.

In this phase of revision your aim is to ensure that you have copies of all that you require close to hand, and to make sure that it is well organised so that you can consult what you need, quickly:

❑ Check that you have all the lecture notes and make arrangements to download or copy them, if you do not have these things in place.

❑ File your notes in sequence.

❑ Buy or borrow the textbooks that support your course (check the reading list in the course handbook). Alternatively, look these up in your library catalogue and place reservations on them if they are available only on limited access.

❑ Gather together all other materials that might be relevant, such as completed coursework with feedback.

❑ Bookmark any online resources that you might be expected to consult.

❑ Obtain copies of past papers and model answers, if available.

❑ Find out where the learning objectives or outcomes are published (for example, in the course handbook), and make a copy of them.

❑ Look in your course handbook for any special guidance notes on the exam and its format.

 Managing the time taken for information gathering

You must not let the information gathering phase take up too much of your revision time - recognise that it can be a displacement activity and limit the time you allocate to it within your revision timetable (Ch 8).

There are many potential sources of information about any topic, and a key aspect of your early university education is that you are guided by your tutors as to what is important and reliable, and what is not. Students at higher levels are expected to carry out elements of this task for themselves, as autonomous learners. Working out exactly how much and what kind of extra information you require is closely linked to how you will need to process it.

What is autonomous learning?

At university, you are normally expected to frame your own learning within the context of your course. This self-management is often referred to as 'autonomy' and means that you need to be able to work on your own, defining the knowledge and understanding that you need to achieve goals, solve problems and create new outcomes. The ability to learn autonomously develops over time. As you become more experienced as a student, you will recognise and develop skills and approaches that will make you an independent learner.

● Information processing

This revision phase involves analysing and manipulating the material you have gathered, with the learning objectives and past exam papers in mind. The principle is not to study passively, for example, by reading through the written material, but to try to do something active, to help you to memorise it (Ch 11 and Ch 12).

Thinking about thinking

It is important to recognise that university teaching is not solely about information transfer where you just accumulate information and memorise a series of facts from lectures and other source material. You must be able *use* information. In short, you must develop skills in critical thinking. The facts are still required, but it is what you do with them - the critical thinking - in response to the exam or assessment instruction that is important (Ch 15). Benjamin Bloom, a noted educational psychologist, and colleagues, identified six different stages involved in the acquisition of learning and the process of thinking. These are popularly listed as:

- Knowledge
- Comprehension
- Application
- Analysis
- Synthesis
- Evaluation

Bloom *et al*. (1956) showed that students were expected to progress through this scale of thought-processing during their studies (Table 1.1). Looking at this table, you may recognise that your school or college work mainly focussed on knowledge, comprehension and application, while your university tutors tend to expect more in terms of analysis, synthesis and evaluation. These expectations are sometimes closely linked to the instruction words used in exam questions. Table 1.1 provides a few examples. However, take care when interpreting these instructions, as processes and tasks may mean different things in different subjects. For example, while 'description'

Table 1.1 **A classification of learning objectives derived from the work of Benjamin Bloom and colleagues (1956)**

Taxonomy of learning objectives (in ascending order of difficulty)	Typical question instructions
Knowledge. If you know a fact, you have it at your disposal and can *recall* or *recognise* it. This does not mean you necessarily understand it at a higher level	• Define • Describe • Identify
Comprehension. To comprehend a fact means that you *understand* what it means	• Contrast • Discuss • Interpret
Application. To apply a fact means that you can *put it to use*	• Demonstrate • Calculate • Illustrate
Analysis. To analyse information means that you are able to *break it down into parts* and show how these components *fit together*	• Analyse • Explain • Compare
Synthesis. To synthesise, you need to be able to *extract relevant facts* from a body of knowledge and use these to *address an issue in a novel way* or *create something new*	• Compose • Create • Integrate
Evaluation. If you evaluate information, you *arrive at a judgement* based on its importance relative to the topic being addressed	• Recommend • Support • Draw a conclusion

might imply a lower-level activity in the arts, it might involve high-level skills in subjects such as architecture.

When you analyse the instructions used in exam questions, you should take into account what type of thinking process the examiner has asked you to carry out, and try your best to reach the required level.

Thinking about learning

When starting out at university, it may be useful to consider or reconsider the ways in which you learn best. This is a personal matter: people differ greatly in their preferences for processing and retrieving information. For some students, developing an understanding of this aspect of their character makes a huge difference to their levels of attainment. Chapter 4 considers various types of learning personality, different methods of diagnosing your learning style, and the best ways of approaching study and revision once you know where your learning preferences lie.

Understanding the university exam system

Your department or school will provide plenty of helpful information about assessment. You can find it in course or programme handbooks, printed or online. Accessing this material will help you process the course material and your notes appropriately.

● **Learning objectives/outcomes.** These signify what your tutors believe you should be able to accomplish after participating in the different parts of the syllabus and carrying out the further studies they have recommended. They are a vital resource to you when revising, as they will help you interpret the course materials correctly and gain clues about the sorts of exam questions that will be set (Ch 9).

Keys to successful information processing

As part of an approach based on active revision, you will probably wish to reduce or 'distil' the notes you have made (Ch 11). This can only be done effectively with a clear idea of the sort of questions that will be asked and an indication of the depth at which you will be expected to deal with the material. In part, this information can be obtained by studying the learning objectives or outcomes and past exam papers.

- **Design of exam papers.** To process information effectively as part of your revision, it is essential to look at past papers. These will be valuable in three respects:
  - **Type of exam.** Tutors use different forms of assessment, depending on which aspects of your learning they wish to evaluate (Ch 17 and Ch 21). If you understand why they have chosen a particular form, you can adjust your revision strategy to take this into account.
  - **Style of questions.** The ways in which you will be expected to process the information you have collated can be deduced from the style of questions in past papers. For example, you can figure out the scope of knowledge and depth of understanding that will be expected by relating each question to the learning objectives and the syllabus as taught (Ch 9).
  - **Weighting of marks.** Information about the proportion of marks allocated to different questions or sections of a paper will give you an indication of the effort you should put into each topic within your revision timetable (and during the exam). As a rough guide, the proportion of time spent revising, or answering specific questions in exams, should match the proportion of marks allocated. However, you may wish to adjust this balance if a particular topic is difficult for you (Ch 8 and Ch 15).

If past papers are not available in any of your subjects, you should consider meeting with others in your class to see if, together, you can come up with ideas about potential questions and styles of question (Ch 6 and Ch 9).

 Beware of changes to the syllabus or to the construction of exam papers

It is worth remembering that courses may change over time, as can the staff teaching them. This can have a considerable impact on content and the course structure. These should be flagged to you within the course handbook, or by tutors, but it might be worth confirming with the course leader or departmental administrator if you sense a mismatch between the syllabus as taught and the learning objectives or question papers. The same applies to checking whether you can assume that this year's exam papers will be constructed in the same way as in previous years.

- **Marking criteria.** These statements indicate the levels of attainment that tutors expect for different grades (Ch 2). They are the benchmarks for assessing the evidence of your learning, as shown in your responses to assessments and exams. The marking criteria are useful to look at before you start revising: allied with an understanding of Table 1.1, they will give you a better feel for how deep your understanding should be and for the standards that apply to your work.

Using feedback from past exams and assessment

Feedback you have received about your previous exam and assessment performances (Ch 10) should affect how you carry out information processing during revision. For example, this might indicate that your answers have lacked relevance or sufficient depth. You should therefore adjust your approach to reflect any comments, perhaps by ensuring that you are applying higher-level thinking skills (Table 1.1) or have committed relevant facts to memory (Ch 12).

● Information retrieval and delivery

The important part of this phase will occur within the exam hall as you answer the specific questions that have been set, but it is vital to recognise that you can practise the skills involved. By doing so, you can reduce nerves and enter the exam hall with confidence. Ways of doing this are considered throughout this book, and include:

- refining the techniques you employ for memorising (Ch 11 and Ch 12);
- testing yourself on individual elements you feel you need to know (Ch 12);
- practising answering exam questions in mock exams (Ch 9);
- discussing how you would approach exams and potential exam questions with a 'study buddy' (Ch 6);
- in quantitative subjects, practising numerical problems (Ch 18).

Having an exam strategy (Ch 15) is essential to ensure that you balance your efforts when 'delivering' information in your answers.

Practical tips for making the most of your revision time

Plan your time. Recognise that you will need to allocate time to study 'out of hours', that is, in the evenings and over weekends – at least in the short term.

Create a revision timetable. The two most important things you can do to make the most of your revision time are to create a plan for your work quickly and to stick to it in a disciplined way (Ch 7 and Ch 8). Without this underpinning, all the other tips given in this book will be reduced in their effectiveness. Remember that you do not need to make your timetable into a work of art as there is always a danger that this becomes a displacement activity that prevents you getting down to real work – a common but flawed strategy that achieves a lot on paper but not much in terms of learning.

Map out the gathering, processing and retrieval aspects of revision within your revision timetable. You should set aside time for each activity.

- Information gathering must occur at the start (or should already have been accomplished), but should not take too long.
- Information processing will probably be the longest phase, and it is worth punctuating it with sessions where you deliberately cross-reference your efforts to learning objectives and past exam papers.
- Allocate some time close to the exams for practising your information retrieval skills.

Spend some time reflecting on past exam performances. Think about changes that you could make to your revision approach that might improve your future performance.

Sort out your non-academic life. You will need space and time to revise properly. Adjust your social commitments as appropriate; ask friends and family to help you out temporarily, perhaps with shopping, cooking or washing. Tidy up your working space so you can study in an organised way.

GO And now . . .

1.1 Find out where learning objectives and past papers are located. Obtain copies at an early stage, and read them as the course material is presented, making notes about how you might wish to adjust your revision strategy to take account of them. For example, you might feel you will need to delve more deeply into certain areas, making extra notes. Alternatively, you might see that there is an expectation for you to read about a specific topic by yourself.

1.2 Create a suitable filing system. If you can develop this as your course proceeds, rather than during your revision time, you will be able to spend less time organising your notes prior to the information processing stage, and will therefore be able to spend as much time as possible understanding and learning the material.

1.3 Take the time to look into your learning personality. Consult Ch 4 for further information. If you already have a good feel for what your learning personality is, then consider what changes to your previous revision approach you could make to take account of this.

Presenting to others

Many people are terrified of presenting to a group at first. Most, with practice, come to enjoy it, though usually with an element of nervousness. This chapter looks at the necessary skills and suggests ways in which you can improve your skills as a presenter. You may not become brilliant at it – such people are rare – but you can become good enough to get high marks and impress employers.

Learning outcomes

By the end of this chapter you should:

- be alert to the things that can go wrong with presentations
- have assessed your own strengths and weaknesses in this area
- be able to structure a presentation in a way that is appropriate to your audience
- be developing your delivery technique
- be using visual aids to good effect
- be confident in handling questions from your audience
- be able to control nervousness.

The final face-to-face communication skill you need is that of making a presentation to a group. Poor presentations can be an ordeal for speaker and audience; good ones can be a delight for both. Furthermore, both good and bad presentations are *remembered*. Whether you are presenting your research results to a group of potential collaborators, talking to a group of senior managers in your own organisation, making a pitch to a potential major client or giving an after-dinner speech for a professional association, it is important to make a good impression. You may pay an invisible price for years to come if you do not. On the other hand, if you do well, unexpected opportunities may come your way far into the future. You will also have an immediate feeling of power and euphoria from having had your audience exactly where you want them.

→ Ch 2, 6, 9 This chapter addresses the problem of nervousness and the skills that you need to make a good presentation. Again, these overlap with skills already covered. Being clear about your objectives, understanding your listeners' (albeit now in the plural) needs, expressing yourself appropriately and clearly and checking understanding will be as important as in one-to-one talking or in making a contribution to a group discussion. But additionally you need to know how to ensure that your audience can see and hear

From Chapter 11 of *The Business Student's Handbook: Skills for study and employment*, 5/e. Sheila Cameron.

you, to gain and hold their attention and to use visual aids to good effect. The bulk of the chapter looks at presenting formally to a captive audience. However, there is a short section on presenting more informally via a poster display with a passing audience.

THE RISKS IN PRESENTATION

Presentations, like written papers or reports, need to be carefully ordered. They need a clear message and should, where possible, use graphs, tables or other illustrations to reinforce the verbal argument. However, the fact that you and your audience are operating in real time makes the risks far greater. If something is difficult to express in writing, you can keep trying until you get it right. If your reader finds that concentration has lapsed, they can go and make a cup of tea, then try reading again from where they 'switched off'. In a live presentation, neither presenter nor audience has a second chance.

There is normally less interchange between speaker and listeners in a formal presentation than in one-to-one or group discussion. Keeping the audience awake, interested and involved is therefore a considerable challenge. You probably know all too well how easy it is to stop concentrating in a lecture and have found sitting still and being 'talked at' a fairly stressful experience. Unfortunately, the older you get, the harder it becomes to be a member of an audience.

As in other areas, the best way to become more aware of what is required is to look at what other people do less than well. You can then look at how those who are more competent do the same thing. Once you are more alert to the different dimensions required, you will be better able to reflect on, and develop, your own skills.

ACTIVITY 11.1

Think of an unsatisfactory presentation that you have attended recently (lectures are fair game here, as well as presentations by fellow students). List all the factors which contributed to your dissatisfaction. Now think of an experience of a good presentation. List any additional features which distinguished this. (You can go on to do this again at the next presentation you attend.)

Good features: _____

_____

Bad features: _____

_____

If your experience is anything like mine, your list of bad practice might include occasions when the speaker did some or even all of the following:

- read a prepared speech in 'written' rather than 'spoken' English
- mumbled, whispered, went too fast or was otherwise inaudible
- used illegible visual aids – perhaps with far too much text in the smallest font
- faced away from you, perhaps while writing on the board or flipchart
- used a hypnotic monotone making sleep irresistible, probably with no visual aids at all
- distributed handouts during the presentation, so that you read these rather than listened
- was muddled incomprehensible, or said nothing you did not already know
- 'lost the thread' by responding at length to barely relevant questions
- went on long beyond the scheduled end
- got into an argument with a single member of the audience.

The remainder of the chapter addresses these common faults as well as covering features which may well have appeared on your list of 'good' points.

ACTIVITY 11.2

→ Ch 1

Did you mention presentation skills as a strength in your SWOT in Chapter 1? If not, use the following questionnaire to assess your skill level (score 5 if the statement is completely true, 4 if mostly true, 3 if it is neither true nor untrue, 2 if it is not very true, and 1 if it is totally untrue)

I have lots of experience in giving presentations   _____

The presentations I give are usually very well received   _____

I always think carefully about what I need to communicate, and how best to do it to any particular audience   _____

I am good at thinking of how to use visual aids to reinforce my message   _____

I am confident in using PowerPoint to produce effective overheads   _____

I think it is really important to watch the audience, and modify a presentation if it does not seem to be working   _____

Total   _____

If your score is 25 or above you should not need this chapter – assuming your assessment of your skills is accurate. Below this, you might think about developing an action plan to improve aspects of your skills.

STRUCTURE

The importance of structure was emphasised in the context of written communications, but it is even more important in a presentation. It is very easy for your audience to lose the thread of what you are saying and very hard for them to find it again if they do. They cannot go back and read the difficult bit again. So the classic advice of 'Say what you are going to say, say it, then tell them what you have said' still holds good.

Introduction

You need to settle your audience, so say who you are, what you are aiming to achieve, how long you will be talking and how you plan to operate. Do you want to save all questions except those for clarification to the end, for example, or are you happy to take questions at any point? Will you be handing out copies of your overhead transparencies (OHTs) at the end or do people need to take notes? Once the ground rules have been established, you then need to outline the main points that you will be covering during your presentation. If you can say something that catches your audience's attention at the outset and makes them *want* to hear what follows, then the presentation is likely to go well.

Good presentations:
- have a clear structure
- are clearly signposted
- are clearly delivered
- use varied visual aids
- interest the audience
- do not overrun.

Main presentation

As with a written report, you need to make clear what situation or topic you are addressing and use evidence to support the arguments you are making. Because of the difficulty of following a spoken argument, you need to make your structure absolutely clear and give your audience as much help as possible on this: 'What I have established thus far is . . . (brief summary). The next point I want to make is . . .'. If you give such pointers at regular intervals, perhaps with OHTs to reinforce them, your audience will find it easier to maintain concentration and to stay with your argument.

Conclusion

This is the 'tell them what you have said' section. You need to summarise the points you have made, again using visual aids to reinforce them if possible. If you are making a proposal, then it is worth emphasising the main points of this again. It is also good practice to thank the audience for their patience and to invite questions or discussion.

DELIVERY TECHNIQUE

If you do come across good presenters, study them carefully to see if there are ways in which you could improve your own performance. Even if you are not exposed to skilled practitioners, the following guidelines will give you a good foundation.

Relate to your audience

Talking to a point on the back wall, in an impersonal style, will put an unhelpful distance between you and your audience. Try to sound human in your introduction. Look at people. Say things in the way that they are most likely to understand. Check with them that you are on the right lines: 'Was that point clear?', 'Can you all see this slide?', 'Am I going too fast?'

Make it easy for people to hear

Speak clearly, not too fast, and vary your tone. Use short sentences and straightforward language, avoiding unnecessary jargon. Use 'spoken language' not 'written language'.

If you have ever heard someone (literally) read a paper they have written, you will probably be all too aware of the difference. If not, try reading part of a journal article out loud, then rephrase it using words you would normally use in talking. Avoid turning your back on your audience (whiteboards are a real hazard here) or being hidden by equipment.

Try to be interesting

Vary your pace and use a variety of visual aids if there are appropriate ones. Even something as simple as showing a pile of ten books on a subject can reinforce the point that there has been a lot written on it. Occasional humour can be useful, but don't overdo it (unless you are making an after-dinner speech, when a high proportion of jokes seems to be the norm). Above all, make the relevance of what you are saying clear. It may be less obvious to your audience why something is significant than it is to you: you need to *work* at making sure that they see it too.

Beware of becoming bogged down in detail

It is far harder to absorb detail from a spoken presentation than from a written report. More often, the detail merely obscures the main point. Try to give only as much detail as you need to make your point. If a fine detail is crucial, it is probably better to give this as a handout for later perusal.

Avoid giving handouts while you speak

The distribution of handouts while you are talking distracts people, and you will lose your audience. It doesn't matter how often you say of a handout 'don't read this now' – the temptation to look at it immediately seems universally irresistible. If you distribute handouts before you start, early arrivals will have something to do while they wait. It will also be clear to them how many additional notes (if any) they need to take. Handouts distributed at the end can be a good way of concluding, but you need to tell people at the outset that you are going to do this, otherwise they can feel annoyed if they have taken careful notes which the handout makes superfluous.

Keep your notes brief

Particularly if you are new to giving presentations, you are likely to be tempted to write out the whole thing. Then you know you can avoid grinding to a stop because all you have to do is keep reading. Writing it out can be helpful, and the reassurance of knowing you *could* read it if absolutely necessary is very comforting. But try to keep that as an emergency measure. Even if you do write out a full-text version, you should also write briefer notes from which, barring the onset of total panic, you will actually speak.

These notes should indicate the key points to be made, in order. Such notes are ideally made on index cards. Number them or join them with a treasury tag just in case you drop them. Trying frantically to reorder a hopeless jumble of cards while facing an audience can be deeply embarrassing. Indicate in your notes each point at which you need to use a visual aid. And cross-refer to your transcript so that you can easily switch to that if necessary. (After a few presentations, when you have never used the full notes, you will probably feel confident enough to dispense with them.)

Watch your audience

You need feedback on your delivery and people may not tell you in words. But you will be able to see, if you look, whether a glaze of incomprehension is stealing over your audience. If so, you may need to slow down and explain more, or perhaps check understanding by asking a question. If eyelids are drooping, you may be going too slowly already or have underestimated the prior knowledge of people there. Or you may need to vary your delivery more. If people are tense, tapping feet or fingers with restrained force, you are seriously getting on their nerves and need to find out why. As soon as you pick up signals that all is not well, try to work out why. Unless you are fairly sure what you are doing wrong, *ask* what the problem is – and adapt your presentation in the light of the answers.

Be honest

Trying to fool people seldom works. If there is a weakness in your case, admit it rather than hoping that no one will notice. If they do notice, they will not think well of you for seemingly failing to spot the weakness yourself. But if you admit to it and have formed a good relationship with your audience, they may help you to strengthen the point. Similarly, pretending to know something when in fact you don't may make you look foolish. But admitting your ignorance may allow someone in the audience who does know to contribute their knowledge – to everyone's advantage.

Manage your time

Inexperienced presenters are often surprised at how little it is possible to communicate in a specified time. This is because they do not allow for speech being slower than reading, for questions of clarification, for introductions, for interim summaries or for use of visual aids. It is important to judge how long a presentation will take and adjust it if a dry run shows that your guess is wrong. Aim to undershoot slightly. It is generally better to risk allowing slightly too long for questions than to run out of time, and to finish a little early rather than overrun.

EFFECTIVE VISUAL AIDS

Communication will be far more effective in either writing or speaking if you use images to reinforce your words. Visual aids have already been mentioned several times: this should have indicated that they are essential in formal presentations of any length or complexity. Such aids have three main functions: they can help the audience *understand* a point; they can help the audience *remember* a point; and they can keep your audience *awake*. To make good use of visual aids, you need to think about how each of your points could be reinforced by an action, an object or a picture, and then how best to achieve this reinforcement. The best visual aid to use will depend on both the point you are making and the audience to whom you are making it.

Visual aids can:
- reinforce key points
- clarify meaning
- aid retention
- keep audience awake.

Some things can be conveyed far more effectively by means other than words alone. Relationships are more clearly shown in diagrams, whereas trends are clearly demonstrated in graphs. Other chapters cover representing data visually and diagramming other aspects of a situation, also incorporating the results in written reports. The same principles apply, though within the restrictions of what can be seen from a distance. Revise these principles if you are in doubt. But although you will probably use visual aids similar to those suitable for a report for most of your points, your scope in a spoken presentation is potentially far wider.

Video clips of products, processes, people or places can be hugely effective. Concrete objects can also make a lasting impression. To take an example, when I am running open events to attract potential Open University students, one thing I need to explain is how distance learning works. It is not always obvious that a subject like management can be studied effectively at a distance. So I *show* the audience a course pack, with all the CDs and written units. I *show* them course assignments, covered in teaching comments from the tutor. I may *show* them extracts from teaching videos or a video of a tutorial. This allows me to convey far more about the course than would a mere description. If I wanted to make a point about the volume of reading on a conventional course, I might show the audience a pile of the books on the recommended reading list.

I have seen speakers hold up broken items to make a point about quality, or a new product to make a different point. Cognitive psychologist Stephen Pinker held up a comb to make a point about the innate distastefulness of using a comb to stir coffee. Such images make a lasting impression – though the point they demonstrated is not always clearly remembered. If the image is too strong, then it may overshadow the point (what *was* the significance of this particular distaste?). But this slight caution aside, apart from points which are made better by use of visual aids, people also tend to remember what they see better than what they hear. It is therefore worth using visual aids even to reinforce points which can be made adequately in words in order to aid their retention.

It is also important to incorporate variety to keep people awake and interested. For any presentation longer than, say, half an hour, it is worth using a range of visual aids for this reason alone. You can mix PowerPoint slides (or prepared OHTs) with diagrams you draw on a board or flipchart at an appropriate point (do this quickly and avoid talking while drawing). If appropriate and you have the facilities, video clips and animated PowerPoint slides (used selectively) can help to enliven the presentation.

If your talk is short, you do not need to work so hard at keeping people's attention, and too much variety in visual aids can be counterproductive. It is better to reserve them for points that are best made visually, plus those which you really wish to emphasise. More will be a distraction.

It is now normal to use presentation software: PowerPoint is virtually the standard in management presentations, although other packages are available. This allows far more flexibility than was available before the invention of the laptop. Suppose you are talking with potential clients prior to a presentation and discover that they have concerns that you had not realised when you prepared your presentation. In a couple of minutes you can add a slide or two to address these. You can easily edit the slides you used on one occasion to provide a modified presentation for another occasion. You can easily incorporate charts and graphs from a report into your presentation, or

→ Ch 7, 14 diagrams from your presentation into a report. The use of PowerPoint was discussed in

Chapter 5, and you should aim to become proficient in the use of presentations software if you are not already.

Whatever the kind of visual aid you are using, consider how to maximise its impact and the message it conveys. Your aim is to communicate, and your visual aids are a tool for this, not something to be considered in isolation. Overcomplexity, too many animations and sound effects and too many slides may actually interfere with communication. Fancy backgrounds distract and reduce clarity. Animations may look impressive but are similarly distracting. While it is sometimes extremely useful to build up a picture a bit at a time, you should restrict use of the facility to such times. Words continually flying in from left and right will seldom help your audience to grasp and retain the points you are making. And now that everyone can use PowerPoint, being expert in its use is less impressive than once it might have been. Remember at all times that you are trying to communicate effectively, and use the tools at your disposal to this end alone.

There are less obvious, but perhaps more serious hazards with PowerPoint in terms of the way that it can easily constrain your presentation to an endless series of bullet points. As Naughton (2003) pointed out, PowerPoint was conceived in a software sales environment, so it tends to turn everything into a sales pitch. There was a version of the Gettysburg address doing the email rounds a while ago that demonstrated this limitation (see **www.norvig.com/Gettysburg** for some light relief on this topic). But Tufte, a Yale professor and expert on visual communication, goes further in his criticism, arguing that PowerPoint's ready-made templates tend to weaken verbal and spatial reasoning and corrupt statistical analysis. He attributes the Columbia space shuttle disaster to a slide that led Nasa to overlook the destructive potential of the crucial loose tile (see 'PowerPoint does rocket science', on Tuft's website **www.edwardtufte.com**). His analysis may also add to your understanding of the idea of argument mapping outlined in Chapter 4.

→ Ch 4

General requirements for visual aids

It may sound blindingly obvious, but many people ignore the requirement for an audience to be able to *see* visual aids if they are to be of use. Even experienced speakers have been known to show slides which reproduce a full-page table from a book, with perhaps 200 numbers in invisibly small type. The amount of effective information you can convey on a slide is surprisingly small. Before finalising your visual aids, check that they will be visible to the normal eye from the same distance as the back of the room in which you will make your presentation. A good rule of thumb is to aim at no more than four points per slide.

Colour can either enhance or hinder clarity. Think about how you use it. I have seen tasteful but totally useless slides in shades of blue on blue, the words invisible from more than three paces. Use both colour and light/dark contrast to enhance legibility and emphasise key points. And be careful about fancy backgrounds: they may look good in themselves but they obscure your message.

For 'transient' presentations, for example on group work, where all you are seeking is to convey your thought processes to fellow students, it is fine to use flip charts or acetates. But it is still important that you manage the amount of information per chart, and ensure that charts will be legible from the farthest seat. (Avoid using red pen, or any light colour, as these are not easily visible at a distance.) You can prepare flipchart sheets in the same way as slides and ask a fellow student to be responsible for displaying the right one on cue. (Trying to talk and manage a flipchart is possible but not easy. It helps considerably to split the responsibility.)

If you are still using OHTs, another obvious point (well, I wish it *were* obvious) is always to use photocopying, not write-on, acetate in a copier. Photocopier acetate is firmer and the box should be clearly labelled as suitable for copying. The write-on sort melts in the machine, making a mess which only the engineer can sort out, and which will make you unpopular all round.

ACTIVITY 11.3

You can easily assemble an exhibit for your portfolio that addresses both your ability to use images and your ability to read and respond to materials. Take as the basis for this a presentation you make in class, perhaps summarising something you have studied. Your presentation needs to include appropriate visual aids. You also need a way of obtaining feedback from your tutor and/or those present. The exhibit should include the notes for your talk and copies of the images used, together with a description of how you selected both content and images, feedback on their effectiveness and what you would do differently next time in the light of this feedback.

HANDLING QUESTIONS

Sometimes questions are helpful, but I have seen them wreck a presentation completely. Until you are fairly experienced, and feel confident that you can handle questions during your talk, it is safer to take substantive questions at the end. Make it clear at the outset that during your presentation you will deal only with requests for clarification and that there will be time for questions at the end. Otherwise, you risk being completely sidetracked from your main argument or disconcerted by challenges to what you are saying before you have completed your case. If you want to postpone a question, either take a note of it so that you do not forget or, better still, ask the questioner to ask it again at the end. This means that your brain is not distracted by trying to remember the question while giving the talk.

When you do accept a question, your listening skills will be important. It is hard to listen carefully when you are nervous, particularly if someone is asking a complex multiple question. If this happens, jot down the key parts of the question, otherwise it is easy to answer the first part and forget all the rest. If you are at all uncertain what the question means, clarify this with the questioner. You may feel that it makes you look stupid if you don't understand. But if the questioner is far from clear it is sensible to pick up on this. You may tie yourself in knots if you try to answer a question that you have only partially understood: this does not look all that impressive either.

If a question challenges what you have said, resist the temptation to become either defensive or aggressive. Take the contrasting view seriously, looking for ways to develop your position in the light of it, unless you are convinced that the questioner really has missed the point of what you were saying or is misinformed. If the point has been missed by the questioner, it is possible that others missed it too, and finding another way of making it may be helpful. But if you cannot quickly satisfy the questioner, it is usually better to suggest that you discuss it after the presentation is finished, rather than get into an argument that will be of little interest to most of the audience.

People ask questions for many reasons. In work presentations, there will be some who are trying to make an impression on the audience, perhaps with a view to establishing themselves as a rival expert or advertising their own business. Or they may simply like being the centre of attention. Where questions are clearly being asked in the questioner's personal interest, it is simplest to thank them for raising their point, agree with as much of the point as you can, perhaps suggest a discussion outside the meeting and move on to the next question.

If questions reveal a genuine weakness in your presentation, it is usually better to accept this and ask for suggestions from the questioner and the audience for ways around the difficulty. You may find that someone can suggest a way forward. If, however, the difficulty seems to you to be much less significant than the questioner is suggesting, you will need to make sure that the audience does not end up devaluing the bulk of what you have said.

POSTER PRESENTATIONS

Thus far the chapter has addressed formal presentations to a (normally) seated audience. At conferences it is common to supplement the formal presentation programme with less formal poster presentations. A large space will be made available, and each presenter will be allocated wall space for a poster. The audience will wander round the room, looking at the various displays and stopping to discuss those of particular interest with the 'presenter', who will be standing by the poster ready to answer questions.

This allows participants access to a much greater number of presenters than would otherwise be the case, and is often used to allow students to present their research. If you are doing a dissertation you may have the opportunity to take part in a poster session within the university or at a larger conference. This sort of presentation is also sometimes used in organisational contexts, at meetings between members of different project groups, so it is worth extending your presentation skills to include this format. In either case the poster presentation tends to be aimed primarily at peers and/or colleagues.

Poster presentations present different communication challenges to the presenter. The 'talking' part tends to be less intimidating: you are talking to people individually or in very small groups. On the other hand, these conversations are equivalent to the 'questions' part of a formal presentation, which is in many respects the most challenging part as much of the control passes to the questioner.

The real challenge for most, however, is in poster design. Typically you will have a space 1 metre high, and 1.5–1.75 metres wide. This space has to work hard for you. As with any communication, your first task is to clarify your objectives. What do you want the poster to achieve? Clearly this will depend on what you are presenting upon and the context in which you are presenting. Are you simply aiming to inform as many participants as possible? If so, what are the key points you are trying to get across? Are you trying to sell yourself or your research, and if so, to whom? Are you aiming to engage colleagues in conversation? If so, what would you particularly like to talk with them about? Are you seeking like-minded people from other universities with whom to network? If so, what would be most likely to interest such people? This is not an exhaustive list. It merely indicates the sort of objectives you might have. You need to be absolutely clear of your objectives on each occasion.

Posters aim to:
- attract
- inform
- start conversations
- advertise your work
- summarise achievements.

Clarity is paramount because 1.5 square metres is not very big, and anything within this space has to be visible from around 1.5 metres away. So every word needs to count, and you need to use pictures (or graphs or whatever) as much as possible. Aim to 'show' rather than 'tell'. A good rule of thumb is 20 per cent text, 40 per cent graphics and 40 per cent space. This last 40 per cent is not a 'waste of precious space'. You could cram more into it, but the overall effect would be far less than the impact of what you can communicate via the 60 per cent if it is well laid out.

Given this limitation on what you can effectively include, there are some important questions to answer.

- What are your (very few) key points?
- How can you convey these graphically?
- How can you lay these out on a poster so that they will communicate to someone walking past at a distance of up to 2 metres?

Remember, you may be in competition with dozens of other posters, and participants will not look in any detail at more than a small proportion of these. You will not have time to talk to everybody even if you attract them. So how can you ensure that you engage those people with whom you are likely to have the most profitable conversations, prime them to ask the most useful questions, and leave a favourable impression both of you personally and of the work that you have done?

If you Google 'poster presentations' you will find a wealth of information on how to lay out posters for maximum impact. The essential messages are:

- You need to say who you are, where you come from and the topic covered by your poster – IN VERY LARGE WRITING.
- You need to have a clear 'path' through the poster so that people can follow the narrative easily.
- You cannot afford to waste a single word – 'Findings' or 'methodology' do not convey information by themselves. Something like '80% misunderstand age

legislation' carries a message. Think newspaper headlines here. Writ large, and with bar charts or other simple graphics to support them.

- You need a way of continuing the exchange when you have 'engaged' someone's interest. At the very least show your email address clearly on the poster. But it is even better to have a handout expanding on key points, with your email address on it. Safest of all, particularly if your key aim is to network, is to have people write *their* email address (or write it for them) and email a more substantial document – the text behind the headlines – a couple of days later, with a note saying how much you enjoyed talking to them.

Figure 11.1 shows two possible layouts for poster presentations for a standard research presentation. You may be able to be far more creative – but do remember the need for clarity from 2 metres distance. Messy and cluttered do not, on the whole, attract.

CONTROLLING YOUR NERVES

It is natural to be nervous when standing up in front of a group of people, whether in formal presentation or in a poster display. The adrenaline it generates can give your performance an excitement that it would otherwise lack, so do not aim to become totally blasé about it. But excess nerves can be a liability, drying your throat and making you physically and verbally clumsy. If you think that you are worrying more than is reasonable, there are several things that can help considerably: get as much practice as you can; concentrate on exposing yourself to similar situations; practise deliberate relaxation; and prepare for each specific presentation.

Increase your confidence in presenting by:
- frequent practice
- relaxation techniques
- thorough preparation.

If you *are* over-nervous, you probably avoid all situations where you need to talk in front of people, or to strangers one to one. But the best way to reduce nervousness is to seek out such situations and force yourself to talk. Find the least threatening situations first – talking to a small group of students before addressing the whole class, getting used to the class before giving a paper at a conference. But *do* it. Each time you will feel less nervous.

This is one form of practice which 'desensitises' you to the general trauma of the situation. Another form is to have one or more 'practice runs' of a specific presentation. This will mean that you are confident about the structure of the talk, have practised some of the phrases you will use, know where to use your OHTs or other visual aids and have checked how long it takes, so that you are not worried about having too much or too little material.

→ Ch 2   Relaxation techniques, discussed as part of stress management in Chapter 2, can help reduce this sort of stress too, though you need to be familiar with the techniques for best effect. If you have not yet practised them, a short period of deep breathing will help. And a *small* alcoholic drink can sometimes be useful.

But your best weapon against nerves is the knowledge that you have done everything possible to prepare for the event, that you have carefully researched your subject and audience, your talk (or poster) is well structured and your notes are well organised,

Sheila Cameron
The Open University

LEADERSHIP: THE ANSWER TO EVERYTHING?

Introduction
xxxxxxxxxxxx
xxxxxxxxxxxx
xxxxxxxxxxxx
xxxxxxxxxxxx
xxxxxxxxxxxx
xxxxxxxxxxxx

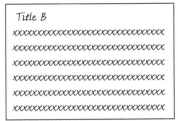

Title C
xxxxxxxxxxxx
xxxxxxxxxxxx
xxxxxxxxxxxx
xxxxxxxxxxxx
xxxxxxxxxxxx
xxxxxxxxxxxx

Title A
xxxxxxxxxxxx
xxxxxxxxxxxx
xxxxxxxxxxxx
xxxxxxxxxxxx
xxxxxxxxxxxx
xxxxxxxxxxxx

Title B
xxxxxxxxxxxxxxxxxxxxxxxxxxxx
xxxxxxxxxxxxxxxxxxxxxxxxxxxx
xxxxxxxxxxxxxxxxxxxxxxxxxxxx
xxxxxxxxxxxxxxxxxxxxxxxxxxxx
xxxxxxxxxxxxxxxxxxxxxxxxxxxx
xxxxxxxxxxxxxxxxxxxxxxxxxxxx

Conclusion
xxxxxxxxxxxx
xxxxxxxxxxxx
xxxxxxxxxxxx
xxxxxxxxxxxx
xxxxxxxxxxxx
xxxxxxxxxxxx

Sheila Cameron
The Open University

LEADERSHIP: THE ANSWER TO EVERYTHING?

Context
xxxxxxxxxxxxxx
xxxxxxxxxxxxxx
xxxxxxxxxxxxxx
xxxxxxxxxxxxxx
xxxxxxxxxxxxxx

2
xxxxxxxxxxxxxx
xxxxxxxxxxxxxx
xxxxxxxxxxxxxx
xxxxxxxxxxxxxx
xxxxxxxxxxxxxx
xxxxxxxxxxxxxx
xxxxxxxxxxxxxx
xxxxxxxxxxxxxx

4
xxxxxxxxxxxxxx
xxxxxxxxxxxxxx
xxxxxxxxxxxxxx
xxxxxxxxxxxxxx
xxxxxxxxxxxxxx
xxxxxxxxxxxxxx
xxxxxxxxxxxxxx
xxxxxxxxxxxxxx
xxxxxxxxxxxxxx

1
xxxxxxxxxxxxxx
xxxxxxxxxxxxxx
xxxxxxxxxxxxxx
xxxxxxxxxxxxxx
xxxxxxxxxxxxxx
xxxxxxxxxxxxxx

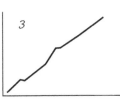

3

5
xxxxxxxxxxxxxx
xxxxxxxxxxxxxx

Fig 11.1 Possible layouts for poster presentations

your visual aids well chosen and you have at your fingertips supporting evidence and examples. Dry runs, described above, can be part of your preparation. Remember, a presentation is a challenge, but it can be exciting and rewarding, and can provoke interesting discussion on a subject dear to your heart. Preparation is so important that more detail is given below.

Even if you have prepared, you may well experience an initial onrush of nerves when you stand up to make a formal presentation. To get you over this, make sure that you have your introductory remarks written out in full, preferably learned by heart. Take a sip of water and a deep breath, go over your introduction and by then you will have calmed down enough to enjoy yourself.

PREPARATION

Preparation is the key to successful presentation and you cannot afford to cut corners if you want to do well. You need to have thought carefully about what to communicate, how to structure it and how to add impact to your arguments by examples and visual aids. For important presentations, you will want to rehearse your arguments several times. Much of this can be done piecemeal, for example while exercising or in a waiting room, *sotto voce*. But you will need one full-scale, real-time rehearsal to check timing, use of aids and flow of arguments – or responses to a poster and likely questions. Ideally, find colleagues or friends to act as an audience and ask them to give you feedback afterwards. If this is impossible, then, for a formal presentation, tape yourself and replay the tape after a decent interval, listening critically and noting points where you need to change something. For a poster, come back to it a few days later and try to pretend that you know nothing about the topic.

If you are giving a presentation at work, to clients or potential customers, or a paper at a conference, your preparation needs to extend to ensuring that the location is set up as you want it, temperature is appropriate and equipment working properly. You do not want to be hunting for porters or chasing around for a fresh bulb for the projector while half the audience has arrived and is watching your increasing panic. So arrive early and make all the necessary checks.

 Preparation for your *next* presentation should be informed by feedback from the last, so it is important to capture as much feedback as possible. Make a note of your immediate reactions in the light of audience response. Do this as soon as possible after the event, noting in your learning journal your feelings and points for future action. If possible, have a friend in the audience charged with giving you their reactions and suggestions. You may even be able to design and distribute a short questionnaire for the audience to complete on leaving. If the presentation is one of a series, this can be extremely useful in helping you to adjust future events to meet audience needs more effectively. If you are likely to have the chance to participate in more than one poster display, feedback may have the same benefits. If you are preparing an exhibit on your presentation skills, it will be important to include all such feedback.

SUMMARY

This chapter has argued the following:

- Presentation skills are an important part of communication in the work context and may indeed be tested during selection procedures.

- During your studies you will have many opportunities to develop these skills and they may even influence some of your marks.

- Successful presentation depends on adequate preparation. You need to be clear on your objectives and those of your audience, and structure is even more important here than with written communications.

- Good visual aids help audience concentration, comprehension and retention. Using PowerPoint or a similar package to project slides from your PC is flexible and looks professional.

- Audibility, visibility and ability to pace your delivery to suit your audience and your content are essential.

- Questions can be an asset or a disruption. Substantive ones are probably best taken at the end.

- Poster displays present major challenges of distilling the core message into words and graphics visible from 1.5–2 metres away.

- Extreme nervousness can be disabling but lower levels can help. Practice, relaxation and preparation will help you to reduce excessive nerves.

Further information

- Bradley, A. (2006) *Successful Presentation Skills*, 3rd edn, Kogan Page.
- Collins, J./Video Arts (1998) *Making Effective Presentations*, Kogan Page.
- Conradi, M. and Hall, R. (2001) *That Presentation Sensation*, Financial Times Prentice Hall.
- Leech, T. (2001) *Say it like Shakespeare*, McGraw-Hil. This gives an interestingly different slant on presenting.
- Manchester Open Learning (1993) *Making Effective Presentations*, Kogan Page.
- Williams, J.S. (1995) *The Right Way to Make Effective Presentations*, Elliot Right Way Books.
- **http://www.ncsu.edu/project/posters/NewSite/** – there are many useful websites but try this one.

SKILL *LEARNING*

- Making Oral and Written Presentations
- Essential Elements of Effective Presentations
- Summary and Behavioral Guidelines

SKILL *PRACTICE*

- Speaking as a Leader
- Quality Circles at Battle Creek Foods

Making Oral and Written Presentations

SKILL DEVELOPMENT OBJECTIVES

- MAKE IMPACTFUL AND ENGAGING ORAL PRESENTATIONS
- WRITE CLEARLY AND PERSUASIVELY
- RESPOND APPROPRIATELY TO QUESTIONS AND CHALLENGES

SKILL *LEARNING*

Making Oral and Written Presentations

Taylor Billingsley was hired as a sales representative in the Apex Communications Corporation in 1972. With training and hard work, she advanced through the levels of the corporation, finally landing the position of senior vice president in charge of personnel. Although she had anticipated this position would require some adjustments, she was surprised at the kinds of challenges she faced during her first few weeks on the job. Taylor had a lot of ideas about how to make the personnel division work more efficiently, but she realized almost immediately she had to convince others to adopt them. In addition, she had to establish her own credibility—to make her employees and interested outsiders understand and appreciate her personal commitments and management style.

In the first few days on the job, Taylor had several opportunities to communicate her philosophy and expectations during a number of meetings with the departments in her division. Some of these meetings were formal, such as when she first accepted the position; others were more informal, including lunch meetings with the division heads. Immediately following the announcement of her appointment, she also wrote a memo to her division heads and their employees outlining some of her ideas for moving the department forward. In separate memos she addressed the personnel development and financial benefits departments, introducing a new project and encouraging them to move ahead full speed to develop a new policy on research teams.

Then Taylor began a round of visits with people who worked in her division. She talked individually with several workers and responded to the questions posed by informal groups. She was asked to write up her evaluation of morale among workers in her division and forward it to the corporate chief executive officer. The latest financial reports released by the company's controller's office revealed that quarterly figures were down unexpectedly; it seemed certain costs had risen dramatically. Taylor was concerned and adjusted a report she had written for a scheduled meeting with the region's top executives to reflect these new developments. Later, she spoke to an assembled employee group in the cafeteria in an effort to calm their fears about job cuts. At another facility located in a tough urban environment, the task proved more difficult. Workers were outspokenly critical of the company and challenged much of the information she presented. Following these meetings, Taylor was the featured dinner speaker at a regional Chamber of Commerce meeting.

Taylor Billingsley was experiencing the challenges of management in her new position. During her first two weeks, she addressed dozens of groups on a broad range of subjects; she wrote even more reports and memos. In most of this communication, Taylor was not simply presenting facts. Instead, she was conveying support, pointing a new direction, generating enthusiasm, communicating a sense of caring, building goodwill, and underscoring the value of teamwork. Some situations called for polite, ceremonial messages; others were confrontational. Some covered familiar material; others stretched her ability to find the right words to convey her ideas. At the end of her first two weeks, Taylor began to appreciate the importance of communication skills.

Managers have to master the basic elements of public communication and be flexible enough to adapt them to varying situations (Barrett, 1977; Mambert, 1976; Peoples, 1988; Sanford & Yeager, 1963; Wilcox, 1967). Like Taylor Billingsley, you may find yourself addressing many different audiences through speeches and in writing. Like Taylor Billingsley, you will probably discover very quickly your effectiveness as a manager depends in large part upon your ability to communicate with your coworkers and customers. Unfortunately, new managers are often lacking in these skills. According to a survey of major business recruiters, the biggest deficiencies in college graduates were the lack of good oral communication and writing skills (*Endicott Report*, 1992). Researchers have observed elaborate training programs are ineffective if basic skills, such as writing, are not present (Maruca, 1996). Considering that speaking and writing skills are central to good management and many new employees are also relatively weak in these areas, we should turn our attention to how managers can improve these two critical skills. Let's focus first on the core ingredients of good communication and then examine the specific requirements of speaking and writing.

Essential Elements of Effective Presentations

How can one person meet all of the communication demands confronting a good manager? There are five basic steps to making effective presentations—we'll label them the Five *S*'s. These five *S*'s are sequential in the sense that each step builds upon the preceding steps. Good communication depends heavily on adequate forethought and preparation. As shown in Figure A.1, the first three steps involve preparation, the fourth and fifth focus on the spoken or written presentation itself. Adequate preparation is the cornerstone of effective communication (Collins and Devanna, 1990; Gelles-Cole, 1985; Wells, 1989).

1. Formulate a *strategy* for the specific audience and occasion. This is the phase in which you develop your purposes in relationship to the audience and situation.

2. Develop a clear *structure*. This step translates your broad strategy into specific content.

3. *Support* your ideas with examples, illustrations, and other material adapted to your audience. This will reinforce your ideas.

4. Prepare your material to create a presentation *style* that will enhance your ideas. How you present your ideas is often as important as what you present.

5. *Supplement* your presentation with confident, informed responses to questions and challenges. Your performance in a spontaneous, free-flowing discussion or exchange of memos should be as impressive and informative as your prepared presentation.

We have maintained throughout this book that effective personal performance is a function of skill, knowledge, and practice. This is especially the case with communication. The key to gaining confidence in making oral and written presentations is preparation

and practice. If you follow the basic five steps, you should be on your way to delivering effective messages. Specific guidelines for implementing these five steps are presented in the following sections.

FORMULATE A SPECIFIC STRATEGY

Identify Your Purpose

Michael Sheehan, a leading communications consultant whose clients include CEOs of major firms and presidential candidates, lists as his number one rule for effective communication: "Know your objective, know your audience. It sounds easy, but it's really the hardest art of communications" (Reingold, 2004). In line with this recommendation, before collecting information or writing notes, you should clarify your general purpose for speaking or writing. Are you trying to motivate, inform, persuade, demonstrate, or teach? Your general purpose is to inform if you are providing information, demonstrating a technique, or delivering a report. When your purpose is to inform, you are concerned with the transmission and retention of ideas and facts. On the other hand, if you are motivating workers for higher production, convincing others to adopt your ideas, or stimulating pride in the company, your general purpose is to persuade. Persuasion requires the use of motivational language, convincing argument, and audience adaptation. Your general purpose may affect how you structure your message and how you supplement your ideas as well as your style of presentation. That is why it is important to identify your general purpose first.

Your specific purpose should be easier to determine once you have identified your general purpose (see Figure A.2). You can discover your specific purpose by asking, "What do I want my listeners to learn?" or "What behaviors or attitudes do I want my listeners to adopt?" You may answer, "I want my listeners or readers to learn the six steps in our new accounting procedure" or "I want them to spend more time with customers." Each of these is a specific purpose. It determines how

---

Figure A.1 | **The Five *S*'s Approach to an Effective Presentation**

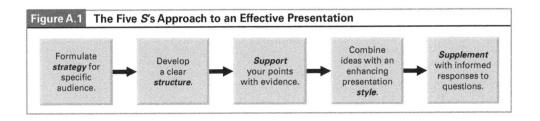

Formulate **strategy** for specific audience. → Develop a clear **structure**. → **Support** your points with evidence. → Combine ideas with an enhancing presentation **style**. → **Supplement** with informed responses to questions.

Figure A.2 Determining Your Purpose

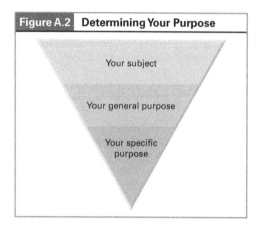

Your subject

Your general purpose

Your specific purpose

you will tailor the remainder of your preparation to your audience and the demands of the situation.

Tailor Your Message to Your Specific Audience

The success of your communication is partially dependent on your audience's understanding and receptivity.

The key to developing an audience-appropriate message is to understand their knowledge of the topic, their attitude toward your message, and their expectations of your presentation. If they already know what you are trying to teach them, they'll become bored and possibly hostile. Start with what they already know, then expand on it. If you are teaching a new accounting procedure, begin with the one your listeners currently

use, then add the new steps. Remember audiences retain more information if the material is associated with something they already know, rephrased and repeated, reinforced with visual aids, and limited to three to five new ideas. Motivated listeners retain more, so, early in your message, explain how they can use the information.

Your audience's attitudes toward your message are also critical to consider. Hostile receivers don't learn as readily as eager receivers. If your audience is hostile, start by setting realistic goals. If you try to do too much, you might trigger a boomerang effect in which your audience becomes even more hostile. Emphasize common ground by sharing similar values or parallel goals. For example, you might point out that increased profits are good for everyone in the company or everyone has a stake in improving plant conditions.

For hostile or uncommitted listeners it is important to develop a two-sided message (see Table A.1). Present both sides of the issue. Use strong arguments built on logic and extensive evidence (Sprague & Stuart, 1996). Choose neutral language as you develop your ideas. In these situations, it is also important to build your credibility. Show yourself to be calm, fair, reasonable, and well informed. Use humor directed at yourself to ease tension (Sprague & Stuart, 1996).

Meet the Demands of the Situation

Your receivers' expectations of your presentation are also important. The situation frequently determines expectations, such as the level of formality. Some situations clearly demand more formal presentations.

Table A.1 One-Sided Versus Two-Sided Messages

You should use a one-sided message when:

• Your audience already favors your position.

• Your audience is not well educated in general or on the topic.

• You require a public commitment from your audience.

You should use a two-sided message when:

• Your audience initially disagrees with your position.

• Your audience is well educated in general or on the topic.

• Your audience will experience counterpersuasion on the topic.

Research suggests the best way to present a two-sided message is to first give the arguments that support your position. Organize those arguments beginning with the weakest and ending with the strongest. Then, present the argument of your opposition. Organize the opposition arguments beginning with the strongest and ending with the weakest. In this way, you take advantage of your listeners' tendency to remember the most recent thing they hear: your strong argument and your opponent's weak argument.

Source: *Adapted from Sproule, 1991.*

If you are expected to address a board meeting, you should prepare carefully. On the other hand, if you are asked for your off-the-cuff comments, a prepared speech is not appropriate or practical. In this case, it is permissible to present more spontaneous remarks. Written communication also involves certain expectations. Invitations to a company picnic can be posted on bulletin boards, but invitations to a board of directors meeting are sent individually. Some situations are tricky. For example, television often appears informal; however, you should carefully think out your comments. Banquets and ceremonies may encourage an informal, friendly atmosphere, but don't be fooled. These aren't the same settings as one-on-one or small-group events.

The settings of business presentations can create a number of constraints you must anticipate. (Remember forethought and preparation are keys to effective communication.) Consider these common occurrences. A meeting schedule runs over so your 20-minute presentation must be condensed to 5 minutes. Be prepared with a short version that highlights information that will serve your strategy. After presenting your committee's proposal for changing customer service procedures, which the committee has studied for three months, an influential nonmember distributes an outline of a competing proposal. Be prepared to answer specific criticisms of your proposal while maintaining a tone of cordial professionalism.

Language is also affected by the situation. More formal language choices and more correct sentence structure are demanded by formal situations. Slang, colloquialisms, contractions, and less rigid grammar can add to the ease of informal settings. Determine your audience's expectations and adapt your language to them. Most experts agree your language should be one step more intense than your audience's.

DEVELOP A CLEAR STRUCTURE

Begin with a Forecast

In general, an effective introduction does three things. First, it catches the listeners' attention and sets a tone for the message. Second, it provides your listeners with a reason for listening or reading. Finally, it gives them a road map or quick sketch of the message.

At a supervisor's meeting, you might start out your talk on a new plan for production changes this way: "Do you realize we have not changed our basic production process in four years? In that time, seven new competitors have entered the market, and we've lost 9 percent of market share. But with three changes, we can get more production, which will generate 3 percent more profits and pay raises in the next fiscal year. First, we reorganize Bay 2; second, we install a track between the parts room and the assembly line; and, third, we set up a phone connection between the parts room and the assembly line. Let me spend a few minutes filling out the details of each change and explaining why these changes will save us money."

This introduction gets your audience's attention because it portrays the immediacy of the problem and shows why your listeners have an important stake in what you have to say. By setting the larger context of increased competition, you intensify their reason for listening and counter possible resistance to change, which is common in organizations.

Choose an Appropriate Organizational Pattern

Organization is critical because it affects comprehension of the message. Learners retain more when messages are organized. Organization also affects your credibility as a speaker or writer. A person who is organized is viewed more positively than one who is not—and organization affects attitude change. Your receivers are more likely to be influenced by your viewpoint if it is organized. Finally, an organized message is more likely to be retained, and thus to influence the listener.

There are many patterns of organization to choose from (see Table A.2). In general, you should order your thoughts using continua such as time, direction, causal process, problem-solving sequence, complexity, space, or familiarity. A related technique is to organize your material as a series of answers to typical questions. Another common technique is called *sandwiching*. This involves three steps. First, you emphasize the advantages of the plan. Second, you realistically assess the risks or concerns associated with it. Third, you reinforce the benefits by showing how they outweigh the costs, demonstrate how risks can be minimized with proposed safeguards, or show how resistance to change can be overcome.

As you plan your message consider your listeners' orientation. The main question to ask is; "What does my audience already know or think?" Start from that point, then move closer to the desired knowledge or point of view.

Written and spoken communication vary in the amount of detailed information that can be conveyed in a single effort. Because a memo or report can be reread, the receiver doesn't have to remember all the information. However, speeches can't be reheard. It's more important to limit the amount of information presented orally. How many points can you make in a speech?

103

Table A.2	Common Patterns of Organization
STRATEGY	**EXPLANATION**
Chronological	Traces the order of events in a time sequence (such as past, present, and future, or first step, second step, and third step).
Spatial	Arranges major points in terms of physical distance (such as north, central, and south) or direction from each other (such as internal and external).
Causal	Develops ideas from cause (such as diagnosing a disease from its causes) to effect or results to cause (such as from its symptoms to the disease).
Topical	Enumerates aspects of the topic (such as size, color, shape, or texture).
Monroe's Motivated Sequence	Follows a five-step process: 1. Gaining attention 2. Showing a need 3. Presenting a solution 4. Visualizing the results when the solution is implemented 5. Calling for action to implement the solution
Familiarity-acceptance order	Begins with what the listener knows or believes and moves on to new ideas.
Inquiry order	Develops the topic in steps the same way you acquire the information or solve a problem.
Question-answer	Raises and answers a series of listeners' questions.
Problem-solution	First establishes that a problem exists then develops a plan to solve the problem.
Elimination order	Surveys all the available solutions and systematically eliminates each possibility until one remains.

Three main points are preferred by most speakers, but many listeners can remember up to five main points. Seven chunks of information is about the limit of a person's immediate short-term memory at any one time. Since people must remember what you have said if they are to act on it, dividing your speech into no more than five major chunks should make your ideas easier to remember (Miller, 1967). If your presentation is long, consider using visual aids, such as PowerPoint slides or handouts, to reinforce the message.

Use Transitions or Signposts to Signal Your Progress

It is important to give your audience a "road map" at the beginning of your message. Don't stop there. Continue to help them follow you through it. To do this, signal when you're moving from one idea to another by summarizing the first idea, then forecasting the new idea. This is especially important in oral communication, since listeners will only hear your message once; it is critical you provide signposts during your speech. You should indicate major transitions between ideas, such as: "We've just seen how the two standard types of data storage operate, now let's look at the advantages and disadvantages of each storage system." In written form, you can signal transitions by indenting, numbering, or using bullets to highlight information. You can call your reader's attention to key words with italicized or bold print.

Conclude on a High Note

Two important psychological concepts are at work in communication—primacy and recency. Primacy is the first impression received and recency is the last. People tend to remember the first and last things they read or hear in messages. It's easy to understand why the most important parts of any presentation are the first and last impressions it creates. You establish an initial feeling in your introduction that colors the rest of the presentation, and the impression created during the conclusion influences the audience's overall evaluation of your message. Since these are the most important segments of your presentation, they warrant the most preparation. You should plan your message with the beginning and end in mind, that is, consider your specific purpose statement as you develop your introduction and conclusion. Some people write the conclusion first because this allows them to organize the rest of their material so it naturally flows into the conclusion.

Reach closure at the end of your speech or written message by summarizing your ideas for a final time. Research shows this kind of reinforcement helps listeners retain information. Normally, people remember less than 20 percent of what they hear or read. If you preview the information in your introduction, reinforce it in internal summaries, and then summarize in the conclusion, you will increase the odds that your audience will remember your ideas.

The last statements you make after your summary should create a sense of closure and add to the memorability of your message. These statements can take a variety of forms. You can call for action, reinforce your audience's commitment to action, or establish feelings of goodwill (see Table A.3 for further suggestions). For example, you might emphasize legitimacy by highlighting several authoritative quotes, emphasize the "I'm here to help" theme, predict conditions in the future, underscore the utility of your proposal by emphasizing its impact on the bottom line, or use an emotional appeal to increase commitment and loyalty.

SUPPORT YOUR POINTS

Choose a Variety of Support

There are many reasons to use supporting materials, or evidence, as you develop your message. Most research concludes that supporting material makes a great difference in the impact of ideas. This is true even if you are not well known to your receivers or if they find your credibility moderate to low. What kind of support should you choose? Table A.4 illustrates some of the many kinds of supporting materials available. Messages are strongest when they are built upon a variety of supporting materials. For example, reinforce statistics on profit sharing with a specific instance, such as how those numbers will affect a person on the assembly line.

Consider Your Listeners When Choosing Your Support

The kinds of supporting materials you choose partially depends on your audience. If the evidence is new to them, it will have more impact. Videotapes, recordings,

Table A.3	Types of Introductions and Conclusions

When you select an introduction or conclusion, ask yourself if it orients your audience to your purposes and clearly signals the beginning or ending of your speech.

1. Refer to the subject or occasion.
2. Use a personal reference or greeting.
3. Ask a rhetorical question.
4. Make a startling statement.
5. Use a quotation.
6. Tell a humorous story.
7. Use an illustration.
8. Issue a challenge or appeal.
9. Use suspense.
10. Appeal to the listener's self-interest.
11. Employ a visual aid.
12. Refer to a recent incident.
13. Compliment the audience or a member of the audience.
14. Refer to the preceding speaker.
15. Request a specific action.

Table A.4	Types of Supporting Materials
Examples	Specific instances that illustrate the point or clarify the idea: For example, "Our plants in Detroit and Sacramento use Quality Circles."
Statistics	Numbers that express relationships of magnitude, segments, or trends: For example, "Currently, a full 32% of our workforce is involved in Quality Circle decision-making, and that is up 17% over the past two years."
Testimony	The opinions or conclusions of others, particularly experts: For example, "After studying our plants, professor Henry Wilson of the Harvard School of Business observed American workers are not group motivated. He concluded 'American workers cannot be expected to respond well to Quality Circles for that reason.'"

or photos also have greater impact. People who are highly dogmatic are more affected by evidence than those who are not so dogmatic. People are likely to believe evidence that agrees with their own position more than evidence that does not. So their initial position determines the extent to which they will find evidence believable. If your receivers find the source or types of evidence to be believable or credible, it will be more effective (see Table A.5).

Use Visual Aids as Support

There are as many reasons to use visual aids as there are types of visual aids (see Table A.6). Visual aids help people process and retain data (Seiler, 1971). In addition to enhancing comprehension and memory, visual aids can heighten the persuasive impact of your ideas if they engage receivers actively in the communicative exchange. Your credibility and your persuasiveness are enhanced by good visual aids. With these functions in mind, remember visual aids should be simple, clear, and professional (see Table A.7). The purpose of a visual aid is to augment your presentation, not replace it or distract from it. Unfortunately, this last point is lost by many professionals who treat presentations as slide shows in which screen displays and even sound effects—not the presenter—become the center of attention.

Table A.5	Using Supporting Materials

There is a great deal of research on the use of supporting materials or evidence in oral presentations. The following patterns seem to emerge:

1. If you have low to moderate credibility, evidence will probably increase your persuasive effectiveness.

2. There seems to be minimal difference between emotional and logical evidence.

3. Using evidence is usually better than not using it.

4. There seems to be little difference between biased sources and objective sources in their final impact on audiences.

5. Good speech delivery may improve the potency of evidence when sources of the evidence are unknown or have low credibility.

6. Evidence can reinforce the long-term effectiveness of persuasion.

7. Evidence is most effective when listeners are not familiar with it.

8. People are more likely to believe evidence that agrees with their own position.

9. Highly dogmatic people are more affected by evidence than are less dogmatic people.

10. Evidence produces more attitude change when the course and source qualifications are provided.

11. Speakers with low credibility are seen as more credible when they cite evidence.

12. Using irrelevant evidence or poorly qualified sources may produce an effect opposite to what the speaker intends.

Source: *From* Persuasion: Reception, and Responsibility *6th edition by Larson.© 1992. Reprinted with the permission of Wadsworth, a division of Thomson Learning: www.thomsonrights.com. Fax 800 730-2215.*

Table A.6	Functions of Visual Aids

According to research, using effective visual aids in an oral presentation:

- Makes your presentation up to 50% more memorable.
- Significantly clarifies complex or detailed information.
- Portrays you as more professional and better prepared.
- Speeds up group decision making.
- Shortens meeting time by up to 28%.
- Makes your message 43% more persuasive.

Sources: *Osborn & Osborn, 1991, and Gronbeck et al., 1992.*

Computer-aided graphics make it easier than ever to supplement your main ideas with visual materials. They also make it easier to create cluttered, excessive visual and sound images that distract the audience from your strategic message. Select and design visual aids to reinforce your strategy and ideas, and to make them clearer. Keep in mind each type of visual aid communicates information in a different way. In general, visual aids such as slides, photographs, and posters can help an audience *feel* the way you do. They enhance the emotional dimension of a presentation. On the other hand, descriptive or written materials help an audience *think* the way you do. Numbers and charts reinforce cognitive processes; photographs reinforce affective processes. Use tables and graphs to highlight relationships and patterns, not to convey comprehensive data. If necessary, use supplemental handouts of comprehensive tables and charts.

USE AN ENHANCING STYLE

Up to this point, the preparation of oral and written messages is very similar. Whether you intend to deliver

LEARNING

Table A.7	Checklist for Using Visual Aids

As you prepare your visual aids, ask yourself the following questions:

❏ Can I avoid making the visual aid the most important aspect of my speech? Will it be more than just an ornament?

❏ Can I translate complex numbers into bar or line graphs for easier comprehension?

❏ Am I comfortable with using the visual aid? Have I practiced with it so using it is natural, and it does not break the flow of ideas in my speech?

❏ Is it large enough to be seen by everyone without straining?

❏ Is all the printing short and neat?

❏ Is the visual aid colorful and involving? Studies show color highlights aid recall of information.

❏ Are my visual aids professional: neat, attractive, and accurate?

❏ Have I made the necessary arrangements for special visual aids in advance?

❏ Can I use the visual aid without blocking my audience's view of it? Will I be able to maintain good eye contact with my listeners while using the visual aid?

❏ Can I avoid reaching across my body or waving the visual aid in front of my face?

❏ Can I avoid distracting my listeners by keeping the visual aid covered or out of sight before and after I use it?

❏ What will I do if the visual aid fails to work? Am I prepared for unexpected contingencies such as a burned-out projector bulb or a room that cannot be darkened?

❏ Have I planned for assistance or volunteers in advance if they are needed?

❏ Will a pointer be needed?

❏ Will all charts be secured so I don't have to hunt for them on the floor in the middle of my speech?

❏ Am I using a variety of visual aids to increase my listeners' interest?

❏ If I'm using handouts, can I adjust to the distraction caused by passing them around? Can I compete with listeners who will read the handout rather than listen to me?

❏ Can I speak over the noise of a projector or other machine?

a speech or write a memo, you need to develop your strategy by identifying your purposes, structuring your message, and supporting your ideas with evidence. The fourth step requires separate treatment of oral and written messages because they are stylistically very different forms of communication. We'll first focus on oral presentations.

STYLE IN ORAL COMMUNICATION

Prepare Your Notes

The mark of effective presenters is the appearance of effortlessness. Some speakers have such command of their material it appears they are ad libbing. Most of us prefer such a conversational style (see Table A.8), but don't be fooled by appearances. Hours of preparation and practice preceded the actual performance. You've already been introduced to the three steps of preparation, but how do you develop the fourth stage of your preparation for oral communication?

After you have carefully considered your strategy, structure, and support, you should prepare your speaking notes. To do this, simply write your key points in a rough outline following the organizational pattern you have chosen. What you do next depends on your method of presentation. Most often, you will speak in a conversational manner that is not memorized or read; this is referred to as extemporaneous speaking. Extemporaneous presentation is desirable because it is natural and flexible; it applies to most situations. To prepare, copy key words on note cards to stimulate your memory; standard pages are often distracting. Write out quotations, statistics, or anything that requires exact wording. Highlight places where you intend to use visual aids, pause for questions, or present an exhibit. To rehearse, go through the speech, phrasing your ideas in language that seems natural. You may find yourself phrasing ideas with different words each time. That is okay. It will increase the conversational quality of your speech because your words will be typical of oral style and natural expression. It will help you develop flexibility, allowing you to adjust to different wording and flow of ideas.

If the occasion is formal and demands precise wording or exquisite prose, you should prepare a word-for-word manuscript to memorize or read. Then you should rehearse with the manuscript, trying to achieve as much natural flow in the dialogue as possible. This form of presentation is rare, but it may be required for discussing legal and financial issues, making announcements to the press, or conducting special ceremonies. Otherwise, avoid using written scripts and memorization for presentations because they disrupt the natural flow of conversational style and break eye contact with your listeners. Because manuscripts are prepared in written form first, they usually take on the style of written language. Unless you are a practiced speechwriter, your manuscript will sound like written rather than oral speech (see Table A.9).

Practice Your Presentation

It is a good idea to rehearse your presentation under simulated conditions—in a similar room, with listeners who can give you suggestions for improvement. Time your presentation so you know if it is necessary to cut or expand your ideas. Research shows practicing a speech for short periods of time over the course of several days is more successful in reducing anxiety and improving memory than concentrated practice. So give the speech to yourself during breakfast, at your morning coffee break, as you walk to a midafternoon meeting, and before bed. Distributed practice is more efficient and yields better results than massed practice.

Table A.8	Differences Between Public Speaking and Conversation

Folk wisdom holds that giving a speech is just like talking to another person. While it is true most people prefer a conversational style of public speaking, there are at least three noteworthy differences between giving speeches and holding conversations:

1. Public speaking is more highly structured. It requires more detailed planning and development. Specific time limits may be imposed, and the speaker does not have the advantage of being able to respond individually to listeners.

2. Public speaking requires more formal language. Slang, jargon, and poor grammar all lower speaker credibility, even in informal speech situations. Listeners usually react negatively to poor language choices. In fact, many studies show some kinds of language, such as obscene language, dramatically lower a speaker's credibility.

3. Public speaking requires a different method of delivery. The speaker's voice must be adjusted in volume and projection, posture is more correct, and distracting mannerisms and verbal habits are avoided.

Source: *Adapted from Lucas, 1989.*

Table A.9	Differences Between Oral and Written Styles

Why do we instantly recognize a memorized speech? Why does a meeting transcript sound funny? The answer to both questions is oral style differs from written style. Memorized speeches from manuscripts reveal their written style, and conversations that are read reveal their oral style. Oral style differs from written style in the following ways:

1. The average sentence length is shorter (about 16 words) in conversations.

2. Vocabulary is more limited in speaking than in writing. "I" and "you" make up almost 8% of the words used in speaking; fewer than 50 words make up almost half of the total vocabulary we use when we speak.

3. Spoken vocabulary consists of more short words.

4. Speakers use more words referring to themselves such as "I," "me," and "we"; listeners rate this as more interesting.

5. More qualifying terms (such as "much," "many," and "a lot") and allness terms (such as "none," "never," and "always") are used in speaking.

6. More phrases and terms indicating hesitation are apparent in speaking, such as "it seems to me," "apparently," "in my opinion," and "maybe."

7. Fewer precise numbers are used in speaking.

8. Speakers use more contractions and colloquial expressions such as "can't," "wouldn't," "wow," and "chill out."

One final note on language: There is some evidence that we use lexical diversity as a cue to a speaker's socioeconomic status, competence, and perceived similarity.

Source: *Copyright 1978 From* Oral and Written Style *by L. Einhorn. Reproduced by permission of Taylor & Francis Group, LLC. www.taylorandfrancis.com.*

LEARNING

Practice Using Your Visual Aids

This will help you get used to managing them and give you some idea of how long your speech will take with the visual aids. Prepare for the totally unexpected. What if the roar of an overhead plane drowns out your voice? What if the microphone goes dead, a window blows open, or the room becomes extremely hot? Compensate for minor disruptions by slowing your rate, raising your volume a little, and continuing. You will encourage listeners to listen to your message rather than be temporarily distracted. For other disruptions, a good rule of thumb is to respond the same way you would if you were in the audience. Take off your jacket if it is too hot, close the window, raise your voice if listeners can't hear you, or pause to allow a complex idea to sink in.

As you practice, think about how you will channel your anxiety. Most speakers report feeling anxious before they speak; it's normal. To manage your anxiety, channel it into positive energy. Prepare well in advance for the speech—develop your ideas, support them, and practice your delivery. Even if you are anxious, you will have something important to say. It may help to visualize the speaking situation. Close your eyes, relax, and think about how it's going to feel and what your audience will look like as they watch you. Expect to feel a little momentary panic as you get up to speak; it will evaporate as you progress into the speech. Remember to think about your ideas rather than how nervous you feel. Focus on your message. Also remember anxiety about speaking never really goes away. Most experienced speakers still get podium panic. The advantage of experience is you learn how to cope by converting your anxiety into energy and enthusiasm. That gives you an extra sparkle as you speak. Above all, don't tell your listeners you are nervous. This will divert their attention from your ideas to your anxiety. Usually, listeners can't tell a speaker is nervous—only speakers know, and they should keep that secret.

Convey Controlled Enthusiasm for Your Subject

When a survey was given to 1,200 people asking them to identify the characteristics of effective presentations (Peoples, 1988), the results contained adjectives such as flexible, cooperative, audience-oriented, pleasant, and interesting. What was striking about these results is that only the last item on the list of 12 outstanding characteristics was specifically related to the content of the presentations. This suggests the preceding discussion of effective format, while necessary, is not sufficient to guarantee your success. Put another way, a rambling, poorly organized presentation will surely produce an overall negative evaluation. On the other hand, a well-organized, highly logical, and easy-to-follow presentation that is poorly delivered will also be viewed negatively. This study suggests style is extremely important in oral communication.

Years of research on student evaluations of classroom teaching performance have consistently shown that enthusiasm is the hallmark of a good teacher. Students will forgive other deficiencies if the teacher obviously loves the subject and is genuinely interested in conveying that appreciation to the students. The same holds true for presenters. Your posture, tone of voice, and facial expressions are all critical indicators of your attitude. Speak standing if you can, move occasionally, and use gestures to convey an attitude of earnestness. Remember, your audience will become infected with your enthusiasm.

Although enthusiasm is important, it must be controlled. Do not confuse enthusiasm with loudness. A good rule is to use vigorous but conversational tones of voice and inflections. Avoid bellowing or preaching at your listeners. Be sure you can be easily heard and your tone is sufficiently emphatic to convey meaning effectively. In general, your speech should resemble an animated or lively conversation.

Use Delivery to Enhance Your Message

Another key to maintaining audience attention is effective delivery. Eye contact is the most important tool for establishing audience involvement. It makes listeners feel as if they are involved in a one-on-one, semiprivate discussion with you. In this culture, we value directness and honesty. One of the expressions of these values is direct eye contact. Effective eye contact means looking directly at members of the audience, one at a time, on a random, rotating basis. Generally, the smaller the group, the longer you can look at each person. Maintaining eye contact is also your primary source of audience feedback as you are presenting. If your audience appears puzzled, you may need to pause and review your key ideas.

It is important to use physical space and body movement to enhance your message. Remember presentations are like movies, not snapshots. Alternate moving and standing still, speaking and listening, doing and thinking. Intersperse your lecture with chalkboard use, demonstration, audience participation, and audiovisual aids so no single activity occupies a large portion of the presentation. Add some spice to your presentation by including personal anecdotes, references to members of the group, unusual facts, vital information, and vibrant images. Whenever appropriate, arrange the podium area to accommodate physical movement. Physical movement can be used to punctuate important points, signal transitions, build rapport with a person who asks a question, heighten the interest of particular segments of the audience, and help your listeners stay alert by refocusing their attention.

Other aspects of physical space affect the quality of your presentation. If possible, arrange the podium area and seating in the room to remove distractions. In more intimate settings, group participants so there is less space between them. Eliminate unnecessary or distracting materials from the podium, such as unused equipment, signs, and displays. Keep your visual aids covered until they are used and keep the chalkboard clean. Focus your listeners' attention on you and your message.

You can use space to convey intimacy or distance. Position yourself roughly in the middle of your audience from left to right and in a spot where you can comfortably maintain eye contact. With this in mind, you can deliberately alter your presentation style to build rapport with members of the audience. Move closer if you intend to build intimacy or tension; move to a comfortable distance when your ideas are neutral.

Gestures can also add to a presentation. They should appear to be spontaneous and natural in order to enhance, rather than distract from, your message. They should be relaxed, not rigid. Use them to accentuate your normal mode of expression. To some extent, when you concentrate on your message, not your movements, the appropriate gestures will come naturally. Remember your gestures should be smooth, relatively slow, and not too low (below your waist), too high (above your shoulders), or too wide (more than two feet from your body). If you are using a podium, step slightly behind or to the side of the podium so it does not block your listeners' view of your movement. The general rules for gestures change as your audience becomes larger. You must adapt to large groups by making larger, more dramatic gestures.

Avoid any gestures or movements that distract from your message. Irrelevant movement such as jingling change in a pocket, toying with notes, shifting from foot to foot, twisting hair, or adjusting eyeglasses are annoying. In fact, any movement repeated too often creates a distraction. Practice using a variety of body movements to illustrate or describe, enumerate, add emphasis, or direct attention. For variety, some gestures should involve the entire upper body, not just your dominant hand.

STYLE IN WRITTEN COMMUNICATION

Like oral communication, written communication is a skill; it can be learned. Written communication follows the same three preparation steps as oral communication. The writer determines strategies, structure, and support before actually putting pen to paper. As with effective presentations, good writing draws on careful analysis of the audience and situation. In a business setting, "every document is a response to a problem or opportunity requiring that some consensus be achieved or action taken" (Poor, 1992, p. 38).

There are significant differences between oral and written communication style. Although it lacks the interpersonal dimension of immediacy, written communication offers one tremendous advantage over oral communication—it lasts. Written documents can be retained, studied, duplicated, and filed for the future. This means they are essentially capable of conveying much more detailed information. While written communication offers these advantages, it also makes different demands on the communicator; written communication demands precision.

Develop Mechanical Precision in Your Writing

Your professional image is judged by the appearance of your written communication. Cross outs, erasures, typographical errors, or other sloppiness detract from your written message, just as awkward mannerisms can distract from your oral message. Grammatical precision is also required—misspellings, punctuation errors, and poor grammar are marks of uneducated writers. This is certainly not an image you want to convey. You may expect a secretary or clerical worker to catch and correct all these things, and many times that happens. However, when you sign or otherwise endorse the final product, you alone are accountable for any errors it contains. It is essential to develop the habit of proofreading final drafts before you sign them.

Violations of the rules of grammar and punctuation may affect more than just your credibility. They can also disrupt your reader. If the reader is distracted by typos, confusing grammar, or ambiguous pronouns, your ideas may become lost; such errors can cripple the impact of your message. Some recruiters toss out résumés that contain mechanical errors. Their reasoning is if job applicants can't take the time to proofread a short résumé, they may be sloppy on the job, too. Some readers are insulted by poor grammar; others automatically consider themselves superior to the writer. While these may not be logical reactions, they occur, and more important, they block your effectiveness. You may argue correct grammar and punctuation are not vital. Maybe not, but you take a chance every time you present careless work to another reader. Consider the campaign of Charles Day for a seat on local government. His campaign flyers, delivered house to house, carried the banner, "Vote Charles Day for School Bord." Would you want a man who apparently can't spell make decisions on academic matters for your neighborhood schools? The impression is if you don't have the time or incentive to check your own writing, you won't pay attention to details in the work of others.

Practice Factual Precision in Your Writing

Getting the facts right is important. If you send a memo calling for a meeting but record an incorrect meeting date, you'll suffer the consequences of inconveniencing others. Accuracy is critical, but that's just the beginning. It's up to the writer to create sentences that make the meaning unmistakably clear to the reader. Many times writers know the facts but omit important details in writing. Omission occurs when you have all the facts or circumstances but as you write, you assume the reader knows the facts. Write with your reader in mind. This assumes you have analyzed who your readers are and understand what information they need and expect. What basic information is important for readers to know in order to understand your message? Instead of starting with the central part of the message, provide the background first, such as: "In response to your memo of February 2, requesting corrections to our policy on grievances, we have taken three actions. First . . . " If you're not sure what to include, ask someone who doesn't know the details of the situation to read what you have written.

Ambiguity is another barrier to clear writing. Many times we write as we speak, throwing in phrases as we would speak them. Unlike speakers, writers can't use nonverbal cues to convey specific meanings or associations. Since readers may not have the advantage of asking questions or getting immediate feedback, they are left to determine associations for themselves. Consider how ambiguity creates a lack of precise factual meaning in this memo:

> The next meeting of the department is scheduled for next week. Matt Olsen has told Leo Robinson to report on the union elections. His report will follow announcements. We will elect new officers at our upcoming meeting.

This memo doesn't pass the standard test of clear writing. If the memo was sent on Friday and received on Monday, which week contains the meeting? Who is giving the report? The pronoun "his" causes confusion since it could refer to either Matt Olsen or Leo Robinson. Which "upcoming meeting" will result in the election of officers? Will it be the meeting called by the memo or another "upcoming meeting"? Because it can breed confusion, annoyance, and wasted time, such a sloppy memo can have an adverse effect on the relationship between the writer and recipients that can affect their subsequent communication. Seen in this light, the memos a manager routinely writes are an important factor in managing relationships strategically and productively.

Construct Written Messages with Verbal Precision

Achieving verbal precision is different from mechanical or factual precision. Verbal precision is based on the accuracy of the words chosen to express the ideas. In an ideal world, words would provide the exact meaning you intended, but words can't replicate reality. Rather, words are symbols of objects and ideas. Add to this inexact representation the reader's own subtle shadings of meaning, and you can see why it's difficult to achieve verbal precision. Put another way, a word has two levels of meaning: its denotation, or the meaning agreed upon by most people who use the word, and its connotation, or the personal dimension of meaning brought to the word by the receiver.

Communication depends on a blend of both denotative and connotative meanings. Consider the noun *Greenpeace*. Its denotative reference is to a specific international environmental organization. The connotative meaning varies widely. For many environmentalists, Greenpeace is leading a worthy crusade. However, for some governments and companies, the organization is, at best, a nuisance. These are the connotative references of a single word. Consider the difficulty in creating the right blend of denotative and connotative meaning in entire documents. You need to be aware of both types of meaning of the words you use. Frequently, you may recognize your own connotative meaning but be unaware of how others may react. While connotation is often a personal matter, you can attempt to judge this meaning by thinking from your receivers' viewpoint. What is their most likely reaction?

The key to verbal precision in writing is clarity. The fundamental questions you must ask yourself are: "Does the word or phrase convey my meaning without confusion?" or "Could anyone reading this memo for the first time understand the ideas directly and simply?" A secondary question is whether the written message conveys unintentional meanings stimulated by connotative meanings of words or phrases. The impact of connotations once more underlines the importance of knowing your audience and of being aware of what is appropriate for one audience or another.

Pay Attention to Tone

The tone of your writing is directly related to your diction, or word choices. For example, compare these two statements: "Our company will purchase the product" and "We'll buy it." The second sounds more informal because it uses pronouns and a contraction. In general, longer words and sentences tend to convey a more formal tone.

Using the appropriate level of formality in your writing calls for you to analyze the nature of the writing situation. An invitation to a reception for the company's board of directors calls for formal language. When you are writing to strangers or up the chain of command, it is safer to be formal. When you are communicating across or down the chain, you may often be informal. However, a letter of reprimand to a subordinate should be formal in tone.

Tone in business writing goes beyond its relative formality. It reflects on the nature of the writer as a person and therefore affects how the reader feels about the writer. Its impact can be significant and often unexpected. For example, a terse letter may be interpreted as sarcastic or angry even if the writer did not intend sarcasm or anger. Consider a customer who writes a long letter expressing problems with a product. What would the customer think if this response were mailed back: "Thank you for your letter of January 12. We always enjoy hearing from our customers." Although this response has the trappings of courtesy, it seems insincere and perhaps sarcastic. It hardly seems that the respondent read the customer's letter—there is nothing about its contents—or that the letter was "enjoyed." Although the response shows factual and mechanical precision, the tone is inappropriate and potentially damaging to the relationship with this customer.

In most cases, even disappointing news can be expressed in a positive way. Consider an employer who responds to a job applicant by writing, "In a company as well respected as ours, we rarely have time to consider applications such as yours." Not only is the news bad, the arrogant tone also needlessly humiliates the applicant. A response with a more positive tone might be: "We read your application with interest but currently do not have any openings in your specialties. Best wishes with your continued search." The news is still bad, but the polite tone shows respect for the applicant and promotes a professional image for the company.

Compare the following sentence and its more positive version: "Because of recent heavy demand, we will be unable to ship the items you ordered until July 15," and "Although recent demand has been heavy, we will be able to ship the items you ordered July 15." A slight variation in wording here changes a tone of helplessness to one of helpfulness.

Under most business writing conditions, you should be cordial. You should express tact and friendliness appropriate to your relationship with the reader. This attitude will have a positive effect on your word choices, which in turn will more likely convey an appropriate tone.

One area of modern business writing where failing to pay attention to tone has cost many bad feelings and lost time is e-mail. By its nature, e-mail encourages rapid-fire exchanges, especially when busy workers face an in-box filled with messages, many of which are ill-considered and unclear. E-mail is not a phone conversation in which tone of voice and other cues can clarify your meaning and in which you can read the listener's vocal cues. However, many e-mailers seem to forget the difference. They don't state the context of their message; they don't give needed background information; they don't organize their message; they don't make careful word choices that convey a cordial tone. By not taking the time to consider their message in light of the situation and the receiver, e-mailers can convey inappropriately demanding tones or disapproving tones if their requests aren't met promptly. The antagonism created by the poor tone of e-mail messages can delay solving the business problem at hand and negatively affect the work relationships of the e-mailers.

Use the Proper Format

Like it or not, first impressions count, even in written communication. Sloppiness suggests the writer doesn't take the message seriously; odd or unconventional formats hint the writer is ignorant or unprofessional. You should become acquainted with the physical layout of letters, memos, proposals, and other common forms of written business communication. Others expect you to have this basic knowledge; many handbooks and computer software programs are available to guide you in the development of these formats. Some companies have style guides that precisely prescribe the formats for all documents representing the company.

While there are several acceptable formats for written communication such as business letters, the reader should be able to pick up specific information at a glance. In the business letter, this information includes: the intended recipient of the letter, the sender, the sender's address for return correspondence, any enclosures, and recipients of copies of the letter. All of this information is separate from the body of the letter and should be clearly visible.

Because memos are intended to communicate within an organization, their format is different from that of letters. Instead of business letterhead, memo letterhead is used. Basic information can also be obtained at a glance. The top of the memo should include: To, From, Date, and Subject headings. Usually, salutations and closings are not considered necessary within an organization.

Proposals are much lengthier and require special attention to supporting information such as tables, graphs, and charts. The best ways to represent such data can be found in readily available resources on business writing.

Whatever the final format, there is one objective in all written business communication: Your message should be simple, direct, and clear. Anything that interrupts your reader's movement through your writing limits its effectiveness. Any imprecision—a mechanical blunder, a factual omission, or a strange word—calls attention to itself and, like an odd gesture in spoken communication, diverts attention away from your ideas. As a writer, you must aim at clear, direct transmission of your message.

SUPPLEMENT YOUR PRESENTATION BY RESPONDING TO QUESTIONS AND CHALLENGES

Prepare Thoroughly to Handle Questions

Answering questions and responding to objections is a vital part of the communication process because it allows us to interact directly with our listeners. We can learn about how our listeners are thinking and their responses to our ideas from their questions; it's a two-way street.

The key to formulating effective responses is the same as the key to developing good speeches—careful preparation. Read broadly and talk with experts in your field. Don't read just the material that supports your point of view but also read what the opposition is saying. The best defense can be a good offense, and this is no exception. Ask your colleagues to critique your material, discuss their questions and objections with them, and collect supporting documentation or evidence. You can also practice your responses. Begin by considering what your listeners might ask or find someone opposed to your position who will list questions for you. Then, practice your responses to these questions.

Despite your best efforts, you may get an overwhelmingly hostile response from your listeners. Don't be afraid to take a stand that disagrees with them. People may not agree with you but they will respect your sincerity. If someone throws you a curve, don't apologize or bluff your way through with an inadequate response. Be honest and direct, tell them if you don't have the answer. Invite them to discuss the problem further at a later time and follow up on your invitation. The next time someone asks the same question, you will be prepared.

Respond to Objections in an Orderly Manner

In general, answer questions as succinctly as possible. Rambling answers may make it appear as though you are hedging or unsure. They also suggest an inability to think concisely. You can answer objections in four steps:

1. *Restate the objection.* This gives you time to think, shows your interest, and makes sure everyone understands the question. Restatement recognizes the objection and clarifies it for everyone in the audience.

2. *State your position.* Give a concise, direct statement of what you believe to make it clear where you stand.

3. *Offer support for your position.* This is the critical part of the response. Provide evidence that shows your position is the right one.

4. *Indicate the significance of your rebuttal.* Show the impact of adopting your position. Offer reasons for doing so.

Following the four steps we've outlined, a good response to an objection might take this form:

1. Joe has stated a management-by-objectives system won't work in our factory because supervisors don't want input from the cutting floor (restatement of the objection).

2. I think a management-by-objectives system will work and it will increase worker satisfaction (statement of your position).

3. I'm basing my position on a group of studies done in our Newark plant last year. Output increased 0.5 percent during the first month, and more importantly, workers reported more job satisfaction. They had fewer sick days, too (support for the position).

4. If our plant is similar to the Newark plant—and I think it is—then I believe our supervisors will notice the same gains here. Until Joe can provide us with a reason to stick with the current system, I think we ought to give the new one a try—we stand to get more output and better job satisfaction (significance of rebuttal).

Practice this format until it becomes automatic. It builds up your own case while responding to the objection. Since this format rationally shores up your position, it increases your credibility as well. And, it increases the chances that others will agree with you.

Maintain Control of the Situation

You need to balance being sensitive to feedback and flexible enough to respond to legitimate concerns with avoiding prolonged, unproductive interchanges. Recognizing everyone's right to ask questions or offer alternative positions is important because it grants audience members respect. On the other hand, you also have every right to decide what is relevant for consideration. You shouldn't allow one or two members of your audience to dictate the pace or direction of your presentation. This places you in a position of weakness that undermines your credibility. If you should alter your position, make certain the majority of your listeners view it as a responsible shift rather than an effort to placate a minority voice.

Keep exchanges on an intellectual level. Arguments and rebuttals can degenerate into name-calling in which little is settled. Effective communication is more likely to occur when the calm voice of reason dominates than when you squabble with your listeners.

You'll soon learn people don't always ask questions just because they want information. Some people crave attention; others may sabotage your position if they perceive your ideas as a threat. Planning for these possibilities will give you more options; foresight enables you to respond appropriately. You might answer hostile questions with further questions, drawing out your interrogator and regaining the offensive. Or you might broaden the discussion. Don't get trapped into an argument with one person. Involve others to determine if this is an isolated concern or a legitimate issue. Finally, you might express your willingness to discuss special or detailed issues but defer extensive discussion until the end of your presentation.

Summary and Behavioral Guidelines

A key aspect of management is communication, and formal presentations are an essential communication tool. Therefore, effective managers must be able to create effective informative and persuasive messages. You can enhance your speaking and writing with thorough preparation and repeated practice. This chapter has outlined a number of guidelines based on the Five S's model:

1. Formulate a *strategy* for the specific audience and occasion.
2. Develop a clear *structure*.
3. *Support* your points with evidence adapted to your audience.
4. Practice presenting your material in a *style* that will enhance your ideas.
5. *Supplement* your presentation by effectively responding to questions and challenges.

Strategy

1. Identify your general and specific purposes.
2. Tailor your message to your audience.
   - Understand their needs, desires, knowledge level, and attitude toward your topic.
   - Make sure your approach is audience-centered.
   - Present both sides of the issue if your audience is hostile or uncommitted.
3. Meet the demands of the situation.
   - More formal situations demand formal language and sentence structure.
   - Informal situations allow slang and less rigid language use.

Structure

4. Begin with a forecast of your main ideas.
   - Catch your audience's attention as you begin.
   - Provide them with a reason for listening or reading.
   - Give them an outline of the message so they can follow along.

5. Choose your organizational pattern carefully.
   - Start with what your listeners already know or think.
   - Use organization to increase your credibility.
   - Move from familiar to unfamiliar, simple to complex, old to new, or use other continua for organizing your thoughts.
   - Make no more than three to five main points in oral communication.
6. Use transitions to signal your progress.
7. Conclude on a high note.
   - Take advantage of greater audience attention at the conclusion of your message.
   - Reach closure by reinforcing through a summary of your ideas.
   - Use your last statements to call for action, reinforce the commitment to action, or establish a feeling of goodwill.

Support

8. Choose a variety of support.
   - The most effective support is not well known to your listeners.
   - Support increases your credibility.
   - You may use a wide variety of supporting material.
9. Consider your audience when choosing your support.
   - New evidence and live videotapes have more impact.
   - The audience's initial position determines the extent to which they find evidence believable.
   - Using evidence is better than not using evidence.
10. Use visual aids as support.
    - Visual aids have a dramatic impact on comprehension and retention.
    - Visual aids also enhance persuasion.
    - Keep visual aids simple and effective.

Style in Oral Communication

11. Prepare your notes.
    - Remember, the crucial effect is conversational style.
    - Extemporaneous presentation requires limited notes combined with frequent delivery practice.
    - Formal occasions demand precise wording that requires a manuscript or memorized speech.

LEARNING

12. Practice your presentation.
    - ❑ Use distributed practice rather than massed practice.
    - ❑ Practice using your visual aids and plan for the unexpected.
    - ❑ Plan to channel your speaking anxiety.

13. Convey controlled enthusiasm for your subject.
    - ❑ Effective speakers communicate excitement about their topics.
    - ❑ Your posture, tone of voice, and facial expressions all indicate your attitude.
    - ❑ Your speech should resemble an animated conversation.

14. Engage your audience with effective delivery.
    - ❑ Eye contact is the most critical tool.
    - ❑ Use physical space and body movement to enliven your message.
    - ❑ Use space to convey intimacy or distance.
    - ❑ Use gestures to accentuate your normal mode of expression.
    - ❑ Avoid any movement that distracts from your message.

Style in Written Communication

15. Develop mechanical precision in your writing.
    - ❑ Project a professional image.
    - ❑ Errors may distract your readers and disrupt the impact of your message.

16. Practice factual precision in your writing.
    - ❑ Accuracy ensures your meaning will be communicated clearly.
    - ❑ Ambiguity prevents factual precision.

17. Construct written messages with verbal precision.
    - ❑ Words cannot replicate reality.
    - ❑ Consider denotative and connotative meanings of words as you write them.
    - ❑ The key to verbal precision is clarity.

18. Pay attention to tone.
    - ❑ Tone is directly related to word choice.
    - ❑ Adjust the tone of your message to the formality of the situation.
    - ❑ Tone affects how readers feel about the writer.
    - ❑ Writing should express appropriate cordiality.
    - ❑ Positive phrasing is preferable to negativity.

19. Use the proper format.
    - ❑ You are responsible for creating an impression of professionalism.
    - ❑ Business letters, memos, and proposals all have special formats.

Supplement: Questions and Answers

20. Anticipate questions and thoroughly prepare responses.
    - ❑ Rehearse answers to difficult questions.
    - ❑ Handle hostile listeners with honesty and directness.

21. Respond to objections in an orderly fashion.
    - ❑ Restate the objection.
    - ❑ State your position.
    - ❑ Offer support for your position.
    - ❑ Indicate the significance of your rebuttal.

22. Maintain control of the situation.
    - ❑ Balance the demands of specific individuals with the interest of the group.
    - ❑ Keep exchanges on an intellectual level.
    - ❑ Plan for the questioner who has a personal agenda.

SKILL *PRACTICE*

EXERCISES FOR MAKING EFFECTIVE ORAL AND WRITTEN PRESENTATIONS

Speaking as a Leader

As illustrated in the opening case about Taylor Billingsley at Apex Communications, one of the major challenges facing leaders is the requirement to deliver a wide range of presentations. Effective communicators must be skilled at both informing and inspiring. They must be able to hold their own with hostile audiences as well as to impress content experts and instill confidence in novices. They must be skilled at building consensus, pointing out new directions, and explaining complex topics. This exercise, adapted from Richard Linowes, provides an opportunity to practice speaking on a variety of leadership topics.

Assignment

To practice playing this important leadership role, prepare a talk and a memo on one of the following topics. Your speech should last from three to five minutes, unless you are otherwise instructed. Your memo should not exceed two pages. Create a context for your communication by assuming a management role in a familiar organization. Before beginning, explain the details of the context to your audience (either orally or in a written summary). Briefly explain your organizational position, the makeup of the audience, and their expectations of your presentation. (For the memo, attach a one-page background statement.) The specific content of your communication is less important than how well it is prepared and how persuasively it is delivered. Prepare to respond to questions and challenges.

In preparing your presentation, review the behavioral guidelines at the end of the Skill Learning section. The checklist in this exercise may also be useful. You will receive feedback based on the criteria shown in the Observer's Feedback Form.

Topics for Leadership Talks

1. **Taking Charge of an Established Group.** The speaker is a manager newly assigned to a group that has worked together under other managers for some time.
2. **Announcing a New Project.** The speaker is announcing a new undertaking to members of his or her department and is calling on all to rally behind the effort.
3. **Calling for Better Customer Service.** The speaker is motivating all employees to be as attentive and responsive as possible to customers.
4. **Calling for Excellence and High-Quality Work.** The speaker is motivating all employees to perform their jobs with a commitment to meeting the highest possible standards.
5. **Announcing the Need for Cost Reductions.** The speaker is requesting everyone look for ways to cut expenditures and immediately begin to slash spending.
6. **Commending a Job Well Done.** The speaker is extolling a group of people who have worked very hard for an extended period to produce outstanding results.
7. **Calming a Frightened Group of People.** The speaker is endeavoring to restore calm and confidence to those who feel panic in the face of distressing business developments.

PRACTICE

8. **Addressing a Challenging Opposition.** The speaker is presenting a heartfelt belief to a critical, even hostile, audience.

9. **Mediating Between Opposing Parties.** The speaker is serving as judge or arbiter between two groups who are bitterly opposed on a key issue.

10. **Taking Responsibility for Error.** The speaker is a spokesperson for an institution whose actions have produced an unfortunate result that affects the audience.

11. **Reprimanding Unacceptable Behavior.** The speaker is rebuffing certain individuals who have failed to perform up to required levels.

12. **Petitioning for Special Allowances.** The speaker is presenting the case for an institution seeking certain rights that must be authorized by some external body.

Checklist for Developing Effective Presentations

1. What are my general and specific objectives?
2. What is the context of my communication? (My audience, the situation, etc.)
3. How will I open and close the communication?
4. How will I organize my information?
5. How will I get and keep the attention of my audience?
6. What supporting materials will I use?
7. What visual aids (graphs, charts, objects, etc.) will I use?
8. How will I tailor the presentation to my audience?
9. What format will I use in my presentation?
10. What questions or responses will likely occur?

Quality Circles at Battle Creek Foods

A management tool made popular in Japan is widely used in U.S. firms. Ironically, Edward Deming, an American, first brought the notion of "statistical quality control," a management tool, to the Japanese in the early post-World War II years. The Japanese combined these ideas with the assumption the person who performs a job is the one who best knows how to identify and correct its problems. As a result, the Japanese, with Deming's help, developed the "quality circle." A quality circle is a group of people (usually about 10) who meet periodically to discuss and develop solutions to problems related to quality, productivity, or product cost.

The purpose of this exercise is to give you an opportunity to make a presentation on this important topic.

Assignment

You are the director of personnel at Battle Creek Foods, a leading manufacturer of breakfast cereal. Productivity has been sagging industrywide, and your organization is starting to see its effect on profitability. In response, you have been asked by the corporate executive committee to make a 20-minute oral presentation (or prepare a five-page memo) on quality circles. The committee has heard that QCs have been initiated at several plants by your leading competitor, and it would like your recommendation as to whether Battle Creek Foods should follow suit. The committee's only previous exposure to QCs is what each member has read in the popular press. Using the following reference material, prepare a presentation on quality circles. Explain the QC structure and process, and the advantages and disadvantages of QCs. The final section of the presentation should include a recommendation regarding their adoption at your plants. Prepare to respond to questions and challenges.

In preparing your presentation, refer to the behavioral guidelines for effective presentations at the end of the Skill Learning section and the checklist in the preceding exercise. You will receive feedback based on the Observer's Feedback Form.

A Look at Some of the Evidence

Quality circles, on balance, appear to be making a positive contribution to product quality, profits, morale, and even improved employee attendance (DuBrin, 1985, pp. 174–185). The widespread attention QCs have received in recent years has led logically to their evaluation by both businesspeople and researchers. Here we will rely on several types of evaluation methods, sampling first the positive evidence, and then the negative.

Favorable Outcomes with QCs

Honeywell, a high-technology electronics firm, has become a pioneer in the application of QCs in North America. Honeywell currently operates several hundred QCs in the United States. Typically, about a half-dozen assembly workers are brought together every two weeks by a first-level supervisor or team leader. "We feel this type of participatory management program not only increases productivity," says Joseph Riordan, director of Honeywell Corporate Productivity Services, "but it also upgrades the quality of work life for employees. Line workers feel they are more a part of the action. As a result, we find the quality of work improves and absenteeism is reduced. With this kind of involvement, we have, in many cases, been able to increase the capacity of a line without the addition of tooling or extra shifts."

Honeywell used the quality circle method to manage the problem of winning a renewable bid for a government contract. "Here was a situation," Riordan relates, "where we already had cut our rejects down, where all of the learning had effectively gone out of the process." The problem was assigned to the quality circle representing that particular work area. "They came up with a suggestion for further automating the process that enabled us to improve our competitive position by about 20 percent and win the contract."

In an attempt to determine the appropriateness of QCs to North American firms, a team of researchers set up a one-year field experiment at a metal fabricating facility of an electronics firm.

Eleven quality circles, averaging nine production employees each, were established. Performance was measured by a computerized monitoring system created from the company's existing employee performance reporting system. Both quantity and quality measurements were taken. Employee attitudes were also assessed, using the Motivating Potential Score (MPS) of the Hackman-Oldham Job Diagnostic Survey.

The major result of the circle program was its positive impact on reject rate, as shown in the top half of Figure A.3. Reject rates per capita for quality circle participants dropped by one-third to one-half of the former rates by the time the program had run three months. Surprisingly, the reject rates for the control group increased during the same period.

An explanation offered by the researchers for these results is circle members tackled the issues of internal communication as a top priority item. For example, one of the initial projects implemented by the QCs was improving training manuals and procedures, including translating materials into a worker's native language if the worker desired. Careful attention to better training in fundamentals prevented many errors.

Circle members also made fewer errors. In addition, the defective parts the circle members did make tended to be less expensive to scrap or rework into usable parts. The explanation given for these results is circle training instructs employees how to prioritize problems on the basis of dollar impact on the company. The cost savings

119

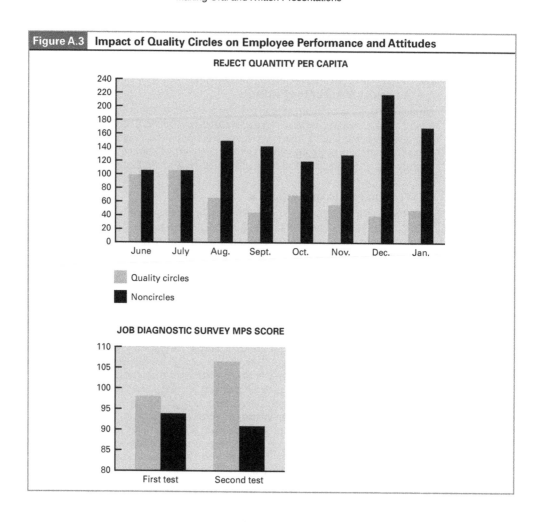

Figure A.3 | **Impact of Quality Circles on Employee Performance and Attitudes**

generated by the lower reject rate represented a 300 percent return on the cost of investment in the program.

The impact of QCs on participants' level of work satisfaction was equally impressive. Results shown in Figure A.3 indicate the Motivating Potential Score (MPS) for the circle participants increased, while the control group showed a decrease. No other changes were present in the work environment that would impact the experimental group differently than the control group. The researchers therefore concluded the improvement in employee job attitudes could be attributed to the circle training program and the problem-solving activity. The job characteristic most influenced by the quality activity was skill variety: the extent to which a job requires a variety of skills.

Negative Outcomes with Quality Circles

Despite the favorable outcomes reported, many negative results have also been reported. A review of the results of the first surge of QC activity in the United States revealed as many as 75 percent of initially successful programs were no longer in operation after a few years. Even Lockheed, one of the American pioneers in this method, had decreased its involvement with quality circles. Robert Cole, a recognized authority on the Japanese workforce, made these pessimistic remarks:

> *[The] fact is that the circles do not work very well in many Japanese companies. Even in those plants recognized as having the best operating programs, management knows that perhaps only one-third of the circles are working well, with another third borderline, and one-third simply making no contribution at all. For all of the rhetoric of voluntarism, in a number of companies the workers clearly perceive circle activity as coercive. Japanese companies face a continuing struggle to revitalize circle activity to ensure that it does not degenerate into ritualistic behavior.*

A study of quality circles in 29 companies, conducted by Matthew Goodfellow, found only eight of them to be cost-effective in terms of gains in productivity. Management consultant Woodruff Imberman investigated the 21 unsuccessful QC efforts and found four major causes of failure. First, in many firms, the employees intensely disliked management. Their antagonism carried over into the quality circles, which some employees perceived to be a management ploy to reduce overtime and trim the workforce by increasing productivity.

Second, most organizations did a poor job of selling the QCs. Instead of conducting individual discussions with employees, they relied on flip charts, booklets, and formal management presentations. The workers were left wondering, "What's in it for me?"

Third, the supervisors chosen to lead the circles received some training in human relations and group dynamics, but they felt little of this information satisfied the specific needs of their own departments.

Fourth, most of the 21 firms regarded the QC programs merely as a way of improving the efficiency of production techniques. They did not realize QCs cannot succeed unless top management is willing to shift its philosophy toward emphasizing good relations among employees and between management and workforce. This last point hints at the importance of establishing the conditions that allow a quality circle program to succeed.

Key Elements of a Successful Program

Quality circle programs show some variation from company to company, whether these companies are engaged in manufacturing or service. They may differ in how frequently they meet, how much authority is granted to the team leader or supervisor, whether they use a group facilitator in addition to a supervisor, and how much coordination there is with the existing quality-control department. Based on the judgments of several observers, the successful programs have certain elements in common.

Quality circles work best in firms where good employee-management relations already exist. QCs are not likely to succeed in organizations suffering from acrimonious union-management conflict or high levels of distrust between employees and management.

Top management is committed to the program. Without commitment from top management, the initiation of a QC program is inadvisable. Instead, the director of a circle project should first prepare reports on other companies where QCs have been successful and present them to top management.

Circle leaders use a participative leadership style. Laurie Fitzgerald, a QC consultant, advocates the "leader as a worker for the members" concept. When the circle leader takes on a highly authoritarian role, the members are usually unresponsive.

The right people and the right area are selected. For quality circles to be effective, the program manager has to be enthusiastic, persistent, and hardworking. The facilitator or team leader must be energetic and cooperative. Also, another important step in getting

PRACTICE

the program off the ground is to select an area of the company where one can expect cooperation and enthusiasm from participants.

Program goals are stated explicitly. Objectives should be made clear in order to avoid confusion or unreasonable expectations from the circle program. Among the goals of QC programs are improving product quality, increasing productivity, improving communications between workers and supervisors, decreasing product costs, improving the quality of work life, and preparing people for future supervisory assignments.

The program is well publicized throughout the firm. Once the program is started, information about it should be disseminated widely throughout the company. Better communication results in less resistance and fewer negative rumors about the program. The content of the communication should be open and positive.

The program starts slowly and grows slowly. A gradual introduction of the program helps expose people to new concepts and helps reduce doubts about its intention and potential merit.

The QC program is customized to meet the needs of the firm. A subtle source of failure in some QC programs is the use of a canned set of procedures that don't fit local circumstances. A QC participant whose work is data processing may have difficulty with the translation of a case from the aerospace industry. A workable compromise is to use standard training as a framework and build on it with the unique problems of the firm in question.

Quality circles are used as a method of employee development. A key purpose of these circles is to foster personal development of the participating workers. If managers intend to install a QC as a tool for their own selfish gain, they would do better not to begin.

Management is willing to grant recognition for ideas originating in the circles. If management attempts to manipulate the circle volunteers or take away from them the credit for improvements, the program will most likely backfire. More will be lost than gained.

Membership is voluntary. As with job enrichment and all forms of participative management, employee preference is an influential factor. Employees who desire to contribute their ideas will generally perform better than employees who are arbitrarily assigned to a QC.

Achievements of quality circles are recognized as results of group, not individual, effort. Recognizing them as such decreases showing off and competitiveness and increases cooperation and interdependence within the group or department. Quality circles, not individual employees, should receive credit for innovations and suggestions for improvement.

Ample training is provided. Program volunteers generally need some training in conference techniques or group dynamics. At a minimum, the circle leader will need skills in group participation methods. Otherwise, he or she will wind up lecturing about topics such as quality improvement and productivity improvement. Leaders and participants will also need training in the use of whatever statistical and problem-solving methods are to be used. Following are eight major problem-solving techniques and their purposes:

1. Brainstorming is used to identify all problems, even those beyond the control of circle members.
2. A check-sheet is used to log problems within the circle's sphere of influence within a certain time frame.
3. A Pareto chart graphically illustrates check-sheet data to identify the most serious problems; that is, the 20 percent of the problems that cause 80 percent of the major mistakes.
4. A cause-and-effect diagram graphically illustrates the cause of a particular problem.

5. Histograms or bar charts are graphed to show the frequency and magnitude of specific problems.
6. Scatter diagrams or "measles charts" identify major defect locations, which show up as dense dot clusters on the pictures of products.
7. Graph-and-control charts monitor a production process and are compared with production samples.
8. Stratification, generally accomplished by inspecting the same products from different production areas, randomizes the sampling process.

Creativity is encouraged. As illustrated above, brainstorming or variations thereof fit naturally into the quality circle method and philosophy. Maintaining an attitude of "anything goes" is particularly important, even if rough ideas must be refined later. If half-processed ideas are shot down by the leader or other members, idea generation will extinguish quickly.

Projects are related to members' actual job responsibilities. Quality circles are not arenas for amateur speculation about other people's work. People make suggestions about improving the quality of work for which they are already responsible. They should, however, be willing to incorporate information from suppliers and customers.

The Arguments For and Against Quality Circles

A major argument for quality circles is they represent a low-cost, efficient vehicle for unleashing the creative potential of employees. In the process, highly desirable ends are achieved, such as improvements in the quality of both products and work life. Quality circles, in fact, are considered part of the quality of work life movement.

Another favorable feature of these circles is they are perceived positively by all—management, workers, unions, and stockholders. A firm contemplating implementing such a program thus runs no risk of either internal or external opposition. (It is conceivable, however, that opposition will be forthcoming if management fails to act on quality circle suggestions.)

Quality circles contribute to organizational effectiveness in another important way. They have emerged as a useful method of developing present and future managers. Recently, a major computing manufacturing firm established a quality circle program. After the program had been operating for two years, the director of training observed the supervisors who were quality circle leaders were significantly more self-confident, knowledgeable, and poised than other supervisors who were attending the regular training program. The director believed the supervisors' involvement in the QC training programs and activities had been the major contributor to this difference.

One major criticism of quality circles is many of them are not cost-effective. Furthermore, even more pessimistic is the criticism that the reported successes of QCs may be attributable to factors other than the actual quality circle program. One explanation is the attention paid to employees by management may be the force behind the gains in productivity and morale (the well-known Hawthorne effect). Another possible explanation of the successes of quality circle programs is the gains are due to improved group dynamics and problem-solving techniques. Therefore, an entire QC program need not be conducted just to achieve these gains.

A discouraging argument has been advanced that quality circles may not be suited to North American workers. Matsushita Electric, a leading user of the quality circle method in Japan, does not use circles in its U.S. plant (located in Chicago) because it does not consider the American worker suited to circle activities. Perhaps Matsushita management believes Americans are too self-oriented to be group oriented.

PRACTICE

Quality circles may prove to be breeding grounds for friction and role confusion between the quality-control department and the groups themselves. Unless management carefully defines the relationship of quality circles vis-à-vis the quality-control department, much duplication of effort (and therefore waste of resources) will inevitably result.

Exclusive reliance upon volunteers for the circles may result in the loss of potentially valuable ideas. Many nonassertive people may shy away from participation in the circles despite their having valid ideas for product improvement.

Some employees who volunteer to join quality circles may do so for the wrong reasons. The circle may develop the reputation of being "a good way to get away from the line for a while and enjoy a coffee break and a good bull session." (To counter such an abuse of the quality-circle program, QC group members might monitor the quality of input from their own group members.)

Guidelines for Action

An early strategic step in implementing a quality circle is to clarify relationships between the circle and the formal quality-control department. Otherwise, the quality-control department may perceive the circle as a redundancy or threat. One effective arrangement is for the quality circle to complement the quality-control department; the QC department thus does not become subject to the loss of authority.

Membership in the circle should be voluntary and on a rotating basis. In many instances, a team member will soon run out of fresh ideas for quality improvement. Rotating membership will result in a wider sampling of ideas being generated. Experience suggests that group size should be limited to nine.

Quality circles should be implemented on a pilot basis. As the circle produces results and wins the acceptance of managers and employees alike, it can be expanded as the demand for its output increases.

Do not emphasize quick financial returns or productivity increases from the output of the quality circles. The program should be seen as a long-range project that will raise the quality consciousness of the organization. (Nevertheless, as noted in the report from Honeywell, immediate positive results are often forthcoming.)

Management must make good use of many of the suggestions coming from the quality circle yet still define the limits of the power and authority of the circle. On the one hand, if none of the circle's suggestions are adopted, the circle will lose its effectiveness as an agent for change. Circle members will become discouraged because of their lack of clout. On the other hand, if the circle has too much power and authority, it will be seen as a governing body for technical change. Under the latter circumstances, people may use the circle for political purposes. An individual who wants to get a technical modification authorized may try to influence a member of the quality circle to suggest modification during a circle meeting.

Training in group dynamics and methods of participative management will be particularly helpful. It may also prove helpful at the outset to appoint a group facilitator (an internal or external consultant) who can help the group run more smoothly.

Observer's Feedback Form

RATING

1 = Low
5 = High

Strategy

_____ 1. Identified the general and specific purposes.

_____ 2. Tailored the message to the audience's needs, attitudes, knowledge level, and so forth.

_____ 3. Met the expectations of the audience by using appropriate language and style.

Structure

_____ 4. Began with a forecast of the main ideas and captivated the audience's interest by giving them an important reason to listen.

_____ 5. Chose an appropriate organizational structure; for example, moved from familiar to unfamiliar and simple to complex.

_____ 6. Used transitions, including internal summaries, to signal progress.

_____ 7. Concluded on a high note; reinforced major points; summarized key actions.

Support

_____ 8. Used a variety of supporting information, examples, and so forth, to increase the credibility and understanding of major points.

_____ 9. Used supporting material (both the content and format of evidence and illustrations) appropriate for the audience.

_____ 10. Used effective, simple visual aids to enhance comprehension and retention of the message.

Style in Oral Communication

_____ 11. Used notes to create a conversational style.

_____ 12. Presentation had obviously been well-rehearsed, including the use of visual aids, and so forth.

_____ 13. Conveyed controlled enthusiasm for the subject through the tone of voice, posture, and facial expressions.

_____ 14. Engaged the audience through effective eye contact, physical arrangement of the room, and appropriate gestures.

PRACTICE

Style in Written Communication

_____ 15. Document was mechanically precise; that is, it contained no errors that detracted from the message.

_____ 16. Document was factually precise; that is, the content was accurate.

_____ 17. The choice of words communicated the message clearly and unambiguously.

_____ 18. The tone matched the topic and the audience (e.g., formality, emotion, directness).

_____ 19. Used the appropriate format for the type of correspondence.

Supplement: Questions and Answers

_____ 20. Handled questions and challenges thoughtfully, candidly, and assertively.

_____ 21. Responded to objections in an orderly manner; for example, restated the objection, restated your position, offered further support for your position, and explained the significance of your rebuttal.

_____ 22. Maintained control of the meeting by balancing the demands of specific individuals with the interests of the group and keeping the discussion focused on the issues.

Team working and leadership

Team working is a key skill on the Quality Assurance Agency (QAA) list and features in almost any job you are likely to want. As a student you are likely to do some of your assignments as part of a team. You may be surprised to find how much difference belonging to an informal study group can make both to your enjoyment of your course and to your performance on it. Leadership is something that more and more organisations are looking for – some graduate management schemes are now renamed 'graduate leadership programmes'. This chapter will help you acquire the skills you need to be an effective team member, and to maximise your learning in group contexts. It will also look at what you can do to become influential in a team and to exercise leadership.

→ Ch 1   Your trawl of graduate recruitment adverts (Chapter 1) should have convinced you that potential employers are looking for 'good team workers': both teamwork and networking are crucial for success in most organisations today. Many issues are discussed in meetings – a group which represents a range of relevant perspectives and skills can potentially take far better decisions that can any individual. If people are involved in taking a decision that affects them, they are far more likely to be committed to making that decision work. Conversely, if a group is ineffective, the cost in terms of poor decisions, poor quality work, time wasted, and demotivation of all those concerned can be substantial.

→ Ch 12, 16 You will almost certainly experience group assignments, both in order to develop your skills and because some things are learned more effectively through discussion. Case study work (discussed in Chapter 12) and projects (Chapter 16) will almost certainly involve group work. Developing your team-working skills will help you to get better grades, and to learn more effectively. If you are doing your degree by distance learning you may be part of a 'virtual' student group. 'Virtual team-working skills' are often necessary at work, too.

Your success in both study and employment will depend on your skill in working with others. It can be hugely satisfying to work in, or even lead, an effective team. Sadly, if you lack team-working skills your working life, and the lives of your colleagues, may be frustrating and stressful. And of course your team is likely to be less than successful. You will have many opportunities to develop your skills while you are a student, both as part of your course and in your social life, any work placements and vacation jobs. Grasp these opportunities and exploit them to advance your development.

TEAM WORKING IN ORGANISATIONS

There are many different sorts of groups which form in organisations. Teams, as opposed to more informal groups, are deliberately formed for a purpose, to perform particular tasks or projects. They have a common goal, and this goal cannot be pursued unless the team members work together.

Teams are essential when inputs from a number of different perspectives or different skills are necessary and where commitment to outcome is important. Teams can be given a considerable degree of autonomy. Output may well be specified and measured by higher management. But the team can be free to decide how best to achieve that output, given prevailing conditions. This way of working offers considerable flexibility, as the team can respond to changes in those conditions far more rapidly than could a group of individuals working on the instructions of those higher in the organisation.

Where decisions are taken only after reference up (and up) the chain of command, they can be very slow. Autonomous team working also provides ideal conditions for high levels of motivation. No wonder team working is so widely adopted.

The nature of such teams will differ greatly, however. Each team's goals will be different. A committee is charged with taking decisions and perhaps seeing that those decisions are implemented. A work group might have the task of producing a particular component or providing a specified service. A project team might be charged with developing an original idea into concrete plans, or with putting those plans into

Successful team working needs:
- clear, shared goals
- agreed ways of working
- effective communication
- support and cooperation between members
- monitoring of progress.

action. Responsibility within the team will also vary. Some teams may have a specified leader who may or may not also have managerial authority. Others may have no such leadership structure. Some teams will contain a wide variety of expertise, whereas others may consist of people with very similar skills.

But whatever the team structure, and regardless of whether the task is sharing information and negotiating a decision, gathering information and making plans, or performing a physical task that requires the skills or labour of more than one person, effective working together is essential for success. And while some of the skills required will be more important than others in any situation, the requirements for success are remarkably similar across the spectrum. Success will depend on:

- clarity of goals and acceptance of these among team members
- agreement over ways of working towards these goals
- effective communication between team members
- support and cooperation within the team rather than competition
- arrangements for monitoring progress and taking corrective action if necessary.

These factors are not, of course, always present. Calling a group a team does not guarantee success. 'Team' is an emotionally loaded word, standing for all sorts of positive things. Organisations often label groups of people 'teams' and think that this is all they need to do. If you have already experienced a rocky time in some of the groups you work with in class, you know that the label is not enough. Thought needs to be given to the success factors above, and the skills which underpin them need to be present in the 'team' members.

Key factors in team success

Looking at the list above, it is clear that the elements contributing to success can be grouped into three broad classes of factors, as has been done in Figure 10.1 (see later in this chapter). Three sets of skills are important:

→ Ch 1, 2

- **Managing the task** – clear objectives, monitoring progress towards them and taking corrective action are as important for team working as for managing yourself. The principles are just the same, although applied in a group context.

- **Managing the process** – this is the part that is new. People need to stay committed to the team's goals, motivated to contribute to achieving them. Attention therefore needs to be paid to their support and encouragement. This will be a major topic in this chapter.

→ Ch 9

- **Communication** – this will be vital for managing both task and process. You have already developed the basic skills of talking and listening (and being assertive where necessary). Their application in a group context is very similar to their use one to one. By practising communication skills in group work, you will become better at communicating in other contexts.

Whatever the type of task a team is addressing, success will depend upon a combination of communication skills and management skills relating to both task and process. The emphasis will differ depending on the nature of the task, as the following exploration of the different contexts for group working shows.

DISCUSSION GROUPS

Because they are a natural extension of the previous chapter, and because almost any group will at times need to have informal discussions about the task, it makes sense to focus first on informal group discussions. You will probably be familiar with these from seminar or study groups.

ACTIVITY 10.1

Reflect on a recent group discussion in which you found it satisfactory to take part and another which you have not enjoyed and/or to which you felt you made little contribution. List at least three ways in which the 'good' group differed from the 'bad' group. If possible, compare your list with the lists other people make.

You will probably find that some of your 'bad' experiences have to do with poor task management. Quotes overheard after experiences like this include:

- *We've been talking for over an hour and I still don't know what we are meant to be doing!*
- *Why can't they see that the real problem is . . .*
- *If they hadn't spent 80 per cent of the time talking about the cost of photocopying we might have had time to discuss what was wrong with the business strategy.*
- *I wish we had spent some time thinking about what we had to do and how long we had to do it in . . .*
- *Nobody came up with a single sensible idea.*
- *Jane had a brilliant idea, but no one could see how good it was.*
- *Juan raised a really good issue to pursue, but everyone seemed to want to keep talking about the impossibility of getting anywhere.*
- *We had a brilliant meeting, and agreed lots of action points, but then no one actually did anything.*

Other 'bad' experiences may have had more to do with poor process management – lack of attention to group needs, perhaps conflict or even aggression between some members. Such meetings produce reactions like:

- *I'm useless in groups – I don't seem to have any good ideas at all.*
- *I felt really bad about the way everyone laughed at Srini.*
- *I was pretty sure I could see what was wrong, but I was afraid I might be missing something somewhere, so I didn't like to say.*
- *Everyone was talking across everyone else, and I couldn't get a word in edgeways.*
- *Gerhard had got it into his head that he was the only person who understood the problem, and he just shouted at anyone who thought that there might be another view.*

Informal discussion groups do not necessarily have a 'leader'. All members of the group may be on an equal footing and between them need to ensure that the discussion goes somewhere and that members stay involved. But some of the issues reflected in the quotes above suggest a chair might have been useful. Informal groups without chairs will only work well if most of the members play their part in contributing to both task needs and group needs, and avoiding behaviours which get in their way. This means keeping a focus on what the group is trying to do, contributing to this yourself and helping others to make a contribution, valuing other members and their contributions and not letting your own or others' needs unrelated to the task (for attention, dominance or whatever) get in the way of what the group is doing. (Even if there is a chair, and especially if the chair is not particularly skilled, it will help if you behave in this way.)

Behaviours which help and hinder discussion groups

If you are aware of which behaviours help and which hinder, you will become more aware of your own strengths and weaknesses in this context. The following lists of the most important behaviours in each category may help you reflect on the part you play in group work and to become more effective in future.

Behaviours serving task needs

- *Clarifying objectives* – unless everyone in the group is clear about what the group is trying to achieve the group cannot be fully effective.

- *Seeking information from group members* – often people are asked to join a group because they know something of particular relevance, or have a particular perspective. If they are naturally quiet or diffident they may not offer this unless they are specifically asked.

- *Giving relevant information* – this may apply to you, so if you offer any relevant information which you have, again this will progress the task.

- *Proposing ideas* – these might be ideas about how to address the group task or ideas about possible solutions to a problem under discussion.

- *Building on ideas or proposals contributed by others* – the real advantage in groups is not that members bring lots of ideas but that these ideas can then spark new ones or be developed by others, so that there is a synergy between members' thinking. Acknowledging the person whose idea you are building on is really helpful, as it makes them feel valued rather than inadequate – 'John, that's a really good idea – it would let us do X. But you've got me thinking – if we did Y as well, we could actually achieve this, this and this . . .'

- *Summarising progress so far* – this can be extremely useful in stopping people from covering the same ground over and over, as it helps the group realise what progress has been made. It also helps any note taker.

- *Evaluating progress against objectives* – once progress has been summarised it is easier to see what is left to be done, and plan to achieve it.

- *Time keeping* – most groups usually have a time limit, so it is important to manage the activity to ensure that it is completed within this time.

131

- *Allocating responsibility for any actions* – all too often a group has wonderful ideas and members go away feeling it was a great meeting, but feel no obligation to actually do anything themselves. Agreed actions are far more likely to be taken if individuals commit, in the meeting, to taking them.
- *Setting up review mechanisms* – if actions will go on for some time after the meeting, some way is needed of reviewing progress and taking corrective action where necessary.

Behaviours serving group needs

- *Encouraging members to contribute* – this is linked to the task need of eliciting information, but also helps individuals to feel part of the group. (Some members will need more encouragement than others.)
- *Rewarding contributions with praise or agreement* – again, this is helpful in making people feel that they are valued members of the group, thus increasing their commitment to the group's collective activity.
- *Checking understanding* – it is important to be sure that you understand any contribution, but particularly helpful to check that you have understood a point by summarising that understanding in your own words before giving reasons for disagreeing. Many disagreements are rooted in misunderstandings but become heated before this is discovered.
- *Helping to resolve conflicts positively* – in any group, conflicts are inevitable, and by exploring the reasons for conflict a group may uncover crucial information, but this needs to be done in a way that avoids either party feeling rejected.
- *Changing your own position in the light of arguments or information given by others* – many people see hanging on to their original position as a high priority, but this can greatly reduce the ability of a group to make any sort of progress.
- *Helping to control those who talk too much* – there is often someone in a group who just loves to talk. Since this prevents others from contributing, sometimes a way needs to be found of making space for others. Ideally this needs to be done in a positive way, so that the talker feels appreciated rather than rejected. 'John – I think your point is important, but we really don't have time to go into it in enough depth here, so perhaps some of us could go into it in more depth after the meeting . . .'.
- *Praising group progress* towards objectives – if group members feel that they are getting somewhere they will feel motivated to keep working, so 'celebrating' progress in some way can make an important contribution.
- *Dissuading group members from negative behaviours* – again, in a positive way if possible (see below).

Behaviours interfering with task or group needs

- *Talking too much* – or otherwise focusing attention on yourself for the sake of it.
- *Reacting emotionally* – while emotions may be an important element in a discussion, and it may be worth saying how you feel about something, contributions driven by anger or other emotions are usually unhelpful.

▧ *Attacking others' points by ridicule or other unreasoned statement* – attacks (e.g. 'it won't work') tend to be directed at individuals and are different from reasoned disagreement which is aimed at a point made and which can be extremely valuable.

▧ *Not listening to others* – which is unhelpful for obvious reasons.

▧ *Interrupting others* or talking at the same time as them.

▧ *Introducing a totally different point* in the midst of productive discussion of something else.

▧ *Chatting with others privately during the meeting* – a form of not listening.

▧ *Using humour to excess* – this can distract the group from the task, though a little humour can 'oil the wheels' and contribute to positive handling of conflict.

▧ *Introducing red herrings* – by this I mean wilful distractions rather than genuinely suggesting something that turns out to be irrelevant

▧ *Withdrawing ostentatiously from the group* – for example by turning away, pushing chair back, crossing arms, determined silence. This can make others in the group feel uncomfortable, and generally reduces effectiveness.

How do you behave?

The lists above are quite long: you will find it difficult at first to keep all the behaviours in mind, but they cover much of what helps and hinders group

	JEFF	SABINE	LING PEI	ASAD	YIANI	CLARK	JO
Clarifying objectives							✓✓✓
Giving/seeking info.					✓✓✓✓✓		
Proposing/developing			✓✓✓	✓✓✓		✓✓✓✓	
Summarising	✓						✓✓✓✓✓
Timekeeping	✓✓✓						✓
Encouraging/rewarding							
Conflict reduction		✓✓✓✓					✓✓✓
'Gatekeeping'							✓✓✓✓✓
Interrupting/speaking over			✓✓✓✓ ✓✓✓	✓✓✓✓✓✓		✓✓✓✓	
Attack/defence			✓✓	✓✓✓			
Changing the subject					✓✓		
Excessive humour		✓✓				✓✓	
Withdrawal		✓			✓		

Fig 10.1 **Example of a simplified form used in recording behaviours in a group**

discussion. The more aware you are of your own and others' use of these behaviours, the more effectively you will contribute to group discussions. It is probably best to look at the way other people are behaving before working on your own habits. A useful first step is to observe discussions without taking part in them. (If you cannot officially act as observer, choose a meeting in which it will not matter if you adopt a low profile and take notes surreptitiously.) You may want to use a form to help with this. Figure 10.1 gives an example of one such form already completed. At first you may wish to concentrate on one category of behaviour, as this simplifies the task. Two other people can observe the remaining categories.

ACTIVITY 10.2

Use a form such as that shown in Figure 10.1 to record the sorts of contributions members make to a discussion (a blank is available as a web resource). Reflect on the extent to which the pattern of ticks which emerges explains the effectiveness or otherwise of the group.

ACTIVITY 10.3

Ask someone else to use a similar form to record your own contribution to group work and give you feedback on the sorts of behaviours you used most and any reflection on your effectiveness in the light of this. Such feedback can be a powerful tool in helping you become more effective. If any of the desirable behaviours seem lacking, practise using them in subsequent meetings. For example, decide that you will try to ensure that even the quietest members are encouraged enough to make a contribution, or make a point of summarising the discussion each time progress seems to have been made so that points are not lost. If you are behaving in a way which interferes with the group, think about why you may be doing this and try to notice (and silently rebuke yourself) each time you do this in future. It should eventually become less frequent. Devise an action plan for becoming more effective.

ACTIVITY 10.4

After a while, perhaps a few months, repeat Activity 10.3 to see whether you have shifted your behaviours in the intended direction. File your comments for future review.

FORMAL MEETINGS

Many managers complain that they spend far too much time in meetings. Formal meetings may seem intimidating until you are used to them. There are rituals to do with approving minutes, making remarks through the chair and identifying 'voting members'. You may feel unwilling to contribute because you feel unsure about the

Cartoon by Neill Cameron, www.planetdumbass.co.uk

'rules' or wonder how on earth to take minutes if charged with this task. However, the 'rules' are really only an attempt to avoid some of the things that commonly go wrong in informal discussions. The actual skills involved are much the same, as becomes clear when you understand what the ritual is intended to serve.

Membership lists

Particularly where a meeting is intended to take significant decisions (about costs, policy, progress on an important contract and so on), the informality of a discussion group is not enough. It is important that the right people are at the meeting, so a formal membership list will need to be agreed. Otherwise there may be complaints that the decision was improperly taken. Indeed, if some key players are not there to contribute their information, a bad decision may be taken.

Attendance

Since there was a reason for members to be on the list, it is important that they attend. Normally the minutes of the meeting will log those present so that they cannot later disclaim responsibility for decisions. Absentees, who should have given apologies in advance, can also be contacted by anyone who feels the need to 'fill them in' on something which happened. The secretary may also wish to arrange for absentees to send a representative in their place. (This representative would not usually be able to vote and would be minuted as 'in attendance' rather than 'present'.)

Chair

In an informal group, members usually share responsibility for the behaviours necessary to progress the task and manage the process. They are expected to exercise self-discipline and avoid the unhelpful behaviours listed above. In formal meetings, the overall responsibility for all this is vested in the person chairing the meeting. With a skilled chair this can work wonderfully. People are asked to make

135

contributions at relevant points, the discussion is gently 'managed' to ensure that it is kept to the point, progress is summarised at intervals, conflicts are tactfully explored and resolved and, when as much progress has been made as is likely, the point is drawn to a close and the next item on the agenda is taken so that the meeting finishes on time, with all items having been properly covered. Unfortunately, not all chairs are good at all these behaviours. (Some, indeed, do not seem to be good at any of them.) They may have been chosen for their seniority or some other reason rather than their skills. Provided other group members quietly adopt the necessary behaviours to fill the gap, this does not matter. If they sit back and cheerfully take no responsibility, the meeting can be a disaster.

Agenda

People need to know in advance what will be discussed so that they can consult with those they represent, gather any necessary information and have thought about the issues involved. An agenda lists the time and place of the meeting and the items to be discussed in the order in which they will be addressed. It should be sent to all members well in advance of the meeting. The chair of the meeting is normally responsible for putting together the agenda and will need to think about how long items are likely to take. Too long an agenda is to be avoided. Items will be given insufficient attention or the meeting may go on beyond the point at which those present are capable of thinking straight. (Most people cannot concentrate fully for more than two hours.) As meetings take some time to warm up, one or two short items at the start of the agenda may be a good idea. But the most important items should follow immediately after this, when people are at their most alert. Beware the really important item which appears at the very end of a long agenda. This will be one where the chair is hoping to get a decision to go in a particular way and is more likely to achieve this when everyone is exhausted and hungry. It is possible in this case to ask for the item to be taken earlier on the agenda. If you suggest this, giving your reasons, and others present support you, the chair may have to agree.

Papers

In assembling an agenda it is important to think about how much preparatory information members need beforehand. Small items may not need supporting papers. Their proponents can make a verbal case at the meeting and this will be an adequate basis for discussion. For any complex case, however, where there are reasons for and against a proposal and information which people need to have absorbed before they can discuss it, supporting papers need to be written. Clearly, these papers need to be circulated to members sufficiently in advance of the meeting (ideally with the agenda) for them to be able to study their content in detail. If you are asked to write a paper for a meeting, remember that you are trying to make a clear and fair case without giving unnecessary information. If a paper is too long, it risks not being read properly.

Preparation

Assuming that the chair and secretary have done their preparatory work adequately and circulated agenda and papers in good time, you have an obligation to prepare too. This means setting aside sufficient time to read papers thoroughly, think about them, discuss them with other people who may be involved, gather together any relevant information to which you have access but not everyone else at the meeting does, as well as working out what points you would like to make at the meeting and how best they might be made, given the people who are likely to be there and their possible points of view and counter-arguments. You may not actually make these points, or not in these words, if the discussion goes in an unanticipated direction. Meetings are not best seen as a collection of set speeches. But if you have done this preparation, the points that you *do* make are more likely to be relevant and effective than if you rely on spur-of-the-moment inspiration. (You are also likely to make a better impression on other group members, which may be important if they have the power to influence your future.)

Discussion style

Because the chair is officially responsible for the progress of the meeting, members are normally expected to catch the chair's eye and gain permission to speak. In large meetings this is essential. In smaller ones, provided conduct is reasonably orderly, the chair may let people discuss without this hindrance, intervening only if discussion is becoming disorganised, someone is talking too much or someone else is contributing nothing on an item on which they would be expected to have useful information to offer. The more formal the meeting, the more formal the language that tends to be used in making contributions, but the basics of talking and listening still apply: paying full attention to what others are saying and making sure that you do not undervalue it because of prejudice; 'rewarding' their contributions with agreement; expressing your points clearly; avoiding getting emotional about issues; being sufficiently assertive to make points that have a fair chance of being valid and to make them in a positive enough way that they will be heard; and avoiding time wasting of any kind.

Minutes

Because it is important to know what decisions were reached, and who was involved in reaching them, minutes are usually taken. In addition to listing those present, minutes need to log the basic reasons for a decision, actions agreed and responsibility for progressing these actions. Minutes will normally be circulated soon after a meeting so that any inaccuracies can be spotted, and the corrected minutes are then approved at the start of the next meeting. As the agreed record of decisions, these minutes are extremely important. There can in theory be no ambiguity about what is now agreed policy and it is clear whose responsibility it is to implement it. The practice, alas, may fall short of this. The person charged with taking the minutes often feels that they need to transcribe every word said, so that the minutes become so long that no one has time to read them. Perhaps because of this, the minutes may be put off as an unimportant or difficult job and appear on the day of the next meeting, by which time no one can really remember what happened and some of those who were supposed to have taken action will have totally forgotten about it. Or the minutes may be circulated late on purpose and record what the chair and secretary wanted to have happened, rather than what really did happen. 'Managing by minutes' can be a very effective tool, if an undemocratic one. Indeed, in an episode of the television comedy *Yes, Minister* it was suggested that the minutes should be written *before* the meeting. If you are taking minutes for the first time, model them on previous minutes. Once you are confident with this, discuss with the chair whether there might be better ways of doing it.

Action notes

For slightly less formal or more task-oriented meetings, a scaled-down version of minutes may be taken. These will note who was present and log actions agreed and responsibilities for these actions, but no more. Because they are briefer and focus on action, they can be written extremely quickly, even during the meeting, and people can be given a clear statement of their responsibilities the next day.

ACTIVITY 10.5

Review the formal groups to which you belong. (If you cannot think of any, try to join at least one during the next few months so that you can practise these skills.) List them and note against each how effective the formal structure is in progressing the group's objectives. If elements seem to be ritualistic rather than serve their intended purpose, think about ways in which you might be able to contribute to their effectiveness. Draw up a plan for doing this and check your success against this after each meeting you attend.

ACTIVITY 10.6

Find a way of taking at least some responsibility for a meeting. This might be by chairing it (volunteers for this role are often very welcome), acting as secretary or gaining the chair's agreement that you might act as assistant, joining in agenda-setting discussions and taking some of the responsibility for ensuring that the meeting progresses as desired. Put together an 'exhibit' for your file which describes the purpose of the meeting and the ways in which you contributed to achieving this. An annotated agenda showing which items you suggested and why, any papers you wrote and comments on the interventions you made, together with the minutes and a statement from the chair saying how s/he perceived your contribution, might form a clear demonstration of your ability to function in this context.

Chairing a meeting requires you to think of far too many things at once. You will be so involved in task and process that you will have little brain capacity for reflecting on your own performance. If at all possible, the first few times you act as chair ask someone attending the meeting to act as observer for you and to give you feedback afterwards. This can feel very risky but may be encouraging. You may feel that you totally messed things up, but the observer may have noticed a number of things that you did well. If they *do* see weaknesses, surely it is better to be aware of them and work at improving them. You would not want everyone else to know about them while you remain in blissful ignorance. Such feedback is best given a short while after the meeting, rather than immediately. Chairing is exhausting and frequently traumatic, at least at first, and you are unlikely to be fit for anything, certainly not for constructive feedback, until you have had a recovery period. It can be helpful to write down your own reflections on your performance – what contributed to success and what might, on reflection, have been handled differently – as soon as you feel strong enough and to file these. Comparing your own reactions with feedback from an observer can make future reflection more effective as you will become aware of blind spots, or areas of over- or under-sensitivity.

TASK GROUPS

Task groups are one of the building blocks of organisations. Teams are formed which contain all the skills needed to progress a specific task. Some teams have a designated leader whereas, in others, responsibility for the work is shared equally among members. The former is the classic 'supervisor responsible for a group of subordinates' structure. It has the apparent merits of clarity of responsibility and of power. If things go wrong, the supervisor will have to answer to his or her superior. But because the supervisor can, in theory at least, discipline any member of the team not pulling their weight, things should not go wrong in the first place.

There are less apparent, but equally real, drawbacks, which parallel issues raised in the discussion of the chairing role above. If 'team' members see all the responsibility as lying with their boss, they will feel none themselves. Their goal will be to avoid being disciplined, and any group interaction is likely to be directed not towards progressing the work better but towards outwitting the boss.

The concept of 'autonomous working groups' (AWGs) was one of the organisational breakthroughs of the 1960s, seen as avoiding many of the problems of assembly lines. AWGs were given collective responsibility for a specified task (in one of the classic experiments, for assembling engines for Volvos) with all the tools and materials needed to do this. Supervisors were no longer in charge of coordinating the efforts of individuals, but either seen as resources available for consultation or removed altogether. All decisions about who did what, how quickly and when (including who took holidays when) were the responsibility of the group as a whole. These autonomous groups became very committed to the task and produced measurably higher-quality work. Absenteeism was much lower. There were queues of people wanting to work in this fashion.

There were costs, of course. Assembly lines are a very efficient way of operating: tooling up for group assembly was much more expensive; there was more work in progress at any one time; the training of multi-skilled employees was initially costly. But above all, management felt threatened by the autonomy which the workforce had under this arrangement, even though managers had their roles redefined rather than being made redundant.

In the harsher 1990s the revolution in information technology meant that neither work groups at the bottom of the organisation nor senior management at the top needed layers of intervening managers to filter information up and down. They could now have direct access to it themselves. Such layers were therefore drastically pruned, or removed altogether, and fairly autonomous work groups came into favour again, variously entitled 'flexible work teams', 'cells' or 'high-performance teams', and have remained a common structure. In professional organisations this has always been a common way of working. You are highly likely, therefore, to find yourself working as a member of a group with some responsibility at least for the group's performance.

→ Ch 12

In the meantime, you should have plenty of opportunities to work in task groups while you are a student. Even groups formed to discuss case studies and present conclusions to the class as a whole are task groups as well as discussion groups if some of the work needs to be subdivided between group members. Collective work on an experiment, or on data collection for a topic, offers further possibilities. Project groups of any nature are likely to share many features with semi-autonomous working groups in organisations and offer excellent scope for practising the necessary skills. (There is more specifically on project work in Chapter 16.)

→ Ch 16

The non-study part of your life may offer further opportunities. You may be raising funds for a good cause, organising a social event or planning an expedition to a remote part of the globe. Whatever the task the group addresses, the general principles underlying success are the same as those for a group discussion. All group members need to understand the group's objectives, communication will be vital both at this and at every subsequent stage, progress needs to be monitored, and so on. Unless a formal leader is chosen, group members will need to find some way of ensuring that these aspects are covered all the time.

Additionally, there will need to be discussion about how to split up the work, both in logical terms of sub-tasks which can be progressed independently and with regard to allocating these responsibilities so that you make best use of the group's resources. Clearly, the more that group members can take on tasks which interest them and which they feel play to their strengths, the better the output is likely to be. This may require a degree of negotiation or even a rearrangement of sub-tasks if some jobs prove much more popular than others. People will need to understand their responsibilities (see comments on action notes in the previous section), will need to use self-management skills to progress their own part of the task (including taking corrective action, perhaps in the form of letting people know if there is a problem and seeking help), and will always need to remember to communicate anything which comes up in the course of their work which would be useful for others to know. This is often problematic: as one's own task assumes great importance it is easy to forget the wider group and its needs.

ACTIVITY 10.8

List the task groups of which you are already a member and use the ideas above as a basis for reviewing their effectiveness. Note whether you are clear about group objectives and whether others share your interpretation of these (could you all draw up the same list of what would constitute success and failure?). Similarly, how clear are you about your personal (or subgroup) objectives? Do you know whether or not you are on target? If you know you have done less than you should have, do you know why? Does anyone else know you are behind? Might they be able to help if they did? Do you feel committed to the group and the task? Note down ways in which the group as a whole, and you individually as a member of the group, could be more effective.

ACTIVITY 10.9

In the light of the previous activity, try to be part of an effective group and to document the experience as an exhibit. You will need to address the following.

- **Understanding of collective goals** – who set them, what constitutes success and what failure, what the constraints are, what the timescales are, how closely group members agree on the goals. (Note that it is important to explore reasons for disagreement: the minority view might be the right one.)
- **Allocation of responsibility for subtasks** – what was done to maximise the extent to which these fit people's strengths and preferences, how the group checked that people understood and agreed to their tasks, whether people were clear on interim goals and the timing for these, whether there are arrangements for checking progress and sharing information on an ongoing basis.
- **Support and encouragement** – are there ways of ensuring that people can seek help from others if things go wrong and can 'reward' each other for interim successes? Particularly for long-term projects, such motivational aspects are extremely important.

Your exhibit might include notes of discussions, highlighting your contributions, quotes from others (including your tutor) on the effectiveness of your own efforts, any plans you drew up for group or individual work with progress noted on them, notes of any corrective action or adaptation of plans that was necessary and reasons for this, and of course, if appropriate, the finished product or tutor comments on this.

VIRTUAL TEAMS

Increasingly, work groups are dispersed geographically and need to 'meet' electronically. Students on the (distance learning) programme I teach are often members and/or managers of groups which span several continents. Indeed, my students are similarly distributed. Since travel is expensive of time and energy, as well as money, it is important to find ways of working effectively as a 'virtual team', using ICT for many of the team's interactions. More technical aspects of meetings in 'virtual space' were dealt with in Chapter 7. Here I want to adopt a more 'group behaviour'

→ Ch 7

perspective on online group working. As in Chapter 7, the focus will be mainly on text-based asynchronous interaction.

Effective working in a virtual team requires just as much attention to task and process as in a 'normal' group. Some task issues are actually easier. It is very easy to transmit documents between members, for example. It is easy to communicate your comments, perhaps by annotating the original document and then circulating it to the group.

Some aspects, however, are harder. Members need to be just as clear on, and committed to, the team objectives, as with face-to-face teams, and they need to continue to feel involved. When working remotely, this presents a considerable challenge. You cannot make someone feel better with a smile. If you are conferencing synchronously using Microsoft Netmeeting or other system allowing the group to talk in real time while sharing screens, you will need to work hard at ensuring that 'airtime' is shared fairly. Gatekeeping is essential, and even if you do not have a formal chair you will almost certainly need to designate someone to manage the turn-taking element. If you are working asynchronously in a computer conference this is less of a problem. But it is still very easy for people to feel 'distanced', and to drop out of discussions, so particular attention needs to be paid to process and making people feel involved. You may find the following guidelines for asynchronous conferencing helpful.

Guidelines for asynchronous conferencing

- Meet face to face if at all possible, in order to get to know group members and to start to build trust.
- If you cannot meet, allow some 'social' time in the conference for people to feel comfortable together.
- At the same time, post résumés so that people can check who you are if they forget. Include a photo if you can.
- Obtain members' explicit agreement on what is needed to achieve the group task, and how it will be most effective to operate (times of logging on, deadlines for contributions and so on).
- Break tasks down into constituent parts with deadlines, and be absolutely clear who is responsible for doing what.
- Ensure that someone accepts responsibility for reminding people of incipient deadlines.
- Be particularly careful to give feedback in a constructive and supportive way – and pay attention to making people feel their contributions are valued.
- Summarise discussion at regular intervals and check on progress.

Set aside some short periods when people will all try to log on at once and respond quickly to each other – this can be a useful antidote to the more disconnected and 'measured' asynchronous communication.

It is particularly difficult to work through the earlier stages of team working remotely. Clarifying objectives, deciding on the roles members will play and agreeing ways of working are much more easily done face to face. These tasks *can* be done electronically, but it is less easy to thrash out complex issues and explore areas of disagreement remotely. Nor is it easy to develop the sense of membership and mutual support essential for effective team working.

Most effective virtual teams go through these early and crucial stages face to face. Once members feel they 'know' each other it is much easier to sustain subsequent progress while working remotely. It also becomes easier as you become more familiar with remote working. So if you do get the chance to work in this way during your course you should use the opportunity to develop your remote team-working skills.

DEVELOPING EFFECTIVE GROUPS

Some of the classic research on groups is still helpful when we think about how to make a group effective, regardless of the nature of the task. In case you have not covered this research in a social psychology course, some commonly used frameworks are outlined here. These relate to selection of group members, to the stages which groups go through when they first form and to two main hazards of an established group: groupthink and scapegoating. If you are aware of these aspects of group working, it will increase your chances of being a member of an effective group.

Assembling an effective group

You may well have found that your 'bad' group experiences listed at the start of the chapter arose at least partly because the group seemed 'wrong' in some way. It may have been too big or too small to do the task effectively. Some key skills or perspectives may have been lacking. Perhaps the group got on *too* well and developed its own view of the world which was out of kilter with that of other groups working on a wider task. Or perhaps the group got off to a bad start and people dropped out because it wasn't working. You need to understand some of the features common to groups in order to comprehend and avoid such hazards.

Group size
The optimum size of group will depend on the task. If a large number of perspectives or skills need to be included, or a great deal of work is needed within a short timescale, then obviously a large group will be needed. But the larger the discussion group, the less the scope for individual contributions, and the larger the task group, the greater the task of coordination. And larger groups can present logistical problems as members find it difficult to identify times when they are all free. As a general rule of thumb, if you can do the job with between four and eight people, then stick with a group of this size.

Expertise
Linked to the point above is the need to ensure that the group includes the necessary range of expertise. If you are choosing a group to work with on a project, this can be an important point. Again you may feel most comfortable with like-minded people, but the task may be better done if you deliberately choose to work with a more varied group, with a wider range of backgrounds and knowledge.

Motivation

In forming groups, it is important to maximise the extent to which people *want* to do the task. At work they may not have much choice, but even then there will be issues that seem of burning importance to some and insignificant to others. Where possible, the more commitment you have to a task at the outset, the better the group is likely to perform. If you are choosing a group to work with on an assessed project, it is important to try to find others who have similar goals to your own. If you want to get top marks, you will be very unhappy in a group where no one else cares about doing more than scraping a pass. If you want merely to pass, you may feel out of place in a group of people aiming for a first.

Individual behavioural differences

When you looked at the behaviours that were shown in a group and who was using each behaviour, you may well have found some quite clear patterns. Some people often behaved in certain ways and seldom, if ever, in others. You might, for example, be very good at proposing ideas, but never get involved with making sure that they are implemented. Someone else might be quite the reverse, or do these activities sometimes but spend much more time on, say, clarifying objectives and checking progress. Although if you are aware of the behaviours needed you can make a conscious effort to fill any gaps, you are likely to have natural preferences and to be able to behave in these ways without effort.

Noting this variation, Belbin (1981) suggested that, for a group to be fully successful, a number of roles were needed. He was working with groups doing real tasks in organisations, so although there are clear links with the behaviours seen in group discussions, you will also notice some differences. He originally suggested that eight roles could be identified, as Box 10.1 shows. Later he added a ninth, the specialist.

→ Ch 16

BOX 10.1

Belbin's team roles

- **Chair**, who acts as coordinator, working primarily through others. The role calls for discipline and balance.
- **Plant**, who comes up with original ideas, is imaginative and usually very intelligent, but can be careless of detail and resent criticism.
- **Shaper**, who stimulates others to act.
- **Monitor–evaluator**, who assesses ideas or proposals.
- **Resource investigator**, who brings in resources and ideas from outside. While usually extroverted and relaxed, this person is not usually original. Nor is s/he a driver, relying on the team to take up and develop his or her contributions.
- **Team worker**, who works on process, holding the team together.
- **Company worker**, who is strong on practical organisation, administration and turning ideas into manageable tasks.
- **Completer-finisher**, who does the essential (if unpopular) work of checking details and chasing when deadlines approach.

It is fairly clear that for most tasks to be progressed all these roles will be needed. You will probably be able to think of people who seem to be particularly good at some and less good at others. You may even have a clear idea of your own tendencies. (If not, Belbin includes a questionnaire that, by asking you about your approaches to and feelings about certain situations, enables you to identify your perceived preferred roles. Your tutor may have access to the questionnaire, but as with all such things, it is necessary to have permission to use it.)

If you have the luxury of choosing members of a group according to their preferred Belbin roles, then there is considerable evidence to suggest that it is worth doing this. But the fact that you cannot is no excuse for poor performance. Regardless of preferred behaviours, the roles are necessary and the group will have to find ways of ensuring that there is attention to process and that details *are* checked, even if this means, say, that one or two people who do not score highly on 'finisher' or 'team worker' have to make a conscious effort to take these responsibilities.

Myers-Briggs typing

Belbin's is but one of a large number of approaches to classifying people. One typology which is widely used by organisations for selection and/or team formation is the Myers–Briggs Type Indicator (MBTI). This uses a fairly complex questionnaire (again, your tutor may be able to administer this) to locate you on the four separate dimensions shown in Box 10.2.

BOX 10.2

Myers–Briggs dimensions

- **E or I: Extravert vs Introvert** – this assesses whether you are externally or internally driven. In the first case, as an 'E' you will react to things and people, acting before you think. In the second, as an 'I' you will be more internally focused, more reflective.

- **S or N: Sensing vs iNtuition** – this looks at what you pay attention to. If you are an 'S' this will be your normal five senses, you will focus on the 'real', take a pragmatic approach. If an 'N' you will use your 'sixth' sense, and be more future-oriented, more of a theorist.

- **T or F: Thinking vs Feeling** – this reflects the way you tend to decide or judge. If at the 'T' end, you will reason from principles, using a logical system. If an 'F' you will use heart rather than head, subjectively emphasising values, preferring compassion to justice.

- **J or P: Judgement vs Perception** – this looks at the way you live and work. A 'J' will adopt the planned approach, organised, controlled and with clear goals. A 'P' will be more spontaneous, preferring to 'go with the flow'.

Since the dimensions are independent, this gives sixteen different types, each of which has distinct characteristics. You will hear people proudly declaiming their 'MBTI type'. Many organisations have found this information useful in helping people to understand why they are finding it difficult to work together. For example, if you are an ISTJ person, you might find an ENFP person to be hopelessly disorganised, whereas they might find you hopelessly unimaginative and unadventurous. MBTI types can also be used to help assemble a suitable team for a particular purpose – you would not want all Js on a project requiring high creativity – though you might need one on the team to increase the chances of an output.

ACTIVITY 10.10

If you have not been 'typed' estimate where you might lie on each dimension. Now think of two people with whom you find it difficult to work in a group. Where do you think they might lie? Can you attribute some of this difficulty to their being different 'types' from you? If so, try to think about the strengths their type might contribute and see whether it helps you to work together more effectively in future.

If you have not done the questionnaire, or if you would like to gain further information, it is possible to find many questionnaires online that will give you an indication (of varying reliability) of your characteristics and their impact on team behaviour. You might like to explore the possibilities and compare your results on one or more of these with the results of other group members.

List the task groups of which you are already a member and use the ideas above as a basis for reviewing their effectiveness.

Group life cycles

Often when groups first work together they are far from effective. Sometimes (perhaps if there are no team workers and lots of plants) arguments can become very heated and destructive. Some members may withdraw from the group altogether, either physically if membership is voluntary or mentally if they have to be there but are hating every minute of it. There may be disagreements about objectives and about how the group is to work, two or three people all wanting to be 'in charge' of the group, some people behaving in ways that others find unacceptable. Tuckman (1965) found that groups commonly go through a sequence of stages in becoming effective. Knowing that this is normal may make the stages easier to bear and enable you to find ways of minimising any negative effects.

The stages are nicely rhyming (this may in part account for the continued use of this framework):

■ Forming – this is when individuals are trying to establish their identity within the group and find out what the 'rules' are. Behaviour is often tentative at this stage and extreme politeness may prevail, with no one saying what they really mean. A leadership pattern may start to emerge.

■ Storming – the politeness vanishes and all positions established earlier are challenged. Personal agendas emerge and there may be fierce status battles. This can be an uncomfortable time in a group: sometimes the group may disintegrate totally. But if the conflict is constructive it may generate greater cohesion, a realistic commitment to objectives and trust between members.

- Norming – out of the storm, more enduring norms emerge for how the group will operate, and what is acceptable behaviour within the group is established.

- Performing – provided that the necessary roles are being filled, the group can now really start to perform well.

Some people suggest that it is important to recognise a fifth stage. For groups that have worked closely together there can be unhappiness, even distress, when the group stops working together. Indeed, some groups keep going long after they have achieved their original goals. It is therefore helpful to talk about a stage of:

- Adjourning – here the process of group dissolution needs to be handled with care so that members can move on to other things.

MANAGING DIVERSITY AND CONFLICT

A major advantage of teams is that they can draw on a range of expertise and different sets of assumptions and perspectives. But to exploit this advantage you need to be prepared to work constructively with people whose world view is very different from yours. This diversity can stem from 'type', but also from cultural and other differences. In diverse groups, conflicts will sometimes arise, and you need also to have the skills to manage these.

Workforces (and students) are increasingly diverse. Many organisations now operate around the globe. Many workforces even within a single location draw upon an ethnically diverse workforce. You are likely to work with people from a wide range of backgrounds during your career. Furthermore, different professions have different 'cultures' too – different values and different ways of working. Yet many work teams are interdisciplinary, as are most customer groups. An ability to work effectively in diverse groups is a crucial management skill.

Most people are fairly tribal, and easily adopt an 'us' and 'them' position: 'We are OK, they are not.' This is the comfortable view as it preserves familiar ways of thinking and doing. It is probably barely conscious. I was once assessing teaching quality in the Midlands and commented afterwards that it seemed odd to see students working in such unmixed subgroups. The four West Indian boys worked together. The three West Indian girls, the five Asians and the three slightly older white women formed the other three groups. The lecturer seemed surprised I'd mentioned it. 'But they always do that,' she said.

Yet this micro-segregation was a hugely wasted learning opportunity. Each of these different groups was bringing different viewpoints, assumptions, values and experiences to the task. But because these were not being exchanged and debated, there was no learning about how others see the world. None of the students was finding out what was important to other people, or realising how their own perspectives might be limited. Nor were they learning how to manage the inevitable differences of opinion. Given concerns about global warming, it is a great pity not to exploit the opportunity to understand other people's ways of thinking without impacting upon your carbon footprint.

147

Working in mixed groups takes more effort. It becomes even more vital to check understanding at every stage than it is with a homogeneous group. Words may mean slightly different things within different cultures. Some cultures are less assertive than others: their 'agreement' may be mere politeness. Some cultures express themselves very directly, in ways that may seem almost offensive to others but are just the 'normal' way of saying things to those concerned. Some cultures treat deadlines differently from others.

If you get the opportunity to work in groups from a range of backgrounds, seize it. The potential for learning about others, and about yourself, is great. But to realise this potential you will probably need to make 'understanding each other's viewpoints and backgrounds' an explicit team objective, and to check progress on this regularly. You will also need to pay particular attention to setting 'group rules' – agreed ways of operating. These may need to include procedures for ensuring that less assertive members contribute at regular intervals, and regular checks on how people are *feeling* about how other members respond to their contributions. (Many of the indications of potential for learning will be at the implicit 'feeling' level.) You will also need to accept and examine explicit conflict.

When conflict *does* arise you need to handle it as a phenomenon to be explored rather than as a personal threat. Be assertive, not aggressive. In particular, aim to explore the situation rather than judge right and wrong. What exactly is the *nature* of the disagreement? Are people perceiving *facts* differently, disagreeing about *ways of working*, operating with conflicting *values* or bringing different sets of *assumptions* to the situation? If the latter, are these assumptions based on different experiences, perhaps in different contexts? By exploring questions such as these you may as a team come to a much more comprehensive understanding of the task and its context.

It may also be useful to explore why people feel so strongly about a point on which they disagree. This is a potential minefield, so you need to tread carefully. Think honestly about your own feelings first. Do you feel threatened? Undervalued? Are cherished values being called into question? Do you carry 'baggage' in the form of ingrained negative attitudes about certain groups of people? Where possible, check your feelings against the facts. For example, 'You are always saying my contributions are rubbish' might not match the perception of others in the group. Could you have an observer sit outside a discussion and check how your contributions are actually received?

By exploring such issues for yourself you may come to a much clearer understanding of your own attitudes. By exploring the issues – carefully – with others, you may come to see both how they perceive you, and the strengths and weaknesses of their, and your own, ways of thinking.

Feelings are dangerous territory. But an ability to appreciate how others are feeling, and how they are *likely* to feel if you say or do something, is an important management skill, and a key component in 'emotional intelligence', described shortly . You can go a long way towards increasing your interpersonal sensitivity by treating conflict within groups as a learning experience. Use your talking, listening and assertiveness skills, focus on the behaviour not the person, refuse to 'give up' until an issue is dealt with, and accept that your view may not always be the only, or even the

→ Ch 9

best one. Check your progress at regular intervals as a group, and try to capture what the various members feel they have learned.

DEVELOPING YOUR LEADERSHIP SKILLS

Organisations are increasingly focusing on leadership potential, and you may well be asked about this at interviews. Leadership is commonly defined in terms of the exercise of influence. Often the focus is on influence that derives from other than power or authority. When you are part of a team carrying out a project, or working in a group on a case study, you are unlikely to have a formally designated leader, so you have the opportunity to exercise your (non-authority derived) leadership skills in this context. Developing confidence in taking the lead on such occasions, and knowing how to increase the chances that others will want to follow your lead, will help you show leadership in work and other contexts.

A vast amount has been written on leadership (Amazon.com listed over 160 000 such items at the last count) but there is still substantial confusion as to what constitutes leadership and how it differs from management – you will often find the words used interchangeably. Increasingly the distinction already hinted at is made in the literature: management stems from position, and has to do with conformity and control; leadership comes from other sources and has to do with inspiring people to change. The emphasis on 'leadership skills' for people in positions of authority is therefore interesting. If it is more than mere fashion, it suggests a growing awareness of the importance of internal motivation rather than 'sticks and carrots' – a form of motivation consistent with a team-based organisational structure.

So what skills does leadership demand? Goleman (1998) claims that his research 'clearly shows that emotional intelligence (EI) is the *sine qua non* of leadership'. (Note that he is clearly taking 'leaders' to mean senior managers, here.) He identifies five components of EI at work:

- Self-awareness – the ability to recognise your own emotions and drives and their impact on others, to be honest with oneself and others.
- Self-regulation – the ability to control impulses and moods, to suspend judgement, to think before acting.
- Self-motivation – a passion for the work itself, and energy and enthusiasm to pursue goals.
- Empathy – the ability to treat people according to their emotional reactions (rather than your own).
- Social skills – proficiency in managing relationships and building networks.

If you are working through this book you should be developing most of these components. Reflective learning, as outlined in Chapter 3, should be increasing your self-awareness, and if you are including reflection on feelings, will also impact upon self-regulation. Your work on planning and on motivation will help with self-motivation. So, too, will ongoing emphasis on the need for clarity of objectives. This chapter and

→ Ch 3

→ Ch 2

149

→ Ch 9 the previous one, together with the feedback you manage to gather on your own impact, will help with developing social skills.

If you have the emotional sensitivity Goleman describes, you will be well on the way to being able to influence people – to making them want to follow your lead. I would argue that understanding their motivation is also important for this, and being able to make them feel good about the group task. (The process-oriented group behaviours are a big help here, while being able to listen, both attentively and actively, will help greatly in one-to-one situations.)

A number of writers on leadership emphasise 'authenticity' as a key component. This is a combination of the self-awareness that Goleman lists, and the willingness to be honest with other group members about your own feelings, possible inadequacies and mistakes. If you are working in a group, this kind of honesty can help to build trust with other group members. If you are all honest about your shortcomings and your worries about being able to do a task well enough or to meet deadlines, the group will be much better placed to exercise control in the sense of planning to cope with the problem so that objectives are met despite any deviation from the original plan.

But there are other dimensions to leadership too, which concern the task and the environment. In the sorts of groups that you will be part of as a student, using the task behaviours listed earlier will help you to exercise an influence on a group. At work, the other key dimension will be to do with being the one who has the clearest idea of what will be needed to meet changes in the wider organisation, or its competitive or → Ch 12, 13, 14, 15 other wider environment. Part 4 of this book addresses many of the relevant conceptual skills, though you will be developing these throughout your degree course.

ACTIVITY 10.11

Consider the extent to which you currently influence a team of which you are a member. What are your 'leadership strengths'? List those factors which you think are helping you to exercise leadership – perhaps you are good at making others feel part of the team and wanting to contribute to the task, or good at organising meetings. Make an action plan to become even more effective through these strengths. Look at any possible reasons for your influence being less than it might be. (Feedback from fellow team members can be really useful here.) Make an action plan to develop your skills in these areas too.

ACTIVITY 10.12

Look for an area where you can demonstrate leadership. Ideally this should be something which you already feel passionate about, whether a hobby or a charity. Aim during your degree to have devised a project within this area, got together a group to work on it, and acted as explicit leader. Log the experience in your learning journal and reflect on it as a basis for further learning. Write up a version of it that could form the basis of answers to 'give an example of when you have exercised leadership' on an application form or in an interview.

POTENTIAL HAZARDS OF TEAM WORKING

Much of this chapter has looked at how to get groups to work well enough. Can a group work *too* well? Obviously not; but if the group *process* is going well, and teams become really close, then there are three related things that can go wrong with the *task*. All are variants of the hazard hinted at earlier: of the group becoming the main focus, with the wider task vanishing from awareness.

Dominance of sub-objectives

If sub-objectives predominate, the group may end up in competition with other groups which are supposedly working towards the same wider objective. The group becomes too committed to its own task and to 'winning' in some way (for example, getting the highest production output), and it forgets that it is part of a wider endeavour. Yet often compromise and collaboration might progress the wider task better than competition. (There is more of this in Chapter 12 when systems ideas are introduced.)

→ Ch 12

Groupthink

Where 'groupthink' exists the group develops such a good feeling about itself, with members reinforcing each other's good opinion, that all indications that anything is wrong are disregarded. Any member brave enough to suggest that there is a problem will be made to feel a traitor to the group. This phenomenon is common in organisations. You will often find a board of a company refusing to believe that the signs of major problems are more than temporary blips, even though it is blindingly obvious to everyone outside this group that there is a significant disaster looming. You may find the same thing in project groups where members get on very well together and are sure that they are doing brilliantly despite evidence to the contrary. If they know what 'groupthink' is, you may be able to make progress by asking if they think it is happening. But the tendency to deny it is a strong one.

Scapegoating

If things do go wrong, and this is finally so obvious that the group has to accept it, its members may still try to preserve their positive feelings about the group by finding one individual to accept all the blame. A group that realises that its presentation on a case study was the worst in the class may blame something outside the group, for example the tutor for giving unclear instructions, or a task that was harder than that given to other groups, or a single member of the group (perhaps the one who was trying to alert them to problems earlier).

There are two negative consequences of scapegoating. First, the scapegoat, if s/he is a group member, may be unhappy and lose self-confidence. Second, the group will not learn what went wrong if it does not accept responsibility for there having been a problem. This is common in work situations. A single person will be sacked when a problem arises. Yet often it is the system that is at fault and many people in that position would have behaved in the same way. Indeed, they will go on to behave in that way in future if the real cause of problems is not investigated.

Guidelines for effective team working

- Select members with appropriate skills, knowledge, and, if possible, a mix of preferred team roles and types.
- If working remotely, try to have an early face-to-face meeting.
- Ensure that all members understand and accept the objectives.
- Pay attention to both task and process.
- Accept that feelings may run high during early storming, and when working in a mixed group.
- Explore the reasons for disagreements and conflict.
- Value all contributions.
- Review both task progress and group process at regular intervals.
- Reward success.

SUMMARY

This chapter has argued the following:

- Team-working skills are essential in employment, aid learning, and can be developed in many ways while you are a student.
- All teams need to manage both task and process, and good communication is essential.
- To work effectively in a team, you need to apply your personal management and communication skills in a group context and understand the requirements for effective teams.
- To be effective in a formal group, you need to understand the role of agendas, minutes and a formal chair. This understanding is also relevant to informal groups.
- In establishing a group, group members should be chosen to cover the necessary range of expertise and of roles. Sometimes it will be necessary to agree ways of dealing with missing expertise or handling non-preferred roles.
- A new group can feel uncomfortable, but later performance will actually benefit from early conflict, provided that this is firmly faced and prevented from being damaging.
- Conflict needs to be handled by focusing on the issue not the person, using assertiveness skills to identify the source of the conflict.
- A 'mixed' group can produce better task outcomes and help you increase your interpersonal sensitivity.
- It can sometimes be helpful to designate a group leader, or to allocate responsibility for different aspects of leadership to team members.
- Leadership skills are increasingly valued by employers, and team working gives you an opportunity to develop your skills.

- Key tasks for leaders include identifying requirements, task management and process management, particularly making individuals feel valued and motivated. Relevant skills include 'emotional intelligence' and conceptual skills for problem identification and clarification.

- Groups are at risk of becoming too cohesive and inward looking, competing with others when they should be cooperating, ignoring external signs that things are going wrong and blaming a scapegoat when things have gone badly, rather than accepting responsibility as a group and learning from the experience.

- Team working is a rich and varied area of activity, with many dimensions. You will need to observe others and yourself in groups and ask others to observe you and give feedback if you are to develop your skills.

Further information

- Baguley, P. (1992) *Teams and Team-working*, Teach Yourself Books/Hodder & Stoughton.
- Barker, A. (2002) *How to Manage Meetings*, Sunday Times/Kogan Page.
- Belbin, R.M. (1993) *Team Roles at Work*, Butterworth-Heinemann.
- Hardingham, A. (1995) *Working in Teams*, Institute of Personnel Development.
- **http://www.helpself.com** – for a wide range of materials including a free basic EQ test (to score your emotional intelligence) and (linked from the leadership section) an electronic book on leadership.
- **http://www.similarminds.com/personality_tests** – for a range of free personality tests.

Critical reading and note taking

As a student you will spend hundreds of hours reading. This chapter suggests steps you can take to cut down on these hours while increasing the benefit gained. There are two parts to this. One is to read more efficiently. This can greatly reduce study time, while improving your understanding and retention of what you read. The other is to think differently while you read, by becoming more critical in your reading. This will deepen your learning and develop the critical skills expected of a graduate. Both skill-sets are useful in the workplace. Taking useful notes is important in a wide range of work contexts.

Learning outcomes

Provided you not only read this chapter but *practise* the skills covered as well, you should be better able to:

- select appropriate reading material
- use techniques appropriate to that material in order to make most effective use of time
- reduce physical causes of inefficiency
- take a critical approach to what you read, questioning evidence, assumptions and reasoning
- take useful notes when reading, in lectures, or when using online material.

Whatever your preferred learning medium, much of the information you obtain as a student is likely to be from words. You may well spend more time reading than doing anything else. Despite twenty or more years' experience, you may be a far less efficient reader than you think. Increasing your skills in reading and note taking is therefore an important part of becoming more effective as a student. Note taking is equally important for lectures, and will be important for other contexts such as when interviewing, perhaps for a research project. Developing your skills in reading and note taking will mean that you spend less time reading yet learn more in the process. Reading skills will probably be important throughout your career. Most managers, and those in other graduate-type jobs, claim that they are 'swamped' with reading material. The ability to deal with this material efficiently and to evaluate its worth will contribute significantly to your likely success at work.

From Chapter 4 of *The Business Student's Handbook: Skills for study and employment*, 5/e. Sheila Cameron. © Sheila Cameron 1999, 2010. All rights reserved.

'SIMPLE' READING SKILLS

Gaining information by reading is one of the most sophisticated skills that we possess. Fine-tuned physical skills are required to use our eyes effectively. A wide range of conceptual skills are necessary too. It is not enough for the eye to focus on the word. The 'meaning' of that word must be interpreted and the 'meaning' of the sentence and paragraph and chapter of which it is a part. Your interpretation will depend upon the context, on other things you have read or experienced, and on your judgement of its acceptability and potential usefulness.

Choosing what to read is equally important. Your university library is likely to stock many relevant books and journals, and to offer online access to many more. The Internet gives you access to what feels like an infinity of materials of varying reliability and relevance. A necessary first step is to be able to select sensibly from this overwhelming array of potential reading materials.

Your choice will largely depend upon your purpose. You may need to reply to a letter, to write an essay, to comment on draft proposals for a change at work, to write a briefing document for your superiors based on what you have read about the latest technological developments in your field, or draft a marketing plan based on market research reports. In some cases (such as the letter) there may be no choice over what you read; in others you may have substantial freedom.

Given our reliance on text, it is small wonder that 'read and respond to written materials' is one of the elements in the key skill of 'communication'. And while effective reading is a component of other skills, it depends in turn on a number of conceptual skills exercised at different levels of mental activity, as well as demanding the physical skill of using the eyes.

There is a common (mis)perception that 'speed reading' techniques, which primarily address the physical side of reading, will allow you to perform miracles. (Woody Allen claimed that after such a course he was able 'to go through *War and Peace* in 20 minutes. It's about Russia.') This chapter, however, addresses much broader issues. Sometimes a superficial scanning *will* serve your purpose, and it is a useful skill to develop. But for much of your course reading, and the reading required of you during your career, will need to be far more thorough. The chapter's primary aim is to increase the *effectiveness* of your reading rather than merely its speed. That said, physical techniques for increasing speed are important and make a good place to start.

Using your eyes

It is important that you do the following exercise before reading any further.

READING SPEED TEST

This requires you to time how long it takes to read the next section quickly but carefully, without stopping, aiming to remember any significant information contained in the text. There will be a short test to check how much you have absorbed. Read without a break until you are told to look at your watch again. Look at your watch *now* and note your starting time before reading on.

Most readers are unaware of their eye movements while they read, assuming, if they think about it at all, that their eyes are moving steadily along each line before moving to the next. If this were the case, reading at one line per second (which most people would guess to be a reasonable speed) you would cover 600–700 words per minute. At this pace you would find you could easily cope with the volume of reading materials you are likely to encounter on your course. Eye movements when reading are far more complex, however. The eye makes a series of extremely rapid jumps along a line, with a significant pause, 0.25 to 1.5 seconds, between each jump. Furthermore, many readers do not move straight along a line, even in this jerky fashion. Instead, as Figure 4.1 shows, they indulge in frequent backward eye jumps, fixating for a second or even a third time on a previous word, and at intervals their eye may wander off the page altogether. With erratic eye movements like this and forward jumps from word to adjacent word, many readers achieve reading speeds of only 100 words per minute. At this rate of reading, the volume of work for your course, or that found in many jobs, is likely to prove an impossible task.

At the purely technical level, it is possible to achieve reading speeds of up to 1000 words per minute by:

- reducing the number of fixations per line, stopping every three to six words rather than every one
- eliminating backward movement and wandering
- reducing the duration of each fixation.

If you wish to reach this sort of speed, you will need to work at it. It will require concentration and considerable practice. But as well as improving your ability to get through your course materials and lessening eye fatigue in the process, such a reduction in eye movements will enable you to deal with reading material at work more quickly. This is important when time is at a premium. Any investment in developing your skills will therefore pay off handsomely. Furthermore, although you might expect comprehension to be reduced by more rapid reading, the reverse may well be the case. The pattern of a sentence and its meaning may emerge much more clearly and be more readily absorbed if the sentence is read in phrases rather than one word at a time. Your interest is more likely to be maintained if ideas are coming at you

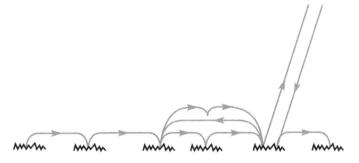

Fig 4.1 Typical eye movements while reading

more quickly and your motivation will be higher if you feel you are making rapid progress, so the rewards of improved reading techniques are many.

→ Ch 3

If practice is all that is needed, you may wonder why we are all reading so slowly. Surely we have been practising reading most of our lives. But remember that learning requires a change of behaviour, usually in the light of feedback. If there is no feedback which suggests the need for improvement, we are likely to establish bad habits more firmly, rather than to develop rapid reading techniques. Breaking such habits is extremely difficult. It takes considerable effort, at least at first, to read at an increased speed. Improvement will be made only through the practice of exercises specifically designed for that purpose. Even when you have developed efficient reading techniques, you may still find that you have to make a point of consciously practising them at intervals, to prevent yourself from falling back into less efficient habits.

READING SPEED CALCULATION

Look at your watch again and note the time _____ . Note how long it is since you last noted the time _____ . There were approximately 590 words in that piece of text. Divide that figure by the number of minutes elapsed in order to find your reading speed in words per minute. Write this down _____ .

TEST EXERCISE 4.1

The activities you have carried out so far have not had 'right' answers, although sometimes the text which followed may have suggested the sort of thing that you might have written. The quiz which follows is the first exercise where your answers can be checked. Answers to test exercises are given at the end of the book.

Now check your comprehension and retention by answering the following questions, saying whether each statement is true or false according to the preceding text. Do not glance back at the text! Cover it so that you cannot. This is a check on what you have understood and can remember. Do the whole quiz before checking any of your answers. Remember, the information is for your use. It will tell you whether or not you need to do subsequent exercises. If you look back (or forward) before answering, you will lose this information.

	True/false
1 Poor readers fixate once per word.	☐
2 With practice a poor reader can increase from a speed of 100 to 1000 words per minute.	☐
3 A speed reader will fixate only once per line.	☐
4 Once you have mastered speed reading techniques they will become second nature.	☐
5 The only drawback to rapid reading is that it tends to reduce comprehension.	☐
6 The duration of each fixation can range from as little as 0.25 of a second to as much as 1.5 seconds.	☐

The two exercises you have just done will have given you some idea of how well you are reading at present, in terms of both speed and comprehension/retention. If you got more than one of the above questions wrong, you should be aiming to improve your retention while you read. You were specifically directed to remember any significant information in the passage. If all your answers were right and you were reading at 250 words or more (even with a diagram), you may not need to work on your reading skills. This will become a priority only if you are studying a course, or are in a job, with an overwhelming volume of material to be read. If you found your speed to be less than this, or your retention needs to be improved, the following exercises will be extremely helpful in both study and subsequent employment.

Increasing reading speed

The following practice activities have been developed from those suggested by Tony Buzan (2003b). They will enable you to make significant improvements in your reading speed, provided you are prepared to invest the time and effort needed for practice: 20–30 minutes daily for several weeks will probably be required to reach the full speed of which you are capable.

ACTIVITY 4.1

If the speed and comprehension test above suggested that your reading skills need to be developed, the project can provide an excellent portfolio exhibit demonstrating your learning skills. You will need to include your diagnostic information from the previous exercises, as part of your justification for targeting this skill, to set targets for improvement and to keep a record of your progress. Comments in the following text will give pointers to how you can do this, rather than being cast as specific exercises.

Feedback is essential to keep up your motivation and to enable you to see when your rate of improvement is starting to level off. Keep a graph of your progress. Select a single book (not a set of readings) to control for ease of reading – material varies enormously in difficulty. When you start, and every week thereafter, time yourself for five minutes, noting start and finish points in the text. Aim to remember significant content – you can jot down the main points from memory at the end of the five minutes. Check this and give yourself a mark out of 10 to reflect how much you remembered. Count the words you covered. Log both scores in your file.

Many of the following practice activities require you to pace yourself. A metronome is ideal for this, as you can vary the speed of its movement. Failing that, you might be able to find a clock with a loud tick or set your PC to emit beeps at intervals. You will also need to measure intervals – a kitchen timer will be invaluable here.

You need to find suitable practice materials of different text densities. A light novel would be low density. An advanced specialist textbook would be heavy density. The informative parts of a serious Sunday paper, or a periodical like *The Economist* or *New Scientist*, would lie somewhere between. You can vary your practice materials. It is only your test 'feedback' text that must stay the same.

Your final resource will be an 'eye guide'. You need this in order to coax your eyes to fixate less often and more rapidly. Point with it to where you wish to fixate and move it after the duration of fixation required. A finger will do or some other pointer. Perhaps best when you are studying is a highlighter, as it allows you also to highlight key points of the text as you go along. You need to be careful when merely pointing to keep it just *above* the page to avoid spots before the eyes.

Reading practice activities

1 Muscle exercise

Fixate alternately between the top left-hand and right-hand corners of the page, moving your eyes between them as quickly as possible. Then alternate between top and bottom and between diagonals. Aim to speed up slightly at each session. (If using a metronome, note your speed each time.)

2 Page turning

Practise rapid page turning. Turn pages at a rate of three seconds per page, increasing to two seconds per page after about ten sessions. Move your eyes rapidly down each page, aiming to absorb *something*, though it will not be much at first. Do this for about two minutes at a stretch.

3 Reducing fixations

Practise fixating less often. Start by pointing at every third word, or every second one if you find three too difficult, and moving your pointer every 1.5 seconds. After a few sessions, gradually increase both the speed at which you move the pointer and the distance you move it, until you eventually fixate only once per line, for one second only. It will take a while to achieve this. You might then experiment with more than one line per fixation, but this is unlikely to be possible with the density of materials you need for study.

4 Speed reading

Still using your eye guide, practise reading as fast as you can for one minute, regardless of comprehension. Mark start and finish points. Then read for a further minute, aiming for comprehension of significant points, noting your end point. Count and record words per minute. Do this exercise several times per session, using different density materials each time.

5 Progressive acceleration

Using light- to medium-density material, and starting with your fastest comfortable 'reading with comprehension' speed, increase your speed by about 100 words per minute and read for one minute, then by a further 100 words per minute for a further minute, until after four minutes you are reading for a minute at approximately 500 words per minute faster than your starting speed. Calculate the speed at which your eye guide must move to achieve these speeds. Then read for a further minute, aiming for the fastest 'with comprehension' speed you can achieve. It should be higher than in the previous exercise.

6 Pre-scanning

Using fairly light-density material, start at the beginning of a chapter. Estimate approximately where 10 000 words will take you and insert a marker. Scan read to the marker, taking 2–4 seconds per page. Then go back to the beginning and read aiming for *some* comprehension, at a minimum of 1500 words per minute. As you get better, increase both the speed and the density of material scanned.

If you practise the above activities regularly, your speed of reading should increase significantly without loss, perhaps even with some gain, of comprehension. But reading effectiveness depends on more than this. You need at the same time to develop study strategies that will help you to choose appropriate things to read, to select appropriate speeds at which to read them, to think about what they contain while you read and to take good notes to supplement recall. It can also be helpful to index these notes for later reference.

SELECTING MATERIALS AND CHOOSING READING SPEEDS

Knowing what to read can be extremely difficult. Some lecturers may present you with a long list of books and articles, none of which is easy to track down. If you do manage to find them they may be dated or of little use. I did hear of one lecturer who had not updated his reading list in 25 years. I hope the story was a campus myth. But even in less extreme cases you may face a problem in knowing what you need to read for an essay, and an even greater one when doing a literature search for a dissertation.

→ Ch 12
→ Ch 2
→ Ch 13
Sometimes you will not know where to start. Sometimes the list may be impossibly long. In this chapter there is a brief introduction to selecting material. It is a variant of the systematic approach to problem solving covered in detail in Chapter 12, and used in short form in Chapter 2 as the basis for self-management. You will find much more detail on how to search for and select information in Chapter 13.

Define your objectives

→ Ch 13
What are you trying to achieve? Why do you want to read something on this topic? What do you really need to know? Are you seeking facts, ideas, theories or frameworks to help you develop your understanding? (More of this in the next section.) Are you looking for appropriate techniques or background information? Is the information something you may need for an examination? Is it necessary or potentially useful for a written assignment or clarification of something totally obscure from lectures? Is it merely for your own interest? Until you are clear what you want, you cannot start to look for it (though Chapter 13 explores some ways in which you may need to start with a vague idea and, through looking, find out enough to clarify your objectives).

Identify options

What sources exist? How easily can you access them? What does the library have, both hard copy and accessible electronically? Until you are comfortable exploring by yourself, staff will usually be happy to help. Is a text sufficiently important to be worth buying? If so, is there a second-hand source? What does a bookshop have on the topic? While the extreme case described above is rare, some lecturers do not update their lists as often as they ought. There might be something newer and cheaper than a suggested text, though you would need to check that it was as good or better. Ask teaching staff and other students for guidance, particularly before buying your own copy. If you are generating your own source list, look at references at the end of recent or key papers on the topic. See whether there are copies of relevant theses or dissertations in the library – they often have good bibliographies. Search key words. Check whether there are relevant government publications – these tend to be available free of charge online. If relying on a library, do remember that others are likely to want the same books as you do, and at the same time. The early student gets the book!

Identify selection criteria

Obviously it is important that the book or paper covers the topic you are interested in. But other factors need to be considered too. Is the text recent (or a classic)? By a reputable author? Pitched at the right level? Is it in a reputable, refereed journal? If it is on the web, how reliable is it? Is it based on evidence or opinion? How relevant/adequate is the evidence to your purpose? Are there any other factors which are important to your choice in this instance?

Selection itself

Selection is difficult unless you have access to the possible materials and can scan them briefly. Otherwise you will need to accept advice from tutors, librarians or others with knowledge on the subject. In North America in particular, academic tenure depends largely on the length of an academic's publication list, so there is enormous pressure to publish regardless of the density of the ideas or the information contained in the book or article. It pays to be sceptical when selecting. It is all too easy to think that everything in print is worthy of your attention. An important graduate skill is to know how to separate that which has value from that which is flawed, whether in terms of logic or in terms of evidence used.

Choosing your reading speed

Sometimes you will be looking for a highly specific piece of information. Did this research use a particular technique? What sample was used? What does the author have to say on a particular point? If your purpose is to answer such questions, a full reading of the selected text is unnecessary. Instead, use the index, plus rapid scanning of the material to identify the part you need to read in detail. Just as you can hear your name being mentioned at the other side of a crowded room, so you can bring selective attention to bear on written materials. While scanning the page too rapidly to read it, you can still notice the word or phrase you need. This will require serious concentration, however, and a refusal to be side-tracked. Of course, interesting digressions are what true education is all about, so indulge in them whenever you have the time.

The next fastest type of reading after scanning is aimed at getting a picture of the overall pattern of a book, chapter or article. For this, focus first on any contents list, then introductions and summaries, main headings and subheadings. Diagrams and tables of results are useful too. Several rapid passes may help you map the material better than a single slower one.

Slightly slower still is speed reading at your fastest speed. This may be suitable for lengthy materials, where the level of relevance is fairly low, or for background reading. Your aim will be to absorb the main arguments and assess the extent to which these are based on relevant and reliable evidence.

Much of your study will require a slower rate. The exercises you did earlier will still have been useful in eliminating inefficient habits, but where almost every word is relevant and you need to think really hard about the concepts and arguments contained, there will be a limit to how quickly you can work. You will probably need to take notes, both to aid comprehension and for later recall. You may sometimes need to stop reading, think and perhaps consult other sources before proceeding.

Slowest of all is reading to learn by heart. If you need to be able to reproduce an equation, a diagram, an argument or a set of categories, then you will need to spend time on every detail, committing these to memory. If you need not only to reproduce but also to apply what you are learning, you will need to practise this, preferably across a range of applications. There is not much to be gained (except possibly marks in a simple test) from learning something if you do not also learn how and when to use it.

You may find that once you have devoted time to understanding all the details, relationships and possible uses of material, you have in the process learned it. If not, try to devise a mnemonic, this is, something which is easier to remember than the thing itself. Acronyms or rhymes are good for this. You can probably already remember the requirements for objectives because SMART is so easy to remember and it is easy to go from that to what the letters stand for. The stages of group formation introduced in → Ch 10 Chapter 10 are easily remembered as 'form, storm, norm, perform'. Sometimes rote learning may be more efficient, particularly if frequent fast recall is needed. This is the way multiplication tables were once taught, involving going over and over something until it sticks. Rote learning can decay rather more quickly than rhyme or acronym, so it needs refreshing if it is used for something you will need only occasionally.

READING CRITICALLY

→ Ch 3 The idea of questioning the material you read was introduce in the previous chapter in the context of reflection on what you learned from reading. There, the focus was very much on how what you read related to your existing mental models, and whether it suggested that you might be able to enhance or improve them. This is closely related to the process of reading critically, and indeed depends upon it. But here I want to look in rather more detail at the 'critical' element, with a focus shifted towards the material read and its author.

Critical thinking is a key graduate skill, and one increasingly emphasised in learning outcomes for courses. So it is important to get a clear idea of what is meant. 'Critical' is not used in the sense of saying disparaging things about an author. Rather, it means engaging with the materials at a 'deep' level, making sure that you understand the claims that are being made and the arguments and evidence that the author is using to support these claims. It means understanding how these claims relate to those made by other authors, and understanding, too, the context within which the author is writing. There may be cultural, discipline-based or other assumptions which are never made explicit but which underpin the claims made. (As a one-time psychologist I have always had immense difficulty coming to terms with papers written by those with a sociology background: the agendas and the vocabulary and the assumptions made seem to me to differ radically from those with which I am familiar.) When you read critically you need to be alert to these assumptions, and prepared to question them. It is also helpful to know when the author was writing. Some older books and papers offer splendid insights, but it is important to be aware of possible differences in organisations and their contexts at the time of writing, and of the implications of these if drawing conclusions about the present.

The nature of claims

Having established the context in which something was written, the next step to becoming a critical reader is to understand the sorts of claims being made. By claim I mean any idea which someone says is true. Usually they give reasons for this claim. The claim and its associated reasons constitute an argument. Before looking at arguments and how they are constructed, it is helpful to understand some of the terms used. In particular I should like to look at possible differences between concept, model, metaphor, framework and theory. I say 'possible' because these terms are used in different ways by different authors. Even though these words are distinguished differently on occasion, the distinctions themselves are worth noting.

A *concept* is any abstract idea. 'Motivation' is a concept. 'Learning' is a concept. 'Hidden agenda' is a concept. Such concepts can be helpful in making you aware of an aspect of a situation and helping you to understand it. I can still remember my excitement when I first came upon the idea of hidden agendas and started to look for the *real* objectives of people in meetings, something it had never occurred to me to consider before. In the previous chapter I mentioned 'cognitive housekeeping': adding a new concept is one of the ways you can improve your 'cognitive house'. When you are reading something, it is important to understand any concepts which the author uses and with which you are not familiar. Be particularly alert to 'everyday' words or phrases that seem to be being used in a non-everyday manner. ('Critical' is one such example in this chapter.) If you do not understand the specialist sense in which the word is being used then your reading will be of little benefit.

A *model* in everyday language is a simplified representation of something. Thus the map of the London Underground is a model of one aspect of the system itself, namely the relationship between lines and stations on a line. An architect's 3D representation of a building he has designed is another sort of model. When you are diagramming a situation you are creating a model of it, often concentrating on only one aspect of the situation. It is important to remember this uni-dimensionality when dealing with models, and not to confuse them with the reality: 'the map is not the territory'.

164

A *metaphor* is the use of a familiar term to describe something probably less familiar. It carries with it the suggestion that understanding the former will help you understand the latter. Examples include talking about an organisation as a 'well oiled machine', or 'a tight ship'. Metaphors can usefully highlight key features of a situation. Morgan (1986) uses the spider plant as a striking metaphor for one form of organisational structure. But they are only as useful as the similarities contained. The comforting feeling of understanding that they give can be a dangerous illusion if you draw too many conclusions. As with models, you need to remember that metaphors only partially resemble the thing you are applying them to. Metaphors can, however, be a great aid to creativity, as discussed in Chapter 15.

→ Ch 15

Framework tends to be used to indicate a rather more organised abstraction. Frameworks are extremely common in management 'theory'. Thus you may well encounter the 4 (or 7) Ps in your marketing studies, and you have seen the SWOT framework in this book. Such frameworks tend to provide useful checklists for analysing a situation. If you wanted to look at the environment in which you were operating you might use STEEPLE (and look at sociological, technological, environmental (in the physical sense), economic, political, legal and ethical factors surrounding the organisation). You have already tried SWOT and SMART as frameworks for examining yourself and formulating your objectives.

'Management theory' is often used as a loose collective term to refer to any of the above, but it is more useful to think of *theory* as being an organised set of assumptions which allow you to make predictions about a situation. The STEEPLE framework alerts you to a lot of things to look for, but does not in itself allow you to predict anything; expectancy *theory*, however, allows you to make a number of predictions. For example, it suggests that if you reduce the value of outcomes, or link them less closely to performance, or make it appear less likely that effort will produce performance, then less effort is likely to be made. Management theories in this sense are rather less common than frameworks.

Management writing varies greatly. Sometimes the author may be proposing a new theory or a new framework, or may be critiquing some other theory. Or they might be describing a case study, or (in the case of some of the less academic publications) proposing the answer to life, the universe, and everything. When you are reading critically it is helpful to be clear whether the author is proposing – or drawing on – a theory or framework, or using metaphor. Some of the questions you would ask while reading will depend upon the nature of the claim.

Analysing the argument

In most papers you read, the author will be claiming that one or more statements are justified/true/useful, and providing arguments from evidence (which might be other theories, or research data or even armchair observations) to support this case. So before going further you need to work out the main claim that the author is making, and indeed any secondary claims. As an example of this sort of thinking I'll take another classic motivation theory, Herzberg's (1966) 'motivation–hygiene' theory: you are likely to encounter this at some point in your studies and we have already introduced two other theories of motivation so it allows comparison. I shall abbreviate the argument here, for simplicity.

Herzberg claims that man has two sets of needs: one set concerns the need to avoid pain and the other concerns the specifically human need to grow psychologically. This claim is supported by the results of interviews with 200 engineers and accountants 'who represented a cross-section of Pittsburgh industry'. Interviewees were asked to think of a time when they had felt especially good about their jobs, and then to answer questions about why they had felt like that, and its impact on their performance, personal relationships and well-being. This process was then repeated for a time when they had negative feelings about their job. Five factors stood out as strong determinants of job satisfaction: achievement, recognition (for achievement), work itself, responsibility and advancement. Dissatisfaction was associated with company policy and administration, supervision, salary, interpersonal relations and working conditions. Thus satisfaction was associated with the person's relationship to what they do, dissatisfaction with the context within which they do it. A chart showing how responses are distributed is included, which broadly supports the 'two-factor' idea: although most things are cited in the context of both satisfaction and dissatisfaction, mentions in the 'wrong' category are much less frequent than those in the 'right' one.

Remember the original claim: there are two categories of human need operating. The evidence to support it appears plausible. Different circumstances seemed to cause feeling good about your job, and feeling bad. But consider the evidence: is it actually adequate? No detail is given about whether the 'theory' was already known to the person categorising the responses, or whether the experiment was done blind. There is room for subconscious bias in any subjective judgements: the paper I was reading (an extract from a book) did not make this clear, so I would need to go back to the original research paper to check the method. (At this point you would make an action note to do this.) Then what about the sample of people interviewed? You could argue that two professional groups in a single US city is not really a representative sample. Would blue-collar workers respond in the same fashion? Would poor people in other countries be similarly unmoved by money?

Then what about the reasoning? Is the conclusion inevitable from this evidence? Would you get these results *only* if people had two different sets of needs? There is quite a lot of evidence to suggest that in other contexts we tend to take personal credit for good things that happen to us, and blame others for the bad. Herzberg's results could be explained equally well by this human tendency. Alternatively, as indeed Herzberg points out, the 'motivators' tend to be associated with performing the task, the dissatisfiers with the context in which it is performed. Would not expectancy theory, which was being developed at around the same time, predict exactly this? And in a way that enabled further predictions to be made about ways in which strengthening the effort–outcome link could increase motivation?

The next question is the 'so what' one. At the time, Herzberg's theory had a profound influence on organisations. It proposed a whole new approach to improving employee motivation. Instead of pay rises, organisations found ways of increasing responsibility. A whole 'job enrichment' industry grew up, following a very prescriptive approach which Herzberg developed. (Indeed, this is still the thrust of many job redesign exercises today, although because the underpinning theory is less simplistic, the chances of success are arguably higher.)

Did it work? Sometimes. But in other cases the effort–performance link was already weak because the staff concerned did not have the skills to do even what was required of them before the intervention. As expectancy theory would have predicted, the effects of job enrichment in such cases was catastrophic. It might have saved a lot of money in some of the organisations concerned if a more critical reading of Herzberg had been undertaken before job enrichment was embarked upon.

Mapping the argument

In looking at this particular, much quoted and, at the time, highly influential piece of writing, I was trying to do three things:

- identify the claim being made
- evaluate the evidence being used in support of the claim
- evaluate the reasoning used to link the evidence to the claim.

It can be helpful to approach this graphically. You can use the form of a mind map (described later in this chapter) where each branch represents a single 'reason' with the twigs being the pieces of evidence that together form that reason. Figure 4.2 shows an example of an argument map, Figure 4.3 (on page 96) a spray diagram on note taking.

Branches might be in the form of different logical links. Thus one set of twigs might 'prove' something, make it fairly likely to be the case, be consistent with it, be inconsistent with it, or actually disprove it. You could write this on the branch. When

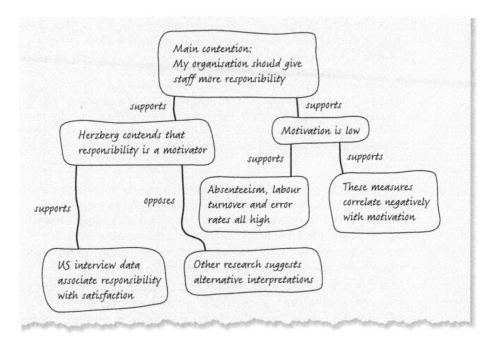

Fig 4.2 **Example of an argument map**

167

you have a complex argument, unless there is actual proof – rare in management research – you will be faced with working out how much weight to give to the different reasons. This will depend upon the strength of the evidence itself, its consistency, and the strength of the evidence–claim links.

Although we have been talking about mapping other people's arguments, the technique is valuable for mapping your own reasoning when you are planning an essay answer. If you are planning a research project or dissertation it can also be invaluable to think about your potential evidence before you finalise your research design, and consider how

→ Ch 8, 16 – however it comes out – it relates to claims you might hope to make in your report.

Software packages which allow you to map arguments can be really useful if the argument is complex. And arguments can be *very* complex, with many reasons operating on several levels. In these cases each twig is in itself a claim, and has supporting reasons (premises), objections to reasons (rejoinders) and objections to objections (rebuttals). By teasing them apart it is possible to evaluate each chain of claim-supporting claims-evidence, by looking both at the logic involved and the evidence (and assumptions) to which this logic is applied. As in the example above, you may find that both the evidence and the reasoning leave something to be desired. If you are interested in this, you can find material online. It may be designed to support – and sell – a particular product, but in the process may provide more detailed teaching than there is room for here (try **www.austhink.com/reason/tutorials**).

Select an article from a business or management journal or professional magazine. Try to identify: the principle claim and any secondary claims. If applicable, it may help to decide whether theory, framework and/or metaphor is involved. Define any new concepts. Ask 'so what'? If the claim is true, what does it imply? If the implications are important enough to justify the effort, try to tease apart the arguments involved. What claims and/or evidence are used to support the claim(s) and what, if any, evidence is used to support any intermediate claims? What are the logical links used? Do they add up to a valid argument provided the evidence is sound (i.e. is the conclusion drawn the only possible one)? Is the evidence adequate? Are there any hidden assumptions being made? If so, how valid are these assumptions?

Hidden assumptions are difficult to identify but may be critical to an argument. There was a hidden assumption in the Herzberg case which you may have seen once the alternative explanation was pointed out. This was that 'no other explanation is possible'. Once this assumption was queried, other possible explanations were looked for, and some found. So when a reason is offered it is always worth asking whether this reason is sufficient in itself to support the claim.

The other difficulty in business research is the complexity of most of the issues addressed, and the variety of contexts in which these issues arise. This makes it very difficult both to obtain convincing evidence and to know how far to generalise from it. Even if the evidence and argument were adequate in their context, would it be reasonable, for example, to draw conclusions about all employees from two professional groupings in one city? It was clear in the example above how difficult it was to interpret the subjective responses given by the professionals concerned. There is a real dilemma faced by many authors between seemingly 'scientific' quantitative data and the richer, but harder to interpret, qualitiative information. More of this in Chapter 13.

→ Ch 13

There are many other useful questions to ask when reading critically. A basic selection, including those already covered, is given in Box 4.1.

BOX 4.1

Useful questions when reading critically

- When/where was this written and what was the author's purpose?
- What claims is the author making?
- What new concepts are introduced, and what do they mean?
- Are they really new or merely a 're-badging' of existing ideas?
- How/when might they be useful?
- What new frameworks are introduced?
- What do they add to existing frameworks?
- How/when might the new frameworks be useful? Are there limitations to their application?
- Is there any new theory introduced?
- Do the 'organised assumptions' that make up the theory hang together logically?
- Does it extend an existing theory? (Sometimes quite small additions can be surprisingly useful)
- Is it consistent with other theories that you already know? If not, what are the inconsistencies? Are they explained/justified?
- How/when might the new theory be useful? Are there limitations to its application?
- Are there ways in which this new theory might usefully be amended?
- Was the author arguing a case to which s/he was personally committed? (This can indicate potential for bias)
- How good is the argument supporting the claim? Are there any shortcomings in the evidence or the logic, or any hidden assumptions which might be questioned?
- If there are inadequacies, is this because the paper is a shortened version of something else? If so, could you find more of the evidence by looking at other sources?

NOTES AND ANNOTATIONS USING WORDS AND DIAGRAMS

Take notes for:
- concentration
- understanding
- retention
- reference
- revision.

Note taking is a crucial study skill, but also invaluable at work. You have probably often taken notes to help you remember something afterwards. But note taking is far more than merely a way to extend your memory. It is a key component in active learning. And if you are one of those who learns best by writing, it will be one of your best 'aids'.

169

In writing notes you are – or should be – *organising* material, and therefore organising your thoughts. By extracting themes and key points, and jotting them down in a way that *makes sense* to you, you are interacting with the material. This interaction engages your mind. It stops your attention drifting off. It is *interesting*. It means that you will *absorb* the key points you have extracted, almost without effort. And good notes are likely to be far more useful to you in essay writing or revision than the original material.

'Good notes' are clearly more than a verbatim record of a lecturer's words or a section of text. Of course there will be times when a diagram or piece of text is so important that you will want to copy (or photocopy) the whole thing, or save it from the Internet. Even if you do, it will normally be helpful to take notes on it as well. When your notes do include direct quotes it is important to make this very clear, so that when you come back to them you know which parts are the author's words and which your own. There are two reasons for this. First, you may want to quote exactly what someone said when you are writing an essay or dissertation, so you need to know which words are a direct quotation. (With this in mind it is always a good idea to note beside it the page number from which the quote is taken – you may be asked to give this when quoting.) Second, and possibly even more important, if you quote without giving credit to an author, this is the deadly (in academic terms) sin of → Ch 8 plagiarism (see Chapter 8). If your notes do not make make clear what is a direct quotation you are in danger of accidental plagiarism when you come to use these notes in writing.

As suggested earlier, the active process of organising material into notes can maintain your concentration and help you sort out the structure of what the author is saying (you might try mapping their arguments). Thus you learn at a deeper level, understand more and remember more than if you merely read passively.

Not only that, good notes can often be far more useful than the original material. They will be easier for you to understand, as you will have organised the material into a form which makes sense to you. You can also include cross-references to relevant material from other sources or other courses. If working on paper, you can use colour to emphasise structure and aid memory. Notes which are briefer than the originals are likely to be much easier to refer to and to revise from. This is particularly the case if you devise an indexing system which allows you to find related topics easily.

As with everything else, you need to be clear about *why* you are keeping notes. If you are working with borrowed materials which will be crucial for a major project later, you will need to keep more detailed notes and to copy quotations and key diagrams as well as any useful references that you may need to explore and/or quote. When accessing materials on the Internet there is a strong temptation merely to copy huge chunks. While such copies may have their uses, remember the advantages of notes just mentioned. Without active 'digestion', condensing and restructuring you are likely to miss major benefits. Keep a full copy for reference, but make brief notes to supplement this. The same applies to photocopying. Apart from the potential expense, copies of papers and chapters will not help you merely by sitting on your shelves. Indeed, if they give you a false sense of achievement they can be a hindrance. They are only any good when you *interact* with them. So how can you do this effectively?

Annotation

If you are working with your own copy of materials, the most basic form of note taking is annotation, highlighting key points or concepts and making brief marginal notes or inserted comments. This will ensure that you are *thinking* as you read, searching for the key ideas, and that you stay awake. When you return to the materials you will be able to extract key points from the highlighting, and the brief notes you have added will remind you of relevant examples from elsewhere or how you finally sorted out a point in the text that was confusing.

Précis

When you cannot annotate materials, or if you want more condensed notes, it can be helpful to make a précis or summary, where you write down key points made. If working from annotated materials, you may merely jot down your highlighted words plus marginal comments. But ideally you are aiming to say something more concise than the original *and in your own words*. The translation process will go far to making the meaning sink in. Normally you will want your summary to be organised point by point, even if the original is less clear.

Diagrammatic notes

In taking notes you will often be looking for *relationships* – between ideas in a text or lecture, or between this material and some other. Diagrams are a particularly useful technique for representing relationships, with huge advantages over linear text for this purpose. A number of diagramming techniques are introduced at different points in the book: you have already encountered argument mapping. This is part of the same 'family' of diagrams as the more general mind-mapping technique, sometimes called brain patterns, described by Tony and Barry Buzan (2003). Variants of this basic form will appear in a variety of contexts and with different names. It is extremely versatile; note taking is just one of its applications.

In drawing a mind map, you start in the centre of the page, with a word or phrase indicating the main idea or central theme, then branch out from this, giving each sub-theme a separate branch. These branches divide further into sub-sub-themes. If you are exploring your own thoughts in this way it is called a mind map. If you are teasing out the content of something else, then it is often called a spray diagram. Figure 4.3 shows an example of a spray diagram on note taking. In the next chapter you will see how a similar diagram can be used to plan the structure of something that you are going to write. Software is readily available for drawing mind maps, and many students find this useful. Computer-drawn mind maps look much neater but they may be less memorable and can sometimes feel more constrained.

Buzan highlights the following advantages of this type of diagram over linear notes:

- The central idea is more clearly defined.
- Position indicates relative importance – items near the centre are more significant than those nearer the periphery.
- Proximity and connections show links between key concepts.

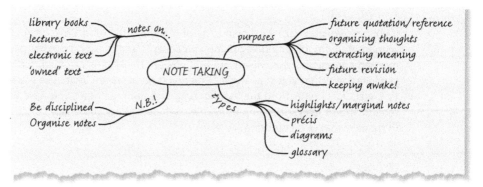

Fig 4.3 **Diagrammatic notes on note taking**

- Recall and review will be more rapid and more effective.
- The structure allows for easy addition of new information.
- Patterns will differ from each other, making them easier to remember.
- (For divergent, creative use – covered later) the open-ended nature of the pattern helps the brain make new connections.

Thus you can see how mind maps help you with both the digesting and structuring of material you are studying and its later recall.

ACTIVITY 4.3

Return to whatever notes you took on Chapter 3 (or to the chapter itself if you did not take notes). Draw a mind map of the main points. Reflect on the extent to which this helped to make the structure clearer. If working with others, compare diagrams and discuss both your diagrams and the extent to which they helped. Draw mind maps for the next five serious chapters or articles that you read. You should be hooked on the technique by then!

ACTIVITY 4.4

Prepare an exhibit showing that you can select, read and summarise in note form an appropriate chapter or paper. Your exhibit will need to document your objectives, the selection process used, the full reference of the text selected and your summary.

Lecture notes

Lecture notes present a particular challenge, as you have to go at the speed of the lecturer and cannot usually ask for a point to be repeated until you have grasped it. A few lecturers make things easy by providing handouts with the slides they use, so that you can make notes against these. More commonly you will simply need to do the best you can at the time and remedy any deficits later. While you do not need to become proficient at shorthand, working out your own abbreviations for frequently repeated words is a great help. If you are taking notes on a lecture, you may eventually become good enough to rely on mind maps, but at first it is better to keep more narrative notes on one page, perhaps trying to build up a mind map in quiet moments on the facing page.

Some lecturers distribute their notes in hard copy. Does this mean you do not need to take notes during the lecture? It does rather depend upon your preferred learning mode. Some people who are strongly auditory may find that taking notes gets in the way, and if notes are to be provided it is best not to make their own. Most people, however, will find that note taking has the same benefits in lectures as it does when reading in terms of maintaining their concentration and forcing them to engage with the key points being made and the relationships between them.

As well as drawing mind maps, try using sketch diagrams. These can sometimes clarify meaning more quickly than words. Space is useful too – leave gaps for things you missed. Leave space, too, for things which will need expansion if they are ever to make sense to you three months later. Indicate as you go along all the points where your notes are not adequate. Then discipline yourself to make good the deficits *as soon as possible*. You will be able to do this relatively easily within 24 hours, while the event is still fresh in your mind. Check with others whose notes, memories or comprehension may be better than yours. If you wait more than a day, the task will be far more difficult, if not impossible.

Discipline and organisation

However you take your notes, whether you use notebooks, loose-leaf files, PDA or laptop, it is vital that you are disciplined about organising your notes. Well organised notes can be invaluable. Dozens of scruffy pieces of paper scattered around your flat, or cryptically labelled documents distributed seemingly randomly between equally cryptically labelled folders, or left unsorted with hundreds of other things in 'My Documents' have little use at all. (Google desktop may provide some sort of rescue in the latter case, but is far from a total solution.) Part of this organisation should include a good index to your materials, so that you know what notes you have on which topics and can easily access them, and related materials, if an assignment or project requires it. A page numbering system is important for paper notes – you need to be able to reorder them if you drop them in a gale or lend them to a friend who mixes them up. If you are keeping electronic notes it is essential to make back-up copies at regular intervals. It can be heartbreaking to lose all your notes, especially if this happens shortly before you need to start your revision. PDAs are particularly prone to being lost, stolen or dropped, so you need to copy your notes to PC at frequent intervals. Hard disks on PCs can fail. So back-up frequently, and keep your back-up copy separate and safe.

For good note taking:
- use words and diagrams
- 'organise' content
- 'improve' within 24 hours
- file systematically.

Discipline is also important when it comes to references to any materials you do not own. Keeping a full reference list (use the format in the list of references at the end of this book if you have not been told to use something different) with your notes will save hours of searching perhaps months or even years later, when you need to use it for a paper or dissertation. It may seem a bother at the time, but it is more of a bother to resurrect an elusive reference when everything you can remember about it is insufficient to identify it.

Organised and disciplined notes will have potential uses beyond the particular course to which they relate. They may be a useful resource for a subsequent dissertation or project, or indeed help in a situation at work. Unless you are very pressed for space, it is therefore worth retaining them. It can be infuriating to need something and then realise you threw it away a year ago.

Similarly, you will have many occasions after your degree when you will need to take notes. Whether you are interviewing potential employees, listening to a speaker at a professional association, reading a lengthy report or sitting in a meeting, you will need similar skills so it is worth developing the skills – and the discipline – to take notes that will be of use after the event.

SUMMARY

This chapter has argued the following:

- Improving your reading skills can make you a far more effective learner, and aid career success.
- Practice can significantly improve reading speeds.
- It is possible to increase your reading speed without loss of comprehension.
- Efficient reading requires you to think more clearly about what you need to read, and why, and about where to find it.
- Lecturers, library staff and other students can help you find and select appropriate reading material.
- Different reading speeds are appropriate for different purposes.
- When reading it is important to adopt a critical approach, asking a range of questions as you read.
- It is important to identify the claims the author is making and to evaluate their internal consistency and the strength of the evidence and reasoning given in support of these claims.
- Mapping the arguments can be a useful approach when evaluating a case.
- It is important to relate your reading to other materials on the same subject, to the author's purpose and to the context in which it was written.
- Taking notes will increase the effectiveness of your understanding and learning and give you something for future reference.
- Mind maps can form a useful part of your notes.
- It is essential to be disciplined in organising and storing your notes.

Further information

- Buzan, T. (2003) *The Speed Reading Book*, BBC Publications.
- Buzan, T. (2003) *Use Your Head*, BBC Publications.

- Buzan, T. and Buzan, B. (2003) *The Mind Map Book: Radiant Thinking – Major Evolution in Human Thought*, BBC Publications.
- Morris, S. and Smith, J. (1998) *Understanding Mind Maps in a Week,* Institute of Management.
- Rose, C. and Nicholl, M.J. (1997) *Accelerated Learning for the 21st Century*, Piatkus.
- Russell, L. (1999) *The Accelerated Learning Field Book*, Jossey-Bass/Pfeiffer.

Answers to test exercises

4.1
1　False. Poor readers fixate more than once on some words. This backtracking is a major cause of slowness and you should have remembered this.
2　True, provided it is specially designed practice.
3　False, according to the text, which claimed three to six fixations per line, although it may well be true as later text will show. You may have *known* that the statement was really true, but it is often necessary to note what is actually *in* a piece of writing, even if it conflicts with what you believe to be true.
4　False. You would still need to practise the techniques at intervals to maintain high speeds.
5　False. Rapid reading may increase comprehension. This was another very important point.
6　True.

Thinking critically

According to the UK's Council for Industry and Higher Education, intellectual ability is one of the top four things that matter most to employers (Archer and Davison, 2008). Intellectual ability is not the same as being able to recall strings of facts. It is the ability to reach informed and valid judgements in complex situations through the use of rigorous analysis and evaluative skills, frequently with the explicit purpose of solving a problem. The nature of that problem may vary between your university work and future graduate employment, but the ability to think critically is the common underlying process in both these settings. This chapter explores some of the essential components of critical thinking which, if you commit yourself to developing them, will help you to achieve higher grades and give you an employment advantage.

In this chapter you will:

1. learn what critical thinking is;
2. find out about argument and some common thinking process and inference errors;
3. explore critical approaches to real-world problems;
4. examine the relationship between critical thinking and professional behaviour.

USING THIS CHAPTER

Estimate your current levels of confidence. At the end of the chapter you will have the chance to re-assess these levels where you can incorporate this into your personal development planner (PDP). Mark between 1 (poor) and 5 (good) for the following:

I understand what the principles of critical thinking are.	I can analyse other peoples' arguments and evaluate their strengths and weaknesses effectively.	I can construct and support my own arguments using evidence and reasoning to reach sound conclusions.	I know what 'critical engagement' with my subject is.	I understand how to synthesise knowledge and ideas as a critical thinker.

Date: _____

1 Why critical thinking is important

I think, therefore I am

René Descartes – (French philosopher, rationalist and mathematician, 1596–1650)

Today's highly interdependent world increasingly requires business students to recognize and understand diverse perspectives. And ... requires ... an understanding of the assumptions on which one's thinking rests (Neville, 2008).

Thinking critically in business and management is important because it is how you rationally question, test and challenge assumptions about the way things are done, then innovate and create new understanding and new solutions to problems. Yet Alter (2006), for example, found 'inadequate critical thinking' in real-world business-oriented system analyses to be one of the shortcomings even in his professional, working MBA students. The way you approach thinking is important if you are to demonstrate the rationale and evidence for your judgements, recommendations and actions. Your lecturers and current/future employers will expect this from you. If you get feedback on your work that says 'You need to be more critical' or 'More critical evaluation required' then you need to stretch and tone your ways of thinking. To get the best from this chapter, you first need to look at Chapter 7 'Reading critically' and Chapter 4 'Getting the most out of lectures', section 7 'Critical listening'. After this section you may then want to (re)visit Chapter 14, 'Improving your business and management studies writing' to develop how you express yourself as a critical writer.

2 What is critical thinking?

In Chapter 7, 'Reading critically', you discovered SMART (**S**kill **M**anagement in **A**cademic work through **R**easoning and **T**hinking) reading and considered the '**R**easoning' and '**T**hinking' aspects involved. As a **critical thinker** this means that for a given situation or context you:

- recognise alternative perspectives;
- analyse impartially;
- evaluate rationally and evidentially;
- judge objectively;
- embrace and respond to critique of your thinking.

Once mastered, this dynamic process drives continuous improvement in your thinking, learning and understanding. Critical listening, critical reading and critical writing are components of this dynamic process and the interaction between these and critical thinking is modelled in Figure 9.1. But 'doing' critical listening or 'doing' critical reading is only part of the bigger picture. Of themselves they are necessary but not sufficient solutions to the challenge of developing critical thinking skills, as the rest of this chapter will explore.

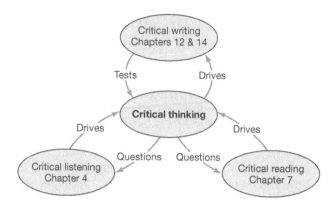

Figure 9.1 The dynamic process of criticality

Being 'critical'

I don't think I can be critical, as I don't like being criticised myself.

Steve, part-time Masters Human Resource Management student

Some business and management studies students confuse academic criticality with *criticism*. Criticism (of someone else's point of view or a friend's preference in music, for example) is usually a negative process of what's not liked about something. Many students assume that being critical means they must find fault, any fault, in the work they are studying. Thinking critically is neither of these: it is a process applied *equally* to all supposed knowledge in a subject area. This process is the constructive, rigorous scrutiny of the strengths and weaknesses of that knowledge (such as theories, models and evidence). The purpose of this is to establish whether and/or how those theories and methods contribute to our broader understanding of, and the solving of, the problems within that knowledge area. So, critical thinking is about demonstrating rigorously to our audience the grounds and reasons as to why we either reject *or* accept something.

I had this, like, sudden flash of inspiration when I was doing a business scenario analysis ... being critical was applying the same questioning framework to different explanations in the literature, trying to judge which provided the better explanation and then showing that in my writing!

Paul, final-year Business Systems student

The right mind frame

We take much every day knowledge for granted. For example, '2 + 2 = 4' is a real-world bit of knowledge that doesn't require constant demonstration of proof (although there will have been a time in prehistory when it was a revolutionary concept!). Some students don't recognise that at degree level they need to distinguish between 'obvious' or 'common sense' knowledge and knowledge which is open to question. If you are a part-time business or management student in employment, you may take for granted the way *your* business/organisation does things. Consequently you may not think outside the box when critically evaluating operational process improvement strategies, for example. Even 'obvious' knowledge in a context may be no more than a deeply embedded belief that has never been questioned, or a legacy from previous changes that no one has thought to review.

> *The other day I heard the saying 'if you do what you've always done then you'll get what you've always got'. As none of my family has ever been to university before I didn't have any experience of other ways to look at the world.*
>
> Serena, first-year Leisure and Tourism student

Many students, like Paul and Serena, discover that thinking at university changes them. The willingness to participate in this change is an important part of the mind frame you bring to your studies as it will push you out of your comfort zone in a number of ways. Look at Chapter 7, 'Reading critically' to review the sorts of approaches you need to develop. Critical thinking is an *'effort applied = results achieved'* relationship where attitude and motivation are important: if you don't put the effort in, then you can't expect to get high grades for your work.

The right thinking skills

The difference between information and knowledge is subtle but important. Knowledge is what you do with information. Knowledge is how you make meaning out of information. And, usually, you gain knowledge through an interactive process – by interacting with someone or by doing some critical analysis or further exploration of information.

(Hilton, 2006)

> *In my first year, for some of my modules I had to learn facts and information, which was fine. In others I thought I'd be told the theory I needed to know and then just write about that. I didn't expect to have to discuss alternative explanations, evidence and points of view and then weigh them up.*
>
> Mark, second-year Management student

There is a big difference between being taught what to think as opposed to learning ways of thinking in order to approach a thinking task. The first requires you to accept that certain things are held as absolutely true under all circumstances, whereas the second demands that you verify the validity of things in their context and test whether they remain valid beyond that context. Activity 1 lets you examine your approach to thinking skills and to consider where you might currently be between these two points.

ACTIVITY 1 Examine my approach to thinking skills

For each of the four **key statements** in the left hand column of the table below, circle the statement in the **response** column that most closely matches your current approaches to thinking about your subject knowledge.

Key statement	Response			
1 How I know about my subject is best described by:	Knowing all the facts.	Knowing what is certain and what is uncertain.	Knowing that everything is uncertain.	Knowing that things might have different meaning depending on context or situation .
2 Where academics have different explanations for something in my subject, this is best described by:	Some of the facts are wrong.	The academics don't agree because some of the facts are uncertain.	The academics all have different points of view.	The academics analyse and evaluate the evidence to reach their conclusions.
3 What I have to do as a student to learn is best described by:	Learning what my tutors tell me.	Applying my understanding of what my tutors tell me.	Developing my own opinions and points of view.	Considering different points of view to analyse and solve problems.
4 Showing my learning is best described by:	Memorising and repeating what I have been taught.	Showing I understand what I have been taught.	Asserting and defending my point of view.	Being able to analyse and evaluate the arguments of others.

Activity 1 is based on Baxter-Magolda's original (1992) Stages of Development of Knowing model and it offers you one way of thinking about your current perception of knowing (about a subject) and the process of learning within it. Baxter-Magolda used research she conducted with US college students to identify four stages of knowing: Absolute/Transitional/ Independent/Contextual. While Baxter-Magolda found certain gender differences, the most successful students **at university** tend to be those who have developed what Baxter-Magolda calls 'contextual knowing'. Contextual knowing is a product of critical approaches to your subject and the topics within it.

See the feedback section for further guidance on what your response pattern to this activity may suggest before continuing with this chapter.

3 Making an argument

Science is built up of facts, as a house is built of stone; but an accumulation of facts is no more a science than a heap of stones is a house.

Henri Poincaré – (French mathematician, physicist and philosopher, 1854–1912)

There is no absolute right or wrong in many of the topics you will study in business and management. There are boundaries set by legal requirements, and there are ethical or social responsibility drivers that will also impose constraints (which is why ethics are considered in Chapter 12). Outside these, you are faced with a range of theories/models and methods that seek to explain business and management phenomena. These theories and models may totally disagree as to the causes or reasons for those phenomena. They may also totally disagree about the solutions or practices necessary to deal with them. However, what these theories and models will each do is make their case on the basis of an 'argument' to seek to persuade an audience (i.e. you or other readers of the text) of their worth. If you and I could each take one of Poincaré's 'heap of stones' and build houses from them, we would likely both end up with different-looking houses. We would then judge each house on how the foundations were laid, how the stones were selected and put together, and how the resultant structure meets expected standards or requirements. An academic argument is in some respects similar to this and has a structure that we can talk about to help us understand how other people have 'built' their arguments.

The structure of an academic argument

At university, 'argument' has a precise meaning and a clear goal which is to present a conclusion based on an argument. When we make an *academic* argument, we combine three components: a starting **assertion**, the **evidence** to support it and the **reasoning** that shows the relationship between the assertion and the evidence (see Figure 9.2). Success at university requires you to understand the difference between these components. Success also depends on you learning how to combine these components as a **process** to show *how* you have approached the thinking tasks most of your assignments will demand of you.

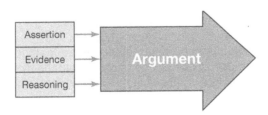

Figure 9.2 Components of an argument

I got very confused when our tutors told us in the first semester that they weren't interested in our opinions. I thought, how can I write anything if they don't want to know what I think?

Suzie, first-year Marketing student

Assertion

Whenever we make a statement about something, we usually say what we think it is, say something about its cause, effect or consequence, or make a judgement about its value or worth. For example: 'Internet shopping will kill off the high street'; 'without some regulation, market principles cannot produce socially responsible outcomes'; 'flexibility is more important than expertise in a modern workforce'. On their own, such statements are *assertions*. An assertion may be based on observation, belief, abstract thinking or research, but even so it is still no more than an opinion expressed by one person. This is really what's behind Suzie's tutor's comments. If you want an opinion on something, you can ask anyone, anywhere, what they think about it and they'll probably tell you. But what they won't do is put effort into researching the evidence and then demonstrating the steps of reasoning that underpin their opinion. All arguments will contain one or more assertions, but it is the further effort of building the argument that turns an assertion into a case to be made. A well-made case, with demonstrated grounds for the conclusion, puts you well on the way to getting good marks. Activity 2 helps you to think a bit more about the nature of assertion.

ACTIVITY 2 Considering assertion and opinion

This activity lets you examine the nature of assertion and opinion.

- First, select a current news topic that is politically, economically or socially significant.
- Second, select three newspapers that are aimed at different audiences and have different political editorial positions. (For example, in the UK, the *Daily Mirror/Sun/Daily Mail* are tabloid papers aimed at the so-called blue-collar audience and the *Guardian/Independent/Times/Telegraph* are broadsheet papers aimed at the so-called white-collar audience. Here they are grouped very approximately to their political persuasion. You might choose one tabloid and two broadsheet papers for example.)
- Next, read how the three different papers present their editorial or 'leader' comments about the news topic you have chosen.
- Now consider the differences in their coverage, perhaps in relation to what they identify as the cause, consequence or solution to the news topic. Use the following **question words** to interrogate what has been written.

Question word	Example
Who	Who are they? E.g. what sort of political agenda might they have? What sort of vested interests might they represent?
What	What are they stating/claiming happened? What do they conclude as an answer?
Why	Why have they picked this issue/topic as a 'leader' item? Why do they reach the conclusions they do?
How	How do they reach these conclusions? How do they present their evidence?
Where	Where else do they get evidence or support for their conclusions?

■ Finally, ask yourself what the different papers want you to accept, to what extent they agree or disagree and what might explain any difference of opinion you observe.

See the feedback section for further comment on this activity.

Evidence

To begin with many business and management students are unsure what is meant by 'evidence'. Whilst there will be some discipline differences, evidence in business and management subjects can be wide ranging. The table below summarises some of the main types and sources of evidence that you might be expected to use in your work.

Type	Examples
Quantitative data	Numerical data and figures from government, academic and trade association sources.
Qualitative data	Surveys, questionnaires, focus groups, observation.
Case studies	Those published in texts, or your own summary and analysis of the business/organisation you are employed in.
Academic texts	Citation from textbooks, journals.
Organisation and business documents	Citation from policies, procedure documentation, memos, meeting minutes.
Professional regulatory bodies	Citation from standards, protocols, codes of behaviour.
Professional/trade journals or magazines	Citation from editorial leaders, articles.
Personal communications	Citation from emails, memos and letters between you and another person.

See Chapter 12, 'Understanding academic integrity: learner ethics and plagiarism' for more about accurate citation.

Hot Tip Your university library will be your major source of good quality evidence; however, online sources are available to widen your research. Use this online tutorial to explore internet research for business and management students: www.vts.intute.ac.uk/tutorial/business/

I didn't pass my first assignment because I hadn't done enough reading, actually I only read the textbook chapter. My personal tutor said: 'If I see only a couple of sources listed in the Reference section of an essay, then I know that no matter how well a student writes, they won't have much to write about'. She was right.

Liu, direct entry second-year International Business Studies student

As Liu found, the type and source of evidence you put into your work will immediately reveal how much or how little independent study and research you have done. You will also reveal much about your skills as a critical thinker from the selection of evidence you use in your work. Be aware that how you *select* your evidence is not the same as being *selective* of your evidence. The critical thinker uses evidence that is relevant and current, and that shows the full range, breadth, depth and authority of evidence about a subject (see Figure 9.3). A non-critical thinker tends to be selective and uses only evidence that 'fits' what they want to say without too much concern for whether it is authoritative, relevant or of sufficient breadth and depth.

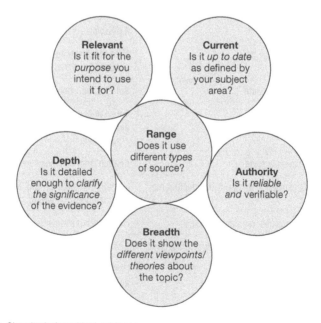

Figure 9.3 Six criteria for critical evidence

Hot Tip

If to begin with you are unclear about what *is* appropriate evidence in your subject area, **ask your tutors for guidance.** They will prefer this to having to write it on your assignment feedback and mark sheet.

Try Activity 3 to identify use of evidence in your subject.

ACTIVITY 3 Using evidence

Choose a text from your subject area. First, look for the types of evidence it uses. Next, use the questions in Figure 9.3 to critically test the evidence. Finally, ask yourself the question: 'Does the evidence presented give me confidence about what the author wants me to accept?'

Reasoning

One way to think about reasoning is to think of it as the glue or cement that holds the evidence together. In doing this it also connects things in certain ways: it shows the *relationship* between things. If we take three of Poincaré's stones, we can assemble them (or not at all!) in a number of ways. Figure 9.4 shows some of these.

There is nothing 'wrong' with any of the combinations in Figure 9.4, but for building purposes some combinations will be better for a certain job than others. There is a relationship between purpose and combination. When we consider the relationship *implied* by the connections, things get a bit more difficult. For example, if on the basis that it rained yesterday and it is raining today I reason therefore it will rain tomorrow, I am connecting my evidence together in a certain way *and* claiming a relationship between two days of rain and what will happen tomorrow. If, however, from the same basis I reason that I cannot predict what will happen tomorrow, I am connecting my evidence differently *and* claiming that there is no relationship between the days of rain. Reasoning is a complex process and there are a

Figure 9.4 Some ways of assembling three stones

number of errors that can creep into it. We look at this a bit more in Section 4, 'Common errors in thinking'.

The argument process

When we put these components of assertion, evidence and reasoning together we can think about the argument *process* as pushing a ball (the assertion) up a slope (the argument to be made). We could then see evidence (one or more pieces of the type identified above) acting like a brake at key points to move the assertion, reasoned step by reasoned step, towards the conclusion at the top of the slope. See Figure 9.5.

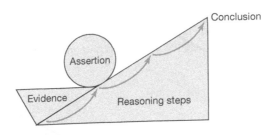

Figure 9.5 The argument process
(This diagram is based on the classical myth of Sisyphus who was destined to eternally repeat the task of pushing his boulder to the top of the slope only to see it roll back to the bottom again)

So an academic argument has three key parts: assertion, evidence and reasoning. We can apply the **A**(ssertion) **E**(vidence) **R**(easoning) approach to test an argument critically to see whether it meets the minimum requirements for an academic argument. Figure 9.6 summarises the AER approach.

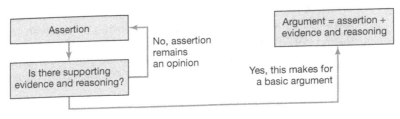

Figure 9.6 The minimum AER requirements for an academic argument

Use Activity 4 to look at the AER approach in a bit more detail

190

ACTIVITY 4 Apply the AER approach to argument construction

Here is a short argument. Read it and then look at the analysis.

'In February 2008 house prices in the UK were at an unsustainable price to income ratio and the market had to readjust. The historic average ratio is around 3.5 (Times, 2006), suggesting the historic ratio is a long-term indicator of what the market can sustain. The last major UK house price cycle saw the ratio peak at 3.9 before falling to 2.1 (Nationwide Building Society). The aggregate UK ratio grew from 3.5 in August 2002 to 5.4 in December 2007 (Nationwide Building Society). Evidence from previous cycles suggests that when the ratio goes beyond certain limits this indicates instability that will lead to adjustment (OED, 2004). Therefore, based on the evidence, the house price market had to readjust.'

Elements of the argument	Analysis
In February 2008 house prices in the UK were at an unsustainable price to income ratio and the market had to readjust.	Assertion
The historic average ratio is around 3.5 …	Evidence
… suggesting the historic ratio is a long-term indicator of what the market can sustain.	Reasoning
The last major UK house price cycle saw the ratio peak at 3.9 before falling to 2.1.	Evidence
The aggregate UK ratio grew from 3.5 in August 2002 to 5.4 in December 2007.	Evidence
Evidence from previous cycles suggests that when the ratio goes beyond certain limits this indicates instability that will lead to adjustment.	Reasoning
Therefore, based on the evidence, the house price market had to readjust.	Conclusion

This activity looks at how an assertion can be built into an argument to reach a reasoned and evidenced conclusion and shows the process of 'pushing the ball up the hill' in a number of steps to achieve this. While this example may appear to be a sound argument, in reality from a critical perspective there are a number of flaws, some of which will be explored later in Activity 7.

My first proper essay got marked down: I was told all I was doing was expressing an opinion, and that I needed to put more critical argument and citation evidence in my work.

Gemma, first-year Business Strategy student

Gemma was not developing her assertions in a rigorous fashion; she was failing to make an argument and therefore to demonstrate a deeper approach (see Chapter 7, 'Reading critically') to her understanding of the subject matter. Furthermore, by not citing evidence sources she wasn't capitalising on the studying effort she had invested in her essay preparation.

Hot Tip
It is a common fallacy that citing other people's work shows you don't know things. On the contrary, it shows that: you've done wider research than just the textbook; you've understood what those other sources are saying in the context of the question set. If you then build arguments based on that understanding, it shows that you can apply that understanding. All these things get marks.

As soon as we are presented with an argument, we can start to examine it in detail. Expert thinkers develop a set of cue questions that they use to test other people's arguments. According to Saaty (2008), the quality of professional decision making also relies on the nature of the information gathered. A systematic method of generating information from reliable, interrogative questions is a transferable skill common to both critical thinking and effective professional decision making. You can use and adapt those questions in Chapter 7 to start to build your own set.

ACTIVITY 5 Develop my critical cue question toolbox

Using the questions from Activity 7 in Chapter 7 as triggers, expand the following toolbox. Some suggestions and prompts are made to help get you started.

Trigger question	Critical cue questions
Who is the author's audience?	Is the audience purely academic, or is it professional or trade? *Consider what the relationship is between the author and audience. Is the audience likely to question or accept the author's authority? How might the audience use the work?*
What are the central claims/arguments of the text?	Are these about solving a problem, identifying new opportunities or proposing new theories? *Consider what stake the author has in the claim/argument. Are they trying to settle an outstanding question or raise new questions? Are they repeating what other people have done? If so, what reason do they give for this?*
What is the main evidence?	How recent is the evidence presented? *Consider its context. Might the regional/cultural origin of the evidence affect its validity in this text? Is the evidence new primary research or is it previously published material?*
How is this substantiated?	Does the author have a wider range of supporting evidence? *Consider the method(s) used to collect that evidence. Is it comparable/relevant to the type of argument being made? Does the author just list other evidence without discussing how or why it supports their main evidence?*

Trigger question	Critical cue questions
What assumptions lie behind the evidence or arguments?	Are these assumptions made clear and discussed in the text? *Consider whether the author has a preference for a particular model or theory. Are they ideologically influenced? Are they sponsored by an organisation with a vested interest in the conclusions reached?*
Is adequate proof provided and backed up with examples of evidence?	Does the author include real-world examples? *Consider the choice of examples. Are they recent? Are they relevant to the context?*
What are the general weaknesses of the threads of the argument/ evidence?	Does the author discuss alternative interpretations of the evidence that might not agree with their final conclusion? *Consider how the author deals with contradictory or 'awkward' evidence. Do they clearly show why they have rejected different explanations? Do they leave threads unconnected? Do they actually answer the question(s) they said they intended to answer?*
What do other leading authors say about the same subject?	Are these leading authors discussed by the author? *Consider the areas of agreement and disagreement between authors on this subject. What conflict or contradictions are there between the authors?*

See the feedback section for comment on this activity.

4 Common errors in thinking

So far we have talked about the process of academic argument. But we haven't talked about the quality of the argument itself. Sometimes arguments appear sound, but it is only when you take a deeper look that flaws are seen. This deeper engagement is vital when dealing with others' work and it is vital that you apply the same approach to your own thinking processes.

> *'When I use a word,' Humpty Dumpty said in a rather scornful tone, 'it means just what I choose it to mean – neither more nor less.'*
>
> Lewis Carroll, *Through the Looking Glass*

Unlike Humpty Dumpty who can make it up as he goes along, critical thinking is about accurate communication of what we mean. We cannot choose and then change what something means when we are making an argument. To communicate clearly and accurately, we also need to be accurate and clear in our thinking process. This is a complex area, but there are some common thinking 'errors' that students make. These errors can get in the way of achieving the advanced expert reading stage 8 (see Chapter 7, 'Reading critically') and of producing critical, written assignments (see Chapter 14, 'Improving your business and management studies writing'). Looking out for these thinking errors will improve your critical thinking and be helpful to your critical reading and writing.

Generalisation

*My seminar tutor told me that I generalised all the time and that it fre-
quently sounded as though I had read something without any thought.*

Sally, final-year Business Studies student

One common error is that of generalisation, for example: 'All good leaders
are good managers.' If this is supported by evidence and reasoning then
it becomes an argument, but as an argument it remains weak. If someone
can find a single case of a good leader who actually isn't a good manager,
then the argument falls over. You can recognise generalisations in your
own thinking and in other people's work as they tend to be introduced by
words or phrases such as: 'All … ', 'It is commonly believed …', 'It is a well-
known fact …', 'Many people would argue …'. None of these provides clear
or accurate communication as far as the critical thinker is concerned. The
table below considers the problems with these phrases.

Generalisation	Issues
'All … '	'All' is generally an unverifiable term. It can be accurate only if it can be guaranteed that every instance of something has been examined. Most of the time this is not achievable.
'It is commonly believed …'	'Common' is an imprecise term. For it to have a sense of accuracy it would have to be a quantifiable majority. But then this quantity gives a more accurate way to refer to the subject. 'Believed' is also unclear as the evidence and reasoning for the belief are not clear.
'It is a well-known fact …'	Like 'common', 'well known' is imprecise. A fact is an indisputable thing. In business and management studies, 'facts' tend to be questioned and argued about in the texts.
'Many people would argue …'	'Many people' is also imprecise. Who those people are, how many there are of them and why they would make the argument are important questions that aren't addressed.

Sometimes a broad assertion is a starting point for an argument, particularly if the topic or subject matter is contentious or uncertain. It can be a
device some advanced thinkers use to set up a target against which they
then argue. This tends not to be encouraged among undergraduates as it
pre-supposes an expert level of knowledge, but you might come across it
in some of your texts. If so, ensure that you apply the trigger and cue questions from your toolbox to test out the author's case.

If you do have to start with a broad assertion, one way to support it is to
provide both necessary and sufficient evidence. Take the example of the

generalisation 'It is commonly believed that taxation in the UK is too high'. To make this an acceptable assertion would require the *necessary* citation of credible, authoritative source and *sufficient* number of such sources to demonstrate the extent of the 'common belief'. The argument still has to be made though!

Hot Tip

Generalisations tend to suggest to your tutor that you haven't given much thought to the subject and/or that you haven't bothered to undertake sufficient reading to fully inform yourself about the subject. It can lose you marks.

Chapter 14, 'Improving your business and management studies writing' looks more closely at the critical writing skills that help you to avoid generalisation and express yourself more clearly.

Cause and effect

Another common error is to simplify or misunderstand cause and effect. The statement 'The implementation of the new business strategy has boosted profits by 12 per cent' sounds very impressive and clear, and might even get its author a pay rise! Figure 9.7 shows this apparently simple cause and effect.

Cause: New business strategy

Effect: Profits up by 12%

Figure 9.7 A simple cause and effect

However, the critical thinker would ask a key critical question:

'How is the observed effect (profits up by 12 per cent) linked to the apparent cause (the new business strategy)?'

It might be that other factors, for example an unrelated change in consumer behaviour or unrelated changes in personnel, caused or contributed to the increase in profits. The critical thinker will start with the observed effect or consequence and then examine the evidence and reasoning in respect of any apparent cause. In the example given, the critical thinker may identify that the suggested cause (the new business strategy) is in fact *not* the only cause. They might produce a very different analysis that reveals a much more complex set of cause and effect events such as that shown in Figure 9.8.

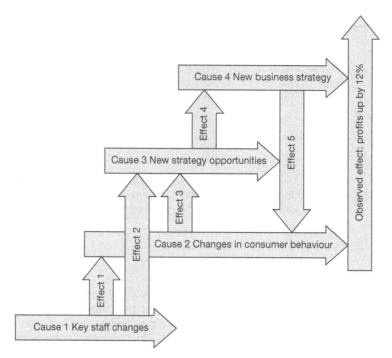

Figure 9.8 A more complex cause and effect

The analysis there shows that the underlying cause, i.e. that of key staff changes, is not *directly* linked to the increase in profits. But it had two effects:

- a related change in consumer behaviour, which can be directly linked to the change in profits; and
- new strategy opportunities (this scenario doesn't examine these, but this would be another set of chained cause/effect events in its own right).

These effects become new causal factors. Changes in consumer behaviour have an effect on new strategy opportunities, and these new strategy opportunities lead to what was seen as the initial *apparent* cause, the new business strategy itself. This in turn had two effects:

- one being a contribution to the increase in profits; and
- one being further changes in consumer behaviour.

This last effect also impacted on the final *observed* effect, the 12 per cent increase in profits. This is a fictitious example, but it demonstrates that one of the key characteristics of a critical thinker is to never take things at face value.

The critical thinker deals with complex chains of events. This is always demanding, but this is precisely where the stretch and challenge of university learning and the resulting personal development opportunities occur for you. Chains of arguments involve more complex thinking approaches and these will be considered in Section 5 below. One final note: sometimes cause and effect may be straightforward: the critical thinker however will ensure that they can demonstrate this by showing the steps they have taken to examine the situation to be able to reach such a conclusion.

> **Hot Tip**
>
> Generalisation and causality statements are common in essay assignment questions. These are designed to test your critical thinking skills by asking you to 'discuss' or 'critically evaluate' the statement (see Chapter 14, 'Improving your business and management studies writing', and for general guidance see Chapter 13, 'Taking control of the writing process'.

Logical conclusions

Logic is a study in its own right beyond this book, but one common logical error some students make is to offer a conclusion that doesn't logically follow from previous statement(s). Consider the following sentence: 'CO_2 (carbon dioxide) is a greenhouse gas as it is emitted from burning carbon fuels.' What is accurate is that CO_2 is accepted as a greenhouse gas and CO_2 results from burning carbon fuels such as coal, oil and petrol. There is a connection between these two, but the relationship needs to be *methodically* demonstrated for the conclusion to be logically linked to the opening statement, as Figure 9.9 shows.

So the problem with the sentence is that it actually says CO_2 is a greenhouse gas *because* it is emitted from burning carbon fuels. The leap to the conclusion has completely missed out the more complex sequence of argument necessary to show the proper relationship. The short-cut results in an illogical and meaningless sentence.

This type of error occurs either because something is not fully understood, or because not enough attention is paid to the way in which it is expressed, or just through laziness. Whatever the case, if you make this type of error in an essay you will lose marks and receive feedback such as: 'You have misunderstood the principles here' or 'You haven't given enough thought to what you are trying to say' or 'You need to critically engage more with this topic.' Activity 6 lets you test your thinking error-recognition skills.

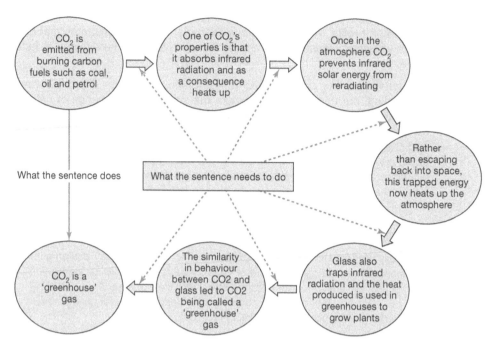

Figure 9.9 Producing a logical conclusion

ACTIVITY 6 Test my thinking error-recognition skills

Analyse each statement, decide whether it contains any error in thinking and identify what needs to be done to correct any error. Note: some statements may contain more than one type of error. The context you assume for the statement may affect your judgement as to the type of error present (or not). In this case you will need to consider how your assumptions have been made and what alternatives exist.

Statement	Error type?
It is generally accepted that communication skills are essential to successful organisational change.	
Assessing the external environment to any organisation is important due to SWOT analyses.	
An increase in scheduled flights has led to a growth in tourist activity.	
All SMEs need to review their IT procurement annually to ensure they have the most cost-effective procedures in place.	
No one under the age of 25 has experienced age discrimination; therefore the company's equal opportunities policy is working.	

See the feedback section for more comment.

5 Developing argument

In the last section we looked at some common thinking errors. These are all based on the key factor that critical thinking at university is about seeking to go beyond what we know using rigorous and systematic means and methods of thinking. Arguments need to be developed in detailed and layered ways using such thinking. And in the process of developing them, we encounter opportunities not just to learn more about what we already know but also to start to see new connections between topics and fields in our discipline. Innovation in business and management depends on the same process.

Chains of arguments

Most academic arguments are built up from a number of chains of arguments. The colloquial saying 'Big bugs have smaller bugs upon their backs to bite them' gives a hint of what this is about. For example, you might need to test some major pieces of evidence (and show your audience this process) before you can rely on it for your own argument. Or, a piece of reasoning needs to be argued for and established before you can apply it to evaluate some evidence. Equally, your main assertion may well be built from a number of contributory assertions. When, in Figure 9.8, we considered a possible cause and effect chain we were actually beginning to build an argument chain (the 'big bug'). And in Figure 9.9 we were actually developing the argument chain to make clear the steps in reasoning (a smaller bug) to support our conclusion. In order to tackle most assignments as a critical thinker you will have to build a clear sense of the whole argument chain that will allow you to answer the question set or the problem posed. Figure 9.10 is an illustration of the argument pathways and branches that a critical thinker might develop for a particular argument.

> I keep getting summative feedback which says 'You need to show more critical engagement' with the topic. I don't know what they mean.
>
> Terry, first-year Hospitality Management student

It is the process of identifying and developing these chains of arguments that will help you to show your critical engagement with a topic. To do this, you will typically:

- identify and summarise the alternative argument(s);
- demonstrate the grounds for accepting/rejecting alternative arguments;
- show the possible limits/implications acceptance of any specific argument implies.

Activity 7 looks at an example of how a chain of argument and critical engagement can be developed.

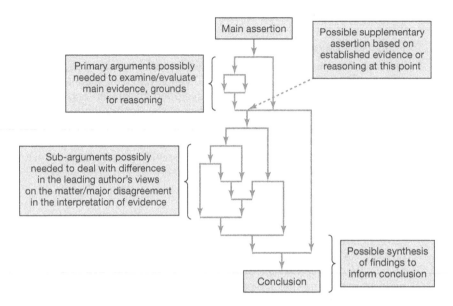

Figure 9.10 A representation of a fictitious argument chain

ACTIVITY 7 Developing chains of argument

Let's have another look at the argument we explored earlier in Activity 4. Let's take one of the pieces of reasoning we used there: '*The historic ratio is a long-term indicator of the sustainable position.*' As critical thinkers we know to use one of our critical trigger or cue questions to test out reasoning. Let's try: 'What assumptions lie behind the evidence or arguments?' By asking this question we're prompted to ask further questions such as: 'Who says so?', ' What's the basis for the assertion?', 'Do authors agree about this?' At this level of analysis, what passed before as 'reasoning' now looks very much like an assertion!

When we answer our critical trigger and cue questions we develop a sub-argument to show our audience the *grounds* on which the reasoning is based. If you refer back to Figure 9.9, you can see how this activity example could be one of the sub-arguments that contributes to the bigger argument chain.

Original 'reasoning'	Elements of a more developed argument chain	Analysis
... the historic ratio is a long-term indicator of what the market can sustain.	Whilst the historic ratio has been generally accepted as a reasonable indicator of the sustainable relationship between house price and earnings, there are a number of factors that are assumed by this.	Assertion
	For example, some observe that the ratio is based on assumptions about average tax or interest levels, but that these need not be taken for granted (OECD, 2004).	Identify/summarise argument

Original 'reasoning'	Elements of a more developed argument chain	Analysis
	This suggests that average interest rates over the last 10 years, if maintained, *could* result in a higher sustainable house price to earnings ratio.	Inference
	This is offset by a view that such short-term analysis of interest levels is the result of temporary monetary and fiscal policy opportunities that are subject to great variability over a longer term (IFS, 2005).	Identify/summarise argument
	On this basis, and without clear evidence that such policy changes may become sustainable,	Rejection/acceptance grounds
	The 3.5 ratio is the best empirical benchmark currently available to judge a sustainable position.	Conclusion with limitation acknowledgement

Now select a text of your choice, analyse it in the same way and make a critical judgement as to how the authors have developed their argument.

See the feedback section for further comment.

Synthesis

I have heard several lecturers say that they don't just want us to present theories and say why one is better than another or why one particular framework would work well here, but another one there. They say they want us to achieve a 'synthesis' – what does that mean?

Asmi, second-year Business Enterprise student

According to a dictionary definition, synthesis is a 'combination of components to achieve a connected whole' (OED). While this answers Asmi's question as to *what* synthesis is, it leaves the process of *how* to synthesise unanswered. Synthesis is opposite to analysis. Analysis is a process of examining something and taking it apart in a systematic way to understand what it is, how it works, why it is like it is, and what its strengths, limitations and weaknesses are. Synthesis is when we are faced with the task of putting something back together from that analysis. Figure 9.11 is a very simplified model of what this might look like at the point we have applied critical analysis and evaluation (in this example) to two theories. At this point we have also evaluated (weighed up) each element against other evidence, explanations or theories to judge how they stand up.

This model suggests that we produce two main results. First, elements of the theories that haven't stood up to our analysis and evaluation, and that we reject. Second, elements of the theories that have stood up to our scrutiny and that we accept. If the thinking process stops here, then the assignment based on it will have some critical engagement. But the assign-

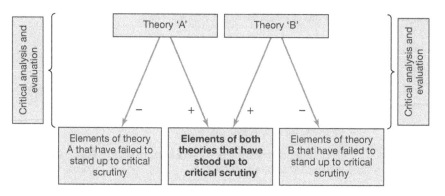

Figure 9.11 The product of a critical analysis and evaluation

ment won't achieve the best marks because it doesn't go on to show the significance or consequence of the *output* of the analysis and evaluation. This is what happens when we 'synthesise'. As an *outcome* of the critical thinking process, synthesis could be one of a number of things, as the table below summarises.

Possible outcome of synthesis	Explanation
Clarification …	… of the core, important factors that different theories do agree about and identify what is less (or not at all) important for your purposes.
New grounds …	… to support the use of thinking or evidence from a related or comparable topic area to the specific one you are working in. This might not otherwise be apparent and which may be innovative.
'Middle way' …	… alternative to the existing positions leading authors hold on a subject.
Confirmation …	… of a different theory or approach that you have already examined, or support your rationale for moving on to consider such a different approach.
Insight into …	… a new way of understanding or explaining a problem or issue (although this is unlikely to happen at undergraduate level except perhaps in the very best final-year dissertations).

Figure 9.12 maps one way of seeing how synthesis is part of a 'system'. Synthesis is probably the hardest idea to grasp in this chapter, as in many respects it is not tangible. Think about getting together the ingredients and utensils for a meal. You can easily define these as *inputs*; they are tangible. Then think about the recipe and activities to prepare and cook the ingredients: you can define the *process*; it is tangible. The product of this process is the cooked meal on the table. The *output* is tangible. The *outcome,* how-

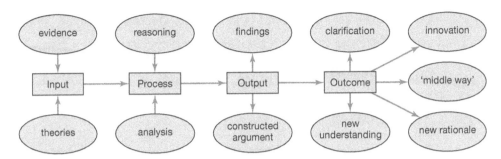

Figure 9.12 Synthesis as part of a critical thinking 'system'

ever, is to do with enjoyment, satisfaction, fulfilment and a range of other real but subtle things about the meal that may vary from person to person; these are less tangible. This is a common, everyday experience, yet even so it shows why synthesis is the ultimate challenge for any critical thinker.

In practical terms, particularly if you are working on an operationally based assignment, synthesis may be the way in which you make the case to 'bespoke' or combine purely theoretical problem solving, analytical or decision-making tools to work for you in a specific real-world context.

ACTIVITY 8 Examining synthesis

Choose a text in your subject that people acknowledge is innovative or offers a new, exciting approach to an existing problem. Using the guidance from all the previous sections, critically analyse and evaluate how the author develops their perspective and how they propose and justify the innovation or new approach they offer in their work.

Chapter 14, 'Improving your business and management studies writing' looks at writing strategies and practices that can enhance your use of synthesis in your assignments as a business or management studies student.

6 Critical approaches to real-world problems and the business or management professional

Real-life problems are messy.

Halpern (1997)

So far we have looked at aspects of critical thinking without thinking about the real world. Real-world problems are complex, with many dimensions, and in business and management terms will frequently involve conflicts of interest. These conflicts may come from competing pressures of a psychological, social, political, legal or regulatory nature that prevent us from acting in certain ways. Some subject areas (in the sciences, for example) avoid 'mess' by not letting real-world consequences interfere with their theorising and experimental demonstration of proof. Business and management students, however, have messiness right at the heart of most of their subjects. Success in your discipline is frequently about understanding and then dealing with the compromises that conflicts of interest force on to business or management practices.

This does not mean that critical thinking has no relevance; in fact, it is even more relevant if you are to achieve the best balance between competing demands *and* be effective. All the critical thinking principles explored so far directly contribute to this. Try Activity 9 to examine a real-world-type problem using a critical thinking approach.

ACTIVITY 9 Rightsizing the sales team

Due to recessionary pressures, you are tasked with restructuring the sales team of the organisation you work for. It is a very successful team of five, but you need to reduce the team to four staff. You must observe legal boundaries in terms of a non-discriminatory approach. Based on the following profiles, and assuming all team members have equal length of service, who would you make redundant and why?

Employee **T** has no dependants and his sexuality is the subject of speculation. He has a wealth of detailed knowledge about the sector and intuitively spots new sales opportunities.

Employee **S** is divorced. She has recently remortgaged her house to support her daughter's university education. Her attention to detail and communication skills make her the best deal-closer in the team.

Employee **Q** has a young family. He previously worked for a blue-chip company in corporate information systems. When this was outsourced, he volunteered for a redundancy package. He is particularly strong in selling to black and minority ethnic-run businesses.

Employee **Z** is 55. He has been in sales all his life and has no formal qualifications. As his wife is disabled, his is the sole household income. He has a portfolio of smaller accounts and meets his targets by spending many more hours on the road than other team members.

Employee **X** is the youngest team member. He is highly motivated and consistently exceeds his monthly targets. He has a cocaine habit.

See the feedback section for further comment on this activity.

For the business or management professional, critical thinking will directly affect how they perform in the tasks and activities of their role, and how they move ahead and stand out for promotion and career progression. Critical thinking offers the business or management professional a systematic method of approaching problem solving and the following observation on methodology is worth considering:

> *Knowledge organised in a discipline does a good deal for the merely competent; it endows him with some effectiveness. It does more for the truly able; it endows him with excellence. (Drucker, 1964)*

7 Critical thinking: putting it all together

In Figure 9.1 we introduced you to critical thinking as part of a dynamic process. Its role 'manages' the connection between the sources of knowledge and information on your course (for example lectures, seminars and texts) and the assessed assignments (for example essays, reports and presentations) you complete to demonstrate your progress as a student.

The central part of Figure 9.1 does not contain convenient linear connections that give you a simple template or set of instructions about critical thinking. Figure 9.13 below represents more closely what it might look like as a 'cloud' with key ideas and elements loosely aligned. The final activity in this chapter is for you to construct your own concept map of the components of critical thinking.

ACTIVITY 10 Your own critical thinking concept map

Using Figure 9.12 and your notes from the activities you have completed in this chapter, construct your own detailed concept map of critical thinking. Make it a 'rich' map with your own ideas and other sources that build it as a personal framework for your understanding. To help you develop your concept mapping, this web link will prove useful:

http://users.edte.utwente.nl/lanzing/cm_home.htm

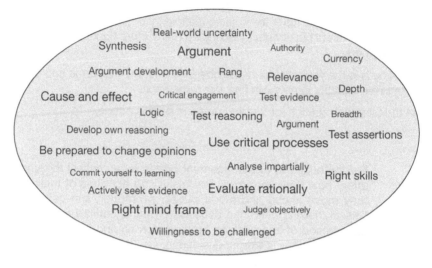

Figure 9.13 The critical thinking 'cloud'

Above all, critical thinking is what Higher Education at university and college is about. How you develop your thinking skills whilst at university, and what this does to your ability to perceive, analyse and interpret the world around you, is the single most marketable skill you will take away with you when you graduate. No book can teach you to be a critical thinker, it can only signpost the way. You have to make the journey.

8 On reflection

If you want to get a good degree and stand out in your graduate career, then this chapter is vital reading. You must develop and enhance your critical thinking skills to allow you to critically apply your learning and show how you connect and construct knowledge in your subject to successfully undertake the assignments you will be set. Knowing **what** and **how** to do something is important. But knowing **why** that something is what it is, the conditions and circumstances under which that holds true and **when** to apply it rather than an alternative, are the essential critical thinking skills that will contribute to your success as a business or management studies student and as a professional. This chapter has introduced you to some of the ways of thinking you need to continue to practise and develop to ensure that in your professional career you are master of your plan for yourself rather than being part of someone else's master plan for you.

Summary of this chapter

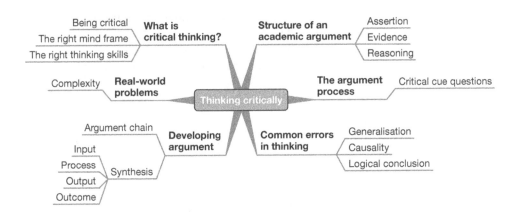

ACTIVITY 11 Update your personal development planner

My developing skills	Confidence level 1-5	Plans to improve
I understand what the principles of critical thinking are.		
I can analyse other people's arguments and evaluate their strengths and weaknesses effectively.		
I can construct and support my own arguments using evidence and reasoning to reach sound conclusions.		
I know what 'critical engagement' with my subject is.		
I understand how to synthesise knowledge and ideas as a critical thinker.		

Getting extra help

- Go to the students union to find out where to go for skills development. Many universities and colleges have tutors who provide this service.

- Be proactive with your seminars or group tutorials. Prepare and participate. These learning opportunities let you practise your critical thinking skills. Direct feedback from peers and tutors is some of the best help you can get.

Consult the following:

- Bonnet, A. (2001) *How To Argue: A Student's Guide*. Harlow, Pearson Education.

- Sussex University's study skills website has helpful information about critical analysis: www.sussex.ac.uk/languages/1-6-8-2-3.html#crit

- Hong Kong University has an extensive website which looks at critical thinking, logic and creativity: http://philosophy.hku.hk/think/critical/

- The Institute for Human and Machine Cognition website gives you an extended background to concept mapping: http://cmap.ihmc.us/Publications/ResearchPapers/TheoryCmaps/TheoryUnderlyingConceptMaps.htm

Feedback on activities

ACTIVITY 1 Examine my approach to thinking skills

If your responses are mainly on the **left-hand side** of this table then you need to review in detail the section on 'Learning in Higher Education' at the beginning of this book and then work through Chapter 7, 'Reading critically' before you continue with this chapter.

If your responses have **no particular pattern** then you need to review Chapter 7 in detail before you continue with this chapter.

If your responses are mainly on the **right-hand side**, then you are already thinking contextually and critically and you should use the rest of this chapter in conjunction with materials from your own independent reading to deepen your approach.

ACTIVITY 2 Considering assertion and opinion

This activity has no right or wrong answer. It sets out to demonstrate that different interpretations/opinions/judgements can exist about something when the **only** point of agreement is that something has happened. The importance of the approach is that you are invited to apply some simple but effective question words (**What/Why/How/ Who/ Where**) that should always inform your critical questioning of any published materials.

ACTIVITY 5 Develop my critical cue question toolbox

The important thing about any toolbox is that it grows to contain a range of tools to deal with a variety of situations. A mechanic sometimes needs a screwdriver and a spanner, at other times a hammer. Sometimes they might need all three, at other times a specialised tool. In all cases they need to know how to use the tools and what to use to complete a particular task successfully. Your critical thinking toolbox is similar to this, and it will grow and develop as your studies progress. You will become more skilled in the use and selection of questions to read, listen and think beyond the words in a text or discussion. This is one of the main things you will learn at university, but this depends on you putting in the effort to maximise this aspect of your learning: no one else can do this for you.

Aim to add a new critical cue question every week. This may come from your reading or from the types of questions that your lecturers pose when they are talking about a topic.

ACTIVITY 6 Test my thinking error-recognition skills

Statement	Error type?
It is generally accepted that communication skills are essential to successful organisational change.	As it stands this is a **generalisation**. If the assertion of 'general acceptance is supported with authoritative citation then this sentence is OK.
Assessing the external environment to any organisation is important due to SWOT analyses.	This sentence does not have a **logical conclusion** as it makes SWOT analyses causal to the importance of assessing the external environment.
An increase in scheduled flights has led to a growth in tourist activity.	As long as **cause and effect** have been established then this sentence is OK.
All SMEs need to review their IT procurement annually to ensure they have the most cost-effective procedures in place.	This sentence is a **generalisation**. As in the first sentence above, it could be 'rescued' with suitable supporting citation.
No one under the age of 25 has experienced age discrimination; therefore the company's equal opportunities policy is working.	This sentence does not have a **logical conclusion** for two reasons. First, the grounds are suspect (*No one under the age of 25*) and second, absence of evidence is not evidence of absence, i.e. even if no one (whatever age) has experienced age discrimination, this does not of itself support the conclusion.

Note that many of the above sentences also need a citation to be acceptable.

ACTIVITY 7 Developing chains of argument

Your examination of the text of your own choice demonstrates that critical engagement is actively going *beyond* what might be seen as the right answer, to show the *basis* upon which it is judged to be the right answer. It demands more of you in terms of research and reading. You have to develop your understanding from that reading. Then you need to write (or verbally present) clearly to communicate that understanding. This is what it takes to get the best marks in your assignments.

ACTIVITY 9 Rightsizing the sales team

This activity demonstrates that there are no absolute answers to many real-world problems; rather, there is a range of possible solutions. The appraisal of those solutions, and the final decision as to what to recommend and/or implement, demands consideration of competing proposals and clarity of rationale. It also illustrates that what is theoretically rational and what is practical or feasible in the real world may be very different. Sometimes the existing frameworks aren't uniquely or singularly up to the job, and this requires a rigorous, critically judged synthesis of such frameworks to fit a new scenario.

References

Alter, S. (2006) 'Pitfalls in analyzing systems in organisations', *Journal of Information Systems Education*, 17 (3), 295–302.

Archer, W. and Davison, J. (2008) *Graduate Employability: what employers think and want*. London, CIHE.

Baxter-Magolda, M. (1992) *Knowing and Reasoning in College*. San Francisco, CA, Jossey-Bass.

Drucker, P. (1964) *Managing for Results: economic tasks and risk-taking decisions*. London, Heinemann.

Halpern, D. E. (1997) *Critical Thinking Across the Curriculum*. Mauwah, NJ, Lawrence Erlbaum.

Hilton, J. (2006) 'The future for higher education: sunrise or perfect storm?', *Educause Review* [electronic version], 41(2), 58–71.

Neville, M. G. (2008) 'Using appreciative inquiry and dialogical learning to explore dominant paradigms', *Journal of Management Education*, 32 (1), 100–17.

Saaty, T. L. (2008) 'Decision making with the analytical hierarchical process', *International Journal of Services Sciences*, 1 (1), 83–98. Available at http://inderscience.metapress.com/media/mftaqnqwxp4t69xrkc3u/contributions/0/2/t/6/02t637305v6g65n8_html/fulltext.html [last accessed October 2009]

Thinking critically

How to develop a logical approach to analysis, synthesis and evaluation

The ability to think critically is probably the most transferable of the skills you will develop at university – and one that it is vital to develop if you wish to gain excellent marks in essays and assignments. This chapter introduces concepts, methods and fallacies to watch out for when trying to improve your analytical capabilities.

Key topics

- Thinking about thinking
- Using method to prompt and organise your thoughts
- Recognising fallacies and biased presentations

Key terms

Bias Critical thinking Fallacy Propaganda Value judgement

Many specialists believe that critical thinking is a skill that you can develop through practice – and this assumption lies behind much university teaching. Your experience of the educational system probably tells you that your marks depend increasingly on the analysis of facts and the ability to arrive at an opinion and support it with relevant information, rather than the simple recall of fact. If you understand the underlying processes a little better, this should help you meet your lecturers' expectations. Also, adopting a methodical approach can be useful when you are unsure how to tackle a new task.

> **Definition: critical**
>
> People often interpret the words 'critical' and 'criticism' to mean being negative about an issue. For university work, the alternative meaning of 'making a careful judgement after balanced consideration of all aspects of a topic' is the one you should adopt.

From Chapter 7 of *How to Write Essays & Assessments*, 2/e. Kathleen McMillan & Jonathan Weyers. © Pearson Education Limited 2007, 2010, 2011. All rights reserved.

● Thinking about thinking

Benjamin Bloom, a noted educational psychologist, and his colleagues, identified six different steps involved in learning and thinking within education:

- knowledge
- comprehension
- application
- analysis
- synthesis
- evaluation

Bloom *et al.* (1956) showed that students naturally progressed through this scale of thought-processing during their studies (Table 7.1). Looking at this table, you may recognise that your school work mainly focussed on knowledge, comprehension and application, while your university tutors tend to expect more in terms of analysis, synthesis and evaluation. These expectations are sometimes closely linked to

Table 7.1 **Classification of thinking processes (Bloom et al. 1956) ('Bloom's taxonomy')**

Thinking processes (in ascending order of difficulty)	Typical question instructions
Knowledge. If you know a fact, you have it at your disposal and can *recall* or *recognise* it. This does not mean you necessarily understand it at a higher level.	• Define • Describe • Identify
Comprehension. To comprehend a fact means that you *understand* what it means.	• Contrast • Discuss • Interpret
Application. To apply a fact means that you can *put it to use.*	• Demonstrate • Calculate • Illustrate
Analysis. To analyse information means that you are able to *break it down into parts* and show how these components *fit together.*	• Analyse • Explain • Compare
Synthesis. To synthesise, you need to be able to *extract relevant facts* from a body of knowledge and use these to *address an issue in a novel way* or *create something new.*	• Compose • Create • Integrate
Evaluation. If you evaluate information, you *arrive at a judgement* based on its importance relative to the topic being addressed.	• Recommend • Support • Draw a conclusion

the instruction words used in assessments, and Table 7.1 provides a few examples. However, take care when interpreting these, as processes and tasks may mean different things in different subjects. For example, while 'description' might imply a lower-level activity in the sciences, it might involve high-level skills in subjects like architecture.

Some disciplines value creativity as a thinking process, for example, art and design, architecture, drama or English composition. In such cases, this word might take the place of synthesis in Table 7.1. Some people also propose that in certain cases creativity should be placed higher than evaluation in the table.

When you analyse the instructions used in writing assignments, you should take into account what type of thinking process the examiner has asked you to carry out, and try your best to reach the required level. To help you understand what might be required, Table 7.2 gives examples of thought processes you might experience in a range of areas of study.

Contexts for thinking critically

Examples of university assignments involving high-level thinking skills include:

- essay-writing in the arts and social sciences
- reports on problem-based learning in medicine and nursing
- case-based scenarios in law
- reports on project-based practical work in the sciences

● Using method to prompt and organise your thoughts

Suppose you recognise that critical thinking is required to address a particular task. This could be an essay question set by one of your tutors, an issue arising from problem-based learning, or a longer writing assignment. The pointers below will help you to arrive at a logical approach. You should regard this as a menu rather than a recipe – think about the different stages and how they might be useful for the specific task under consideration and your own style of work. Adopt or reject them as you see fit, or, according to your needs, chop and change their order.

Table 7.2 **Examples of thinking processes within representative university subjects (Bloom et al., 1956)**

Thinking processes (in ascending order of difficulty)	Law	Arts subjects, e.g. History or Politics	Numerical subjects
		Examples	
Knowledge	You might know the name and date of a case, statute or treaty without understanding its relevance	You might know that a river was an important geographical and political boundary in international relations, without being able to identify why	You might be able to write down a particular mathematical equation, without understanding what the symbols mean or where it might be applied
Comprehension	You would understand the principle of law contained in the legislation or case law, and its wider context	You would understand that the river forms a natural barrier, which can be easily identified and defended	You would understand what the symbols in an equation mean and how and when to apply it
Application	You would be able to identify situations to which the principle of law would apply	You might use this knowledge to explain the terms of a peace treaty	You would be able to use the equation to obtain a result, given background information
Analysis	You could relate the facts of a particular scenario to the principle to uncover the extent of its application, using appropriate authority	You could explain the river as a boundary being of importance to the territorial gains/losses for signatories to the peace treaty	You could explain the theoretical process involved in deriving the equation
Synthesis	By a process of reasoning and analogy, you could predict how the law might be applied under given circumstances	You could identify this fact and relate it to the recurrence of this issue in later treaties or factors governing further hostilities and subsequent implications	You would be able to take one equation, link it with another and arrive at a new mathematical relationship or conclusion
Evaluation	You might be able to advise a client based on your own judgement, after weighing up and evaluating all available options	You would be able to discuss whether the use of this boundary was an obstacle to resolving the terms of the treaty to the satisfaction of all parties	You would be able to discuss the limitations of an equation based on its derivation and the underlying assumptions behind this

- **Make sure you fully grasp the nature of the task.** If a specific question has been given as part of the exercise, then analyse its phrasing carefully to make sure you understand all possible meanings. If you have been given a general topic, rather than a detailed question or instruction, then write down a brief description of the aspects you wish to address – this will help you to clarify the terminology and concepts involved. Revisit the learning outcomes for your module or course and work out how these relate to your topic and the nature of submission required.

- **Organise your approach to the task.** You might start with a 'brainstorm' to identify potential solutions or viewpoints. This can be a solo or group activity and typically might consist of three phases:
  - **Open thinking.** Consider the issue or question from all possible angles or positions and write down everything you come up with. Don't worry at this stage about the relevance or importance of your ideas. You may wish to use a 'spider diagram' or 'mind map' to lay out your thoughts (Figure 6.5).
  - **Organisation.** Next, you should try to arrange your ideas into categories or sub-headings, or group them as supporting or opposing a viewpoint. A new diagram, table or grid may be useful to make things clear.
  - **Analysis.** Now you need to decide about the relevance of the grouped points to the original problem. Reject trivial or irrelevant ideas and rank or prioritise those that seem relevant.

- **Get background information and check your comprehension of the facts.** It's quite likely that you will need to gather relevant information and ideas – to support your thoughts, provide examples or suggest a range of interpretations or approaches. You also need to ensure you fully understand the information you have gathered. This could be as simple as using dictionaries and technical works to find out the precise meaning of key words; it might involve discussing your ideas with your peers or a tutor; or you could read a range of texts to see how others interpret your topic.

Can a methodical approach inspire you creatively?

You may doubt this, and we all recognise that a solution to a problem often comes to us when we aren't even trying to think about it. However, technique can sometimes help you clarify the issues, organise the evidence and arrive at a balanced answer. This should help inspiration to follow.

Sharpening your research skills

The following chapters give further information and tips:

- avoiding plagiarism: Ch 17
- library and web-search skills: Ch 5
- collecting information that will allow you to cite the source: Ch 18

- **Check relevance.** Now consider the information you have gathered, your thoughts and how these might apply to your question. You may need to re-analyse the question. You will then need to marshal the evidence you have collected – for example: for or against a proposition; supporting or opposing an argument or theory. You may find it useful to prepare a table or grid to organise the information (Figure 6.6) – this will also help you balance your thoughts. Be ruthless in rejecting irrelevant or inconsequential material.

- **Think through your argument, and how you can support it.** Having considered relevant information and positions, you should arrive at a personal viewpoint, and then construct your discussion or conclusion around this. When writing about your topic, you must take care to avoid value judgements or other kinds of expression of opinion that are not supported by evidence or sources. This is one reason why frequent citation and referencing is demanded in academic work.

- **Get cracking on your answer.** Once you have decided on what you want to say, writing it up should be much easier.

Value judgements

A value judgement is a statement based primarily on a subjective viewpoint or opinion rather than an objective analysis of facts. It is therefore influenced by the 'value system' of the writer or speaker. Value systems involve such matters as ethics, morals, behavioural norms and religious standpoints that are embedded from a person's upbringing and hence influence their views on external matters, sometimes unwittingly. A value judgement might be detected through the use of 'loaded' language (consider, for example, potentially contrasting usage of 'freedom fighter', 'insurgent' and 'guerrilla'). One aim of academic analysis is to minimise subjectivity of this type by evaluating both sides of a debate and by focussing on the logical interpretation of facts.

● Recognising fallacies and biased presentations

As you consider arguments and discussions on academic subjects, you will notice that various linguistic devices are used to promote particular points of view. Identifying these is a valuable aspect of critical thinking, allowing you to detach yourself from the argument itself and think about the way in which it is being conducted.

Definitions

- **Fallacy:** a fault in logic or thinking that means that an argument is incorrect.
- **Bias:** information that emphasises just one viewpoint or position.
- **Propaganda:** false or incomplete information that supports a (usually) extreme political or moral view.

There are many different types of logical fallacies, and Table 7.3 lists only a few common examples. Once tuned in to this way of thinking, you should observe that faulty logic and debating tricks are frequently used in areas such as advertising and politics. Analysing the methods being used can be a useful way of practising your critical-thinking skills.

One way of avoiding bias in your own written work is consciously to try to balance your discussion. Avoid 'absolutes' – be careful with words that imply that there are no exceptions, for example, *always*, *never*, *all* and *every*. These words can only be used if you are absolutely sure of facts that imply 100 per cent certainty.

 ## Practical tips for thinking critically

Focus on the task in hand. It is very easy to become distracted when reading around a subject, or when discussing problems with others. Take care not to waste too much time on preliminaries and start relevant action as quickly as possible.

Write down your thoughts. The act of writing your thoughts is important as this forces you to clarify them. Also, since ideas are often fleeting, it makes sense to ensure you have a permanent record. Reviewing what you have written makes you more critical and can lead you on to new ideas.

Table 7.3 **Common examples of logical fallacies, bias and propaganda techniques found in arguments.** There are many different types of fallacious arguments (at least 70) and this is an important area of study in philosophical logic.

Type of fallacy or propaganda	Description	Example	How to counteract this approach
Ad hominem (Latin for 'to the man')	An attack is made on the character of the person putting forward an argument, rather than on the argument itself; this is particularly common in the media and politics	The President's moral behaviour is suspect, so his financial policies must also be dubious	Suggest that the person's character or circumstances are irrelevant
Ad populum (Latin for 'to the people')	The argument is supported on the basis that it is a popular viewpoint; of course, this does not make it correct in itself	The majority of people support corporal punishment for vandals, so we should introduce boot camps	Watch out for bandwagons and peer-pressure effects and ignore them when considering rights and wrongs
Anecdotal evidence	Use of unrepresentative exceptions to contradict an argument based on statistical evidence	My gran was a heavy smoker and she lived to be 95, so smoking won't harm me	Consider the overall weight of evidence rather than isolated examples
Appeal to authority	An argument is supported on the basis that an expert or authority agrees with the conclusion; used in advertisements, where celebrity endorsement and testimonials are frequent	My professor, whom I admire greatly, believes in Smith's theory, so it must be right	Point out that the experts do disagree and explain how and why; focus on the key qualities of the item or argument

Appeal to ignorance	Because there's no evidence for (or against) a case, it means the case must be false (or true)	You haven't an alibi, therefore you must be guilty	Point out that a conclusion either way may not be possible in the absence of evidence
Biased evidence	Selection of examples or evidence for or against a case. A writer who quotes those who support their view, but not those against	My advisers tell me that global warming isn't going to happen.	Read around the subject, including those with a different view, and try to arrive at a balanced opinion.
Euphemisms and jargon	Use of phrasing to hide the true position or exaggerate an opponent's – stating things in mild or emotive language for effect; use of technical words to sound authoritative	My job as vertical transportation operative means I am used to being in a responsible position	Watch for (unnecessary) adjectives, noun strings or adverbs that may affect the way you consider the evidence
Repetition	Saying the same thing over and over again until people believe it. Common in politics, war propaganda and advertising	'Beanz means Heinz'	Look out for repeated catchphrases and lack of substantive argument
Straw man/false dichotomy	A position is misrepresented in order to create a diversionary debating point that is easily accepted or rejected, when in fact the core issue has not been addressed	Asylum seekers all want to milk the benefits system, so we should turn them all away	Point out the fallacy and focus on the core issue

Try to be analytical, not descriptive. By looking at Table 7.1, you will appreciate why analysis is regarded as a higher-level skill than description. Many students lose marks in essays and assignments because they simply quote facts or statements, without explaining their importance and context, that is, without showing their understanding of what the quote means or implies.

When quoting evidence, use appropriate citations. This is important as it shows you have read relevant source material and helps you avoid plagiarism (Ch 17). The conventions for citation vary among subjects, so consult course handbooks or other information and make sure you follow the instructions carefully, or you may lose marks (Ch 18).

Draw on the ideas and opinions of your peers and tutors. Discussions with others can be very fruitful, revealing a range of interpretations that you might not have thought about yourself. You may find it useful to bounce ideas off others. Tutors can provide useful guidance once you have done some reading, and are usually pleased to be asked for help.

Keep an open mind. Although you may start with preconceived ideas about a topic, you should try to be receptive to the ideas of others. You may find that your initial thoughts become altered by what you are reading and discussing. If there is not enough evidence to support *any* conclusion, be prepared to suspend judgement.

Look beneath the surface. Decide whether sources are dealing with facts or opinions; examine any assumptions made, including your own; think about the motivation of writers. Rather than restating and describing your sources, focus on what they *mean* by what they write.

Avoid common pitfalls of shallow thinking. Try not to:
- rush to conclusions;
- generalise;
- oversimplify;
- personalise;
- use fallacious arguments;
- think in terms of stereotypes;
- make value judgements.

Keep asking yourself questions. A good way to think more deeply is to ask questions, even after you feel a matter is resolved or you understand it well. All critical thinking is the result of asking questions.

Balance your arguments. If asked to arrive at a position on a subject, you should try to do this in an even-handed way, by considering all possible viewpoints and by presenting your conclusion with supporting evidence.

 And now . . .

7.1 Examine the depth of thinking in your own work. Select a past essay or assignment, then reflect on the thinking processes shown in Table 7.1 and identify the extent to which these are evident in your writing. For example, the early sections may contain descriptive material or cite applications of a concept. Later parts may include deeper analysis and evaluation. If you are appropriately self-critical (itself an important thinking skill), you may recognise that you could perhaps have achieved a better balance between the former 'lower order' and the latter 'higher order' elements. This might connect with tutors' feedback on your work (Ch 20) and reveal how you could improve your marks.

7.2 Practise seeing all sides of an argument. Choose a topic, perhaps one on which you have strong views (for example, a political matter, such as state support for private schooling; or an ethical one, such as the need for vivisection or abortion). Write down the supporting arguments for different sides of the issue, focusing on your least-favoured option. This will help you see all sides of a debate as a matter of course.

7.3 Look into the intriguing world of fallacies and biased arguments. There are some very good websites that provide lists of different types of these with examples. Investigate these by using 'fallacy' or 'logical fallacies' in a search engine. Not only are the results quite entertaining at times, but you will find the knowledge obtained improves your analytical and debating skills.

Academic writing formats

How to organise your writing within a standard framework

Regardless of the type of writing assignment you have to complete, the structure will follow a basic format. This chapter describes this design and explores some features that need to be included as you map your outline plan on to this structure.

Key topics
- Standard format
- Taking word limits into account

Key terms
Citation   Exemplify

This chapter outlines the essential format of any piece of academic writing, namely, introduction-main body-conclusion. It is on this basic framework that different types of academic assignment are constructed, and these are examined in detail in **Ch 9**.

● Standard format

The basic structure follows the convention of moving from the general (the introduction) through to the specific (the main body) and back to the general (the conclusion).

Introduction

Generally, this should consist of three components:

1 a brief explanation of the context of the topic;

2 an outline of the topic as you understand it;

3 an explanation of how you plan to address the topic in this particular text - in effect, a statement of intent.

The importance of the introduction

This is the first contact that your reader makes with you as the author of the text. It has to be well organised and clear. However, to achieve this it is important to see the introductory section as 'work in progress' because, until you complete the entire text, you cannot really introduce the whole work accurately. Indeed, some people prefer to start writing the main body, move on to the conclusion, and then write the introduction.

The introductory section can be quite long as it may take several paragraphs to lay out these three dimensions. It's important to do this with some thought because this indicates to your reader where you expect to take them in the main body of text. The introduction also lays down the parameters that you have set yourself for this piece of text. For example, your topic may be multifaceted and the word limit imposed on the total piece of text will not allow you to give a comprehensive coverage of all aspects. It is better to acknowledge the extensive nature of the topic and note that you are going to limit your discussion to only some of these aspects – usually those you consider to be most important. You need to explain the reasons for this decision at this stage.

Main body

This section lays out your work based on the approach you decide to adopt in organising the content (Ch 9). You will have explained the approach in the introduction and this will mean that you should have mapped out your route for explaining your points.

Sub-headings

For essays in some disciplines, these are acceptable, in others not. For most types of reports, sub-headings are expected. Where sub-headings are unacceptable in a final submission, you may nevertheless find them useful to include in word-processed drafts as they can represent the structure of your writing plan. This will help to prevent you from digressing into irrelevant areas or presenting an apparently rambling paper. You can then delete the sub-headings or 'translate' them into topic sentences (Ch 11) to link between paragraphs or introduce a new theme.

In this section, you may need to generalise, describe, define or provide examples as part of your analysis. Here, it's important to try to keep your writing as concise, yet as clear, as possible. The construction of your paragraphs will be dictated by what you are trying to express at any particular point. Different types of paragraph structures are outlined in Table 11.3.

Conclusion

This summarises the whole piece of work. You should review the entire text in three elements:

1 a restatement of the question or task and what you feel are the important features of the topic;

2 a summary of the specific evidence that you have presented in support of your views;

3 a statement of your overall viewpoint on the topic.

What mainly distinguishes the conclusion from the introduction is language. In the introduction, your explanation should be given clearly, avoiding jargon or technical words as far as possible. In the conclusion, you will be writing about the detail of the content and, therefore, the terminology you use is more likely to contain technical or more sophisticated language because you will have introduced this in the main body. You should avoid introducing new ideas in the conclusion that have not already been discussed in the earlier part of the writing.

Mini-conclusions

As you become immersed in the writing process you will become very familiar with the material and conclusions you have drawn along the way. By the time you come to write the conclusion to the whole work this in-depth awareness may become diluted. To avoid this, it is a good idea, at the end of each section you write, to note down what main ideas you had considered and what your view is about these. If you note these mini-conclusions down on a separate piece of paper or a word-processed file, then this will provide the substance for your final conclusion.

● Taking word limits into account

Word limits are imposed, not to relieve tutors of marking, but to train you to be concise in your writing and to analyse the topic carefully to decide what to keep in and what to leave out.

It's important to note that falling short of the word limit is just as bad as overrunning the maximum. Some students keep a running total of words they have used and as soon as they reach the minimum word limit, they stop abruptly. This is not a good approach because it is more likely to leave a ragged and poorly considered piece of text that comes to an unexpected halt rather than one that is well planned, relevant and concisely written.

It's usually better to plan and write your first draft keeping only a casual eye on word count at this stage. When you come to editing that draft you can prune and reshape your writing so that it becomes a tighter piece of prose that falls within the minimum–maximum word limits imposed by the regulations.

Counting words

Most word processors include a word-count function either for entire documents or selected text. Microsoft Word also incorporates features that allow you to keep a running word total, either in the status bar or as a floating toolbar. The exact details of how to enable these features depend on the program version, so if you wish to use them, consult the help feature or search for online tutorials.

Practical tips for organising your writing within a standard framework

Keep the right proportions in your response. Make sure that the three elements within your writing framework are well balanced in extent. The main body should be the most substantial piece of the writing, whereas the introduction and conclusion should occupy much less space. A common problem for many students is that they devote too much time to outlining the context in the introduction and leave themselves with too little time and space to get to the core of the essay.

Pay adequate attention to the conclusion. By the time that you come to write the conclusion, this is often written at some speed because there may be other demands on your time, or the initial interest in the subject has palled, or you may simply be tired. Thus, conclusions often don't get the attention they deserve; reserve some time to give your conclusion a critical appraisal, and even consider writing this section before finishing the perhaps more 'mechanical' earlier parts. Alternatively, as suggested above, you could 'write it as you go' by keeping detailed notes of key points separately as mini-conclusions, which you can use to frame your conclusion once you have written the main body.

Review the introduction. Once you have completed your draft, go back to the introduction and make sure that you have actually done what you set out to do when defining the parameters of your work and in your statement of intent. The act of writing your text may have stimulated new thoughts and your initial intentions and perceptions may have altered in the process of writing.

Think about appendices. Sometimes the length of your text may be seriously beyond the word limit. This means that some drastic 'surgery' is required. One strategy might be to remove some parts of the text and, while remaining within the word limit, reduce the information contained to bullet-point lists. The detail can then be placed in an appendix or appendices (plural of appendix), making appropriate cross-references in the main text. Clearly, this is a strategy that has to be used sparingly, but it can be useful in some situations, if allowed.

Support your discussion with appropriate citations. In many disciplines you will be expected to include references to recognised authorities within the field you are studying – this helps to validate the ideas and concepts you are discussing. In law, this could be cases; in the arts and humanities, it could be work by a renowned academic. This does not mean that you need to quote substantial pieces of text; you can summarise the idea in your own words and then follow the rules about citation that are given in Ch 18. All this needs to be taken into consideration in planning and drafting your writing.

GO And now . . .

8.1 **Compare textual patterns.** Go back to a basic textbook and identify the proportion of space allocated to introducing the entire book or a specific chapter, and how much is reserved for the conclusion. This should be instructive in framing your own writing.

8.2 **Track the pattern of your writing.** Go back to an existing piece of your own writing and try to identify whether you have the basic elements and sub-elements of the standard writing format in place. Are the introduction, main body and conclusion identifiable? Does the introduction contain the elements of context, specific focus and statement of intent? For the conclusion, is your position laid out clearly and with supporting rationale? If any of your answers are negative, try to work out how you could improve things.

8.3 **Practise converting sub-headings into topic sentences.** Take a piece of your own writing or a section from a textbook where sub-headings have been used. Try to create a topic sentence that could replace that sub-heading. Decide which is more effective - the topic sentence or the original sub-heading. Consider why this is the case. Again, this should be instructive in shaping the style you adopt in your own writing.

Planning writing assignments

How to organise your response to the task

Once you have assembled the information and made notes for your assignment, you will be able to think about how you are going to respond to the set writing task. This chapter outlines some of the different options to consider when structuring the content of your response into an outline plan.

Key topics
- Identifying the key themes in your text
- Adopting a structural approach
- Expanding your outline

Key terms
Brainstorm   Chronological   Hierarchical

The basic framework of an essay was described in **Ch 8**. The next step is to think about the particular assignment that you have to tackle and how you might organise your response to the task. This chapter outlines the key steps in this process.

People and their thought processes are different and so individual approaches to planning an outline response to a writing assignment will vary. For some people, this can be a highly detailed process; for others, it may be a minimal exercise. Too much detail in a plan can be restricting, while too little can fail to provide enough direction. Therefore, a reasonably detailed plan should give some guidance while leaving you the flexibility to alter the finer elements as you write.

● Identifying the key themes in your text

Planning your writing means that you need to return to your 'first thoughts' brainstorm (**Ch 3**), which should have been developed further as you have added key points from your reading and thinking.

Consider whether any themes or recurrent issues are evident. It might be useful to 'colour code' all the items that are related, using a different colour highlighter for each category or theme. Then, you need to reconsider the instruction of the set task to help you construct your plan, that is, on the basis of description, analysis or argument (Ch 3).

 Lower- or higher-order thinking?

While, for some subjects, description would be a lower-order writing activity, for others this would be considered to be a higher-order skill (see Table 7.1). Often written assignments require some initial description of context or process to outline the background to the topic. This is then followed by in-depth consideration of the topic, using more analytical or critical approaches.

● Adopting a structural approach

Your initial brain-storming of your writing topic should give you some indication of how you can construct the content of your paper. You can then frame a logical discussion by considering how it might fit into one of several classic structural models or approaches (Table 9.1).

By adopting one of these models, it should be possible to map out the content of your answer in a way that provides a logical and coherent response to the task you have been set. Note that sometimes it may

Table 9.1 **The seven most common structural approaches for written assignments**

1 Chronological	Description of a process or sequence
2 Classification	Categorising objects or ideas
3 Common denominator	Identification of a common characteristic or theme
4 Phased	Identification of short-/medium-/long-term aspects
5 Analytical	Examination of an issue in depth (situation - problem - solution - evaluation - recommendation)
6 Thematic	Comment on a theme in each aspect
7 Comparative/contrastive	Discussion of similarities and differences (often within a theme or themes)

be necessary to incorporate one of these models within another. For example, within the common denominator approach it may be necessary to include some chronological dimension to the discussion.

Examples of each of these seven approaches are given below.

1 Chronological

An example of the chronological approach would be describing a developmental process, such as outlining the historical development of the European Union. This kind of writing is most likely to be entirely descriptive.

2 Classification

An example of this approach could be to discuss transport by subdividing your text into land, sea and air modes of travel. Each of these could be further divided into commercial, military and personal modes of transport. These categories could be further subdivided on the basis of how they are powered. Such classifications are, to some extent, subjective, but the approach provides a means of describing each category at each level in a way that allows some contrast. This approach is particularly useful in scientific disciplines. The rationale also is sympathetic to the approach of starting from broad generalisation to the more specific.

3 Common denominator

An example of this approach might be used in answer to the following assignment: 'Account for the levels of high infant mortality in developing countries'. This suggests a common denominator of deficiency or lack. This topic could therefore be approached under the headings:

- Lack of primary health care
- Lack of health education
- Lack of literacy.

4 Phased

An example of adopting a sequential approach to a topic might be in answer to a task that instructs: 'Discuss the impact of water shortage on flora and fauna along river banks'.

- **Short-term factors** might be that drying out of the river bed occurs and annual plants fail to thrive.
- **Medium-term factors** might include damage to oxygenating plant life and reduction in wildlife numbers.
- **Long-term factors** might include the effect on the water table and falling numbers of certain amphibious species.

Note that topics amenable to this treatment do not always prompt this sort of response directly by asking for 'results' or consequences of an event; you could decide to use it in answer to a question such as 'Explain why water shortage has deleterious effects on riperian life.'

5 Analytical

This conventional approach might be used to approach complex issues. An example of an assignment that you could tackle in this way might be: 'Evaluate potential solutions to the problem of identity theft'. You could perhaps adopt the following plan:

- define identity theft, and perhaps give an example;
- explain why identity theft is difficult to control;
- outline legal and practical solutions to identity theft;
- weigh up the advantages and disadvantages of each;
- state which solution(s) you would favour and why.

 Adopting an analytical approach

This is particularly helpful in the construction of essays, reports, projects and case studies. It is also useful whenever you feel that you cannot identify themes or trends. This approach helps you to 'deconstruct' or 'unpack' the topic and involves five elements:

- **Situation:** describe the context and brief history.
- **Problem:** describe or define the problem.
- **Solution:** describe and explain the possible solution(s).
- **Evaluation:** identify the positive and negative features for each solution by giving evidence/reasons to support your viewpoint.
- **Recommendation:** identify the best option in your opinion, giving the basis of your reasoning for this. This element is optional, as it may not always be a requirement of your task.

6 Thematic

This approach is similar to the phased approach, but in this case themes are the identifying characteristics. Precise details would depend on the nature of the question, but possible examples could be:

- social, economic or political factors;
- age, income and health considerations;
- gas, electricity, oil, water and wind power.

7 Comparative/contrastive

This is a derivative of the themed approach. For example, consider a task that instructs: 'Discuss the arguments for and against the introduction of car-free city centres'. You might approach this by creating a 'grid', as in Table 9.2, which notes positive and negative aspects for the major stakeholders.

There are two potential methods of constructing text in this comparative/contrastive approach:

- **Method 1.** Introduce the topic, then follow Column A in a vertical fashion, then similarly follow Column B and conclude by making a concluding statement about the merits and demerits of one over the other. In relation to the grid, this would result in the structure: introductory statement, then A1 + A2 + A3 + A4 + A5, then B1 + B2 + B3 + B4 + B5, followed by concluding statement.

Table 9.2 **Model grid for planning comparison-type answers**

		Column A	Column B
	Stakeholders	Positive aspects	Negative aspects
1	Pedestrians	Greater safety, clean	Lengthy walk, poor parking
2	Drivers	Less stress; park and ride facilities	High parking fees; expensive public transport
3	Commercial enterprises	Quicker access for deliveries	Loss of trade to more accessible out-of-town shopping centres
4	Local authority	Reduces emissions	Cost of park and ride
5	Police	Easier to police	Reliance on foot patrols

- **Method 2.** Introduce the topic and than discuss the perspective of pedestrians from first the positive and then the negative aspects; now do the same for the viewpoints of the other stakeholders in sequence. This would result in the structure: introductory statement, then A1 + B1; A2 + B2; A3 + B3; A4 + B4; A5 + B5, followed by concluding statement.

Comparative/contrastive structures

Each method of structuring the points has advantages and disadvantages, according to the content and the context of the assignment. For example, in an exam it might be risky to embark on method 1 in case you run out of time and never reach the discussion of column B. In this instance, method 2 would enable a balanced answer.

● Expanding your outline

Once you have decided what kind of approach is required to cover your written assignment, then you can map this on to the main body of your essay plan and frame an introduction and conclusion that will 'top and tail' the essay. In this way, you can create the outline plan based on the introduction–main body–conclusion model that provides the framework for academic writing (**Ch 8**) in the English-speaking world.

Responding to question words

Not all tasks are based on instructions; some do ask questions. For instance, they may include words such as 'How ... ?', 'Why ... ?' and expressions such as 'To what extent ... ?' In these cases, you will need to think about what these mean within the do-describe-analyse-argue instruction hierarchy. One way to do this is to reword the question.

For example, consider the question: 'To what extent has the disposal of sewage effluence in rivers contributed to depletion of fish stocks over the last decade?'

This might be reworded as: 'Outline the relationship between the disposal of sewage effluence in rivers and the depletion of fish stocks over the last decade'.

This would suggest using a phased approach to organising the content of the answer to the question.

Practical tips for planning the outline of your written text

Return to the outline plan. When you have completed your first draft it is a good idea to go back to your outline plan and check that you have included all relevant points. You can also make sure that the links between sections that you noted in the plan have been achieved.

Achieve balance in your response. Especially in the early years of university study, there is a tendency to adhere to the methods that had succeeded at school or college. This means that written work is often descriptive rather than analytical (see **Ch 7** for explanation). Ensure that the description you give is sufficient for the task, but if the instruction requires you to analyse or argue, then make sure this is the main focus of your response.

Explain your approach. Although the models outlined in this chapter are fairly standard approaches to tackling academic issues, it is still necessary to identify for your reader which approach you intend to adopt in the piece of text. Your reader should learn at an early point in your writing of the route you intend to follow. In most cases this would be in your introduction. This is dealt with more fully in **Ch 8**.

 And now . . .

9.1 Compare textual patterns. Look at a chapter in a basic textbook and analyse the structural approach the author has taken. Identify the proportion of space allocated to 'scene-setting' using description, and to the analysis/argument/evaluation components of the text.

9.2 Identify response types. Look at some of the essay titles or report assignments you have been set. Try to identify which of the approaches given in this chapter might best 'fit' each task.

9.3 Practise converting questions into instructions. If past exam papers' coursework exercises include tasks framed as questions, try converting them into instruction tasks and decide which type they fit into within the 'do-describe-analyse-argue' classification (**Ch 3**).

Improving your grammar

How to avoid some common errors

Many people, not just students, often state that they don't
know much about the grammar of English – but what exactly do
they mean? Spelling? Sentence structure? Parts of speech?
Tense? Word order? The list seems to be endless. This chapter
takes a quick look at some common mistakes and tries to
provide enough in the way of grammatical terms to allow you
to understand the guidance on electronic grammar checkers or
in the feedback you receive on your assignments.

Key topics

- Why grammar is important
- Common grammatical errors
- How to use grammar checkers to best advantage

Key terms
Clause   Preposition   Tautology   Tense

Grammar is the series of rules that governs the use of any language.
It is a vast field and, although intuitively people know many of the
'rules' of grammar when speaking, it is often less easy to apply them
in writing. This chapter cannot provide a complete set of rules, but
gives you enough information to enable you to find what you need in
a specialist grammar book or in a standard dictionary.

● Why grammar is important

Grammar is important to you as a student because it is an integral
and expected component of academic writing. Good grammar is
essential, because without it your writing may be nonsensical, illogical
or ambiguous. In the course of your university studies you will come
across many aspects of language where you need to know exactly
how the appropriate grammar rule needs to be applied.

In the past, there have been two approaches to teaching grammar. The traditional approach teaches the 'technical' terms, for example, 'clause', 'preposition' and 'tense', so that these can be used to explain the mechanics of language; the other, modern, approach encourages people to write freely and then provides them feedback with correct models. For the purposes of this book, we shall use elements of both techniques because we believe that some people do want to know the 'proper grammar', but, at the same time, they may learn best by seeing models of how this works in practice. So, we'll show you some of the more common grammatical errors and explain these as simply as possible, using the grammatical terms only where absolutely necessary.

If you are eager for more information, then you may find it helpful to look at Ch 10 on academic style, Ch 13 on punctuation, Ch 14 on spelling and Ch 15 on vocabulary. These elements are all interdependent in the production of good style, structure and grammar in academic writing.

● Common grammatical errors

There are many common errors that occur in academic writing. Table 12.1 demonstrates how grammatical errors in a weak style of writing can be corrected to produce a more academic form of writing. In order to understand comments or corrections on your written work, it may be helpful to be able to identify some grammar terms. Table 12.2 defines and explains some of the terms you may come across. Table 12.3 gives some examples of errors and their corrections. Highlighting those that could be helpful to you in your writing will help you to create a personal checklist so you can avoid mistakes in future.

Grammatical terms

Grammar has its own particular terminology. This is used as a shorthand reference to allow discussion of more complex ideas. It's rather like the way that knowing the names of the main parts of a car engine helps you to understand the explanation of the mechanic who's fixing your car. The most common grammar terms are given in a very simplified form in Table 12.2. If you can become familiar with some of the basic terms, then this may help you to understand comments written on your assignments. This will also help you when looking up the relevant section in a good grammar book, when you think this might be useful.

Table 12.1 **Comparison of weak and strong academic writing.** This text is part of an answer to the question: 'Did Napoleon achieve most for France at home or abroad?' The original answer, written in a style that is essentially non-academic, is in the left column. The right-hand column is a key to some of the grammatical weaknesses in the use of language, and the final section of the table provides one possible example of how the same text could be written in a more academic style.

Non-academic style (bold text indicates error)	Error and correction analysis
Napolion[1] came up trumps[2] in both French domestic and foreign policies that were many and varied.[3] How you have to think about[4] the value of these achievements is the million dollar question.[5] While his domestic reforms survived after his collapse,[6] most of the affects[7] of his foreign policy necessarily perished with his imperial power. In addition to this,[8] the value of his achievements has to be considered in the light of whether they were achievements for France or achievements in consolidating his own position and popularity. In this essay I will talk about[9] his foreign and domestic policys.[10]	1 Misspelling of key name
	2, 3 Clichés
	4 Personal expression;
	5 Cliché/inappropriate language
	6 Ambiguous
	7 Misspelling
	8 Unnecessary words (phrase not used in corrected version)
	9 Statement of intent: use of personal pronouns – and you cannot 'talk' on paper!
	10 Misspelling
In foreign policy, Napoleon's primary achievement was the Peace of Lunéville (1801) with Austria and subsequent Treaty of Amiens with Britain in 1802. This achievement was significant 'cos[12] it gave both France and Napoleon, not to mention[13] their antagonists, a breathing space[14] in which to collect there[15] resources and reorganise themselves for further hostilities. This initial bargain[16] enabled Napoleon to have a look at[17] the domestic state of France after a decade of almost continuous international squabbling[18] following a major internal political revolution. Applying the same methods to the affairs of state as he did to the tactics of the battlefield.[19] In both two[20] ways he had to take into consideration the outlook and demands of the French people as a hole.[21] This approach he took on the grounds that[22] 'I act only on the imagination of the nation. When this means fails me, I shall be reduced to nothing and another will succeed me.'[23]	11 Add transition sentence to new version to link topic sentence with preceding paragraph
	12 Shortened word (not used in corrected version)
	13 Unnecessary words
	14 Informal language
	15 Misspelling
	16 More appropriate word required
	17 Too informal
	18 More appropriate word required
	19 Incomplete sentence/phrase (hanging participle)
	20 Tautology (same meaning twice)
	21 Misspelling;
	22 Wordy cliché
	23 No reference cited: Harvard method citation added

Table 12.1 continued

Academic style (bold text indicates correction/addition)
Napoleon's[1] achievements[2] in both French domestic and foreign policies **were significant.**[3] However, **the relative merit of these achievements must be considered**[4,5] at two levels. Firstly, although his domestic reforms survived his **downfall,**[6] most of the **effects**[7] of his foreign policy necessarily perished with his imperial power. **Secondly,**[8] the extent to which his achievements were truly for the greater glory of France or were simply strategies for consolidating his own position and popularity has to be taken into account. **The purpose of this essay**[9] **will be to evaluate these two dimensions within his foreign and domestic policies**[10] **in the longer term.**
Domestic and foreign policy in this period cannot easily be separated. In foreign policy,[11] Napoleon's primary achievement was the Peace of Lunéville (1801) with Austria and subsequent Treaty of Amiens with Britain in 1802. The significance of this achievement was that it gave both France and Napoleon, **and their antagonists,**[13] **an interval**[14] in which to collect **their**[15] resources and reorganise themselves for further hostilities. This initial **accord**[16] enabled Napoleon to **survey**[17] the domestic state of France after a decade of almost continuous **fighting**[18] preceded by a major internal political revolution. **He applied the same methods to the affairs of state as he did to the tactics of the battlefield;**[19] in **both**[20] he had to take into consideration the outlook and demands of the French people as a **whole.**[21] This approach he took **because**[22] 'I act only on the imagination of the nation. When this means fails me, I shall be reduced to nothing and another will succeed me' (**Grant and Temperley, 1952**).[23]

Table 12.2 **Grammar toolkit: definitions to help you seek more information**

Grammar term	Definition/model	Example
Adjective	Describes nouns or gerunds.	A red book; an innovative project.
Adverb	Adds information as to how something is done.	The student read quickly.
Articles	There are only three in English: a, an, the. There are particular rules about using these and you will find these rules in a grammar book.	A shot in the dark. An empty house. The Highway Code.
Clause	Part of sentence containing a verb. If the verb and the words relating to it can stand alone, then they comprise the main clause. If the words cannot stand alone, then the verb and the words that go with it form a subordinate clause.	I hate mice which are vermin. *Main* *Subordinate* *clause* *clause*
Conditional	Used to explain a future possible situation; note the comma after the condition.	If I had the time, I would go. *Condition* *Consequence*
Conjunction	Word that joins two clauses in a sentence where the ideas are connected or equally balanced.	The book was on loan and the student had to reserve it.
Demonstrative	There are four in English: this, these, that, those (see Table 12.3).	This house supports the abolition of smoking in public.
Direct object	The noun or pronoun that is affected by the verb.	Foxes kill sheep. Foxes eat them.
Future tense	Explaining things that have not yet happened. There are two forms: will/shall, going to.	I shall work until I am 65. They will come early. He is going to work harder.
Gerund	The gerund acts as a noun and is formed with the part of the verb called the present participle: . . . -ing.	Speaking is easier than writing for most people.

Table 12.2 continued

Grammar term	Definition/model	Example
Indirect object	The person or thing that benefits from the action of a verb.	Tutors give (to) **students** written work. They give (to) **them** essays.
Infinitive	Sometimes called the simple or root form of the verb. This form is usually listed in dictionaries, but without 'to'.	**To work.**
Noun	Term used to refer to things or people. There are different types: e.g. abstract (non-visible), concrete (visible) and proper nouns (names of people, places organisations, rivers, mountain ranges).	**Abstract noun:** thought. **Concrete nouns:** chair, table. **Proper nouns:** Caesar, Rome, the Post Office, the Rhine, the Andes (always begin with capitals).
Passive voice	Used to describe things objectively, that is, placing the emphasis of the sentence on the action rather than the actor. Although some electronic grammar checkers imply that the passive is wrong, it is perfectly correct. Often used in academic writing.	**Essays are written** by students. ↑ ↑ *Action* *Actor*
Past participle	This is usually formed by adding **-ed** to the verb stem. However, in English there are many irregular verbs (see 'tense', below). You will find lists of these verbs in many dictionaries.	Work**ed**. However, there are many irregular verbs: e.g. bent, drunk; eaten, seen; thought; understood.
Present participle	This is formed by adding **-ing** to the simple verb form. It is used to form continuous verb tenses.	The sun is **setting**. We were **watching** the yachts.
Phrasal verb	These are two- or three-word verbs made up of a verb plus a particle (similar to a preposition). These verbs are generally regarded as being less formal in tone than single-word verbs.	**Set down** (deposit). **Pick up** (collect). **Write down** (note). **Look out for** (observe).

Table 12.2 continued

Grammar term	Definition/model	Example
Possessive	Word indicating ownership: my, mine, your, yours, his, her, its, our, ours, their, theirs.	**My** house and **his** are worth the same. **Mine** is larger but **his** has more land.
Preposition	Word used as a link relating verbs to nouns, pronouns and noun phrases. Sometimes these are followed by an article, sometimes not: at, by, in, for, from, of, on, over, through, under, with.	Put money **in** the bank **for** a rainy day or save it **for** summer holidays **in** the sun.
Pronoun	Word used instead of nouns: I, me, you, he, him, she, her, it, we, us, they, them. Also words such as: each, everyone.	I have given **it** to **him**.
Relative pronoun	Words that link adjective (describing) clauses to the noun about which they give more information: that, which, who, whose, whom.	This is the house **that** Jack built. Jack, **who** owns it, lives there. Jack, **whose** wife sings, is a baker. Jack, **to whom** we sold the flour, used it to bake a loaf.
Sentence	A grouping of words, one of which must be a verb, that can stand together independently and make sense.	The people elect their leaders in a democracy.
Subject	The person or thing that performs the action in a sentence.	**Caesar** invaded Britain. **Caterpillars** eat leaves.
Tense	In English, to show past, present and future time, the verb tense changes. This often involves adding a word to show this. Here are three basic tenses; more can be found in a grammar book or language learner's dictionary. Some verbs behave irregularly from the standard rules.	(see table below)
Verb	The action or 'doing' word in a sentence. It changes form to indicate shifts in time (see tense).	I work, I am working, I will work, I worked, I was working, I have worked, I had worked.

Tense example:

	Simple past	Present	Future
I	studied	study	shall study
You	studied	study	will study
S/he	studied	studies	will study
We	studied	study	shall study
You	studied	study	will study
They	studied	study	will study

Table 12.3 **Twelve common grammar errors**

Problem area	Incorrect example (✗) and correction (✓)
1 Comparing Sometimes there is confusion with when to use a word ending in -er or -est rather than using 'more' or 'most'. For grammar book entries, look for **Comparatives** and **Superlatives**.	Comparing two things: ✗ The debit was more bigger than the credit. ✓ The debit was greater than the credit. Comparing three or more things: ✗ China has the most greatest population in the world. ✓ China has the greatest population in the world. Countable and non-countable: ✗ There were less cases of meningitis last year. ✓ There were **fewer** cases of meningitis last year. (Countable) ✗ There was fewer snow last year. ✓ There was **less** snow last year. (Non-countable)
2 Describing Commas can be vital to meaning – misuse can cause fundamental changes to meaning. For grammar book entry, look for **Relative clauses**.	✗ Toys, which are dangerous, should not be given to children. (Inference: all toys are dangerous – not what the author means) ✓ Toys which are dangerous should not be given to children. (Inference: only safe toys should be given to children – what the author means)
3 Encapsulating Using one word to represent a previous word or idea. For grammar book entry, look for **Demonstrative pronoun**.	✗ . . . impact of diesel use on air quality. **This** increases in rush-hour. (Inference: air quality increases in rush hour – not the intended meaning.) ✓ . . . impact of diesel use on air quality. **This impact** increases in rush-hour.
4 Its/it's These two are often confused. For grammar book entry, look for **Possessives (its)** and **Apostrophes (it's)**.	✗ As it's aim, the book describes the whole problem. ✓ As **its** aim, the book describes the whole problem. (Possession) ✗ Its not a viable answer to the problem. ✓ **It's** not a viable answer to the problem (It is . . .) ✗ Its not had a good review. ✓ **It's** not had a good review. (It has . . .)
5 Joining Words such as 'because', 'but' and 'and' join two clauses; they should never begin sentences. For grammar book entry, look for **Conjunctions**.	✗ Because the sample was too small, the results were invalid. ✓ Since the sample was too small, the results were invalid. ('Because' is a conjunction and is used to join two ideas.) ✗ But the UN failed to act. And the member states did nothing. ✓ The country was attacked, **but** the UN failed to act **and** the member states did nothing. ('But' and 'and' are conjunctions that join two separate ideas.)

▶

Table 12.3 continued

Problem area	Incorrect example (X) and correction (✓)
6 Double negative Two negatives mean a positive. Sometimes using a double negative can cause confusion. For grammar book entry, look for **Double negatives.**	X They have <u>not</u> had <u>no</u> results from their experiments. ✓ They have not had any results from their experiments. X The government had not done nothing to alleviate poverty. ✓ The government had done nothing to alleviate poverty. (Intended meaning.)
7 Past participles These are sometimes misused, especially when the verbs are irregular in past forms. For grammar book entry, look for **Past participles.**	X The team had **went** to present their findings at the conference. ✓ The team had **gone** to present their findings at the conference.
8 Prepositions These should not come at the end of a sentence. For grammar book entry, look for **Prepositions.**	X These figures are the ones you will work with. ✓ These figures are the ones **with which** you will work.
9 Pronouns These are used to replace nouns. The singular pronouns often cause confusion because they need to agree with the verb. For grammar book entry, look for **Pronouns.**	**Singular pronouns:** anybody, anyone, anything, each, either, everybody, everyone, everything, neither, nobody, no one, nothing, somebody, someone, something – all take a singular verb. X Each of the new measures are to be introduced separately. ✓ **Each** of the new measures **is** to be introduced separately. **Reflexive pronouns:** X Although disappointed, they only have theirselves to blame. ✓ Although disappointed, **they** only have **themselves** to blame.
10 Specifying Words that are used to identify specific singular and plural items must match. For grammar book entry, look for **Demonstratives.**	✓ **This** kind of mistake **is** common. ✓ **These** kinds of mistakes **are** less common. ✓ **That** result **is** acceptable. ✓ **Those** results **are** not acceptable.

Table 12.3 continued

Problem area	Incorrect example (✗) and correction (✓)
11 Subject–verb agreement Often singular subjects are matched with plural verbs and vice versa. For grammar book entry, look for **Subject–verb agreement.**	✗ The Principal, together with the Chancellor, were present. ✓ The Principal, together with the Chancellor, **was** present. ✗ It is the result of these overtures and influences that help to mould personal identity. ✓ It is the **result** of these overtures and influences that **helps** to mould personal identity.
12 There/their/they're These simply need to be remembered. For grammar book entry, look for **Words that are often confused.**	✗ They finished there work before noon. ✓ They finished **their** work before noon. ✗ We have six places at the conference. We'll go their. ✓ We have six places at the conference. We'll go **there.** ✗ Researchers are skilled but there not highly paid. ✓ Researchers are skilled but **they're** not highly paid.

● How to use grammar checkers to best advantage

Some software packages provide a grammar-checking facility. Although this can provide you with some helpful tips, it is important to recognise that it is not infallible. As an artificial intelligence device, it cannot always fully respond to more sophisticated grammatical logic. For example, in the following sentence, the words 'a lot of' were underlined as grammatically incorrect by an electronic grammar checker:

You get a lot of help for projects from the tutors.

The suggested adjustment was to rewrite the sentence as:

You get many help for projects from the tutors.

This is obviously grammatically incorrect. In another example using the passive voice:

The limitation of feedback from teaching staff was noted by other students to be frustrating.

was 'corrected' to:

Other students to be frustrating noted the limitation of feedback from teaching staff.

This clearly makes nonsense of the original text and meaning. The message is clear: you should not blindly accept all changes recommended by the grammar checker.

If you have had an error pointed out to you, but don't understand it fully, then ask the person who made the correction to explain to you what is wrong. If you are unable to do this or are unsure, then check out some of the resources given below. You can do a little bit of detective work first by looking at your error in conjunction with the grammar definition list in Table 12.2. Once you have an idea of what the problem might be, then you could consult one of the many good grammar books available by looking for the key grammatical term in the index or contents. For example, you could have a look at *Longman's Advanced Learners' Grammar* (Foley and Hall, 2003), which has very useful diagnostic tests to help you identify difficulties. The book gives clear explanations of each grammar point with exercises for practice and an answer key. Another source is *Fowler's Modern English Usage* (Fowler and Winchester, 2002). Other user-friendly sources include the *BBC English Dictionary* (1992) or the *Longman Dictionary of Contemporary English* (2003), both of which give words, meanings and examples of correct usage.

 Practical tips for understanding grammar

Identify and understand your errors. Markers of your assignments often indicate errors on written work, sometimes simply by underlining or circling text, sometimes by restructuring or inserting a correction. It is well worth spending some time looking over your marked work to understand different points that the marker has identified – some will be related to subject matter, some to grammar and some to punctuation. If you can isolate the latter two types, noting the errors and how these have been corrected, then you are well on the way to avoiding them in the future. This could make a real difference to you in your marks on future assignments.

Make your own checklist. Once you have identified an error that you have made, then make a note of it (you could keep a glossary notebook and isolate a few pages for grammar points). It's a good idea to write down the error, its correction and, if you can, a quick note of what is wrong and why.

GO And now . . .

12.1 Get into the habit of consulting reference works when required. The grammar of most languages can be complex, but if you approach it on a 'need-to-know' basis, then you could make a point of learning those things that are most relevant to your need. For example, some students find it difficult to work out when to use a particular tense, so they could look up that section in a grammar book and find out what they need. Other students might have difficulty with working out how the passive operates; again, they could look up that section in a grammar book to find out more (See p. 138 for useful sources on grammar).

12.2 Set up a section in a notebook for keeping a record of errors that have arisen in your writing. Note the error, its correction and also a reference to a source where you were able to find some information on the particular grammar point. The act of writing these details down will help you to memorise the grammar rule – but if you don't, the notebook will act as a useful personal reference.

12.3 Try to learn more grammar with the help of others. It's said that some people have a greater aptitude for understanding language – it's a kind of code, after all, and if no one has ever given you the key then it is not surprising if you cannot 'break the code'. If this is the case for you, and someone has made a comment about your written grammar, then ask friends if they know what is wrong with the word, sentence or paragraph. They may have some more knowledge of the grammar codes and be able to help by explaining to you what is wrong.

Reviewing, editing and proof-reading

How to make sure your writing is concise and correct

Looking critically at your own writing is essential if you want to produce work of the highest quality. These editing skills will allow you to improve the sense, grammar and syntax of your written assignments.

Key topics

- The reviewing, editing and proof-reading process
- The value of reviewing, editing and proof-reading

Key terms
Annotate Syntax Typo *Vice versa*

Writing is a process. It begins with a plan and it finishes with reviewing, editing and proof-reading. This means that you should read your text critically before submitting it for assessment. The effort you invest in this final stage will contribute to the quality of your work and to your assessed mark. Ideally, you should leave a gap of time between completing the writing and beginning the reviewing process, as this allows you to 'distance' yourself from the work and helps you look at it as a new reader would.

● The reviewing, editing and proof-reading process

At this stage you are performing the role of editor. This means that you are looking critically at your text for content, relevance and sense, as well as for flaws in layout, grammar, punctuation and spelling. You should also check for consistency in all aspects, for example, in the use of terminology, in spelling, and in presentational

From Chapter 16 of *How to Write Essays & Assessments*, 2/e. Kathleen McMillan & Jonathan Weyers. © Pearson Education Limited 2007, 2010, 2011. All rights reserved.

features such as font and point size, layout of paragraphs, and labelling of tables and diagrams.

Clearly, there are many aspects to cover, and some degree of overlap in different parts of the process. Some people prefer to go through their text in one sweep, amending any flaws as they go; others, in particular professional writers, take a staged approach, reading through their text several times looking at a different facet each time.

 Definitions

Reviewing: appraising critically; that is, examining an essay or assignment to ensure that it meets the requirements and objectives of the task and that the overall sense is conveyed well.

Editing: revising and correcting later drafts of an essay or assignment, to arrive at a final version. Usually, this involves the smaller rather than the larger details: punctuation, spelling, grammar and layout.

Proof-reading: checking a printed copy for errors of any sort.

There are five aspects to consider in the reviewing process:

- content and relevance;
- clarity, style and coherence;
- grammatical correctness;
- spelling and punctuation;
- presentation.

Table 16.1 provides a quick checklist of key aspects to consider under each of these themes. This has been designed for photocopying so that you can, if you wish, use it as a checklist each time you complete a piece of work. Table 16.2 on pp. 174-75 gives some helpful strategies you can adopt when going through the editing process.

Professional proof-readers have developed a system of symbols to speed up the editing and proof-reading process. You may wish to adopt some of these yourself, and you are certainly likely to see some of them, and other 'informal' marks, on work returned by tutors. Table 16.3 on p. 176 illustrates some of the more commonly used symbols.

Table 16.1 **Quick editing and proof-reading checklist.** Each heading could represent a 'sweep' of your text, checking for the aspects shown. The text is assumed to be a piece of writing produced for assessment.

Content and relevance
❏ The intent of the instruction word has been followed
❏ The question or task has been completed, that is, you have answered all sections or required numbers of questions
❏ The structure is appropriate
❏ The text shows objectivity
❏ The examples are relevant
❏ All sources are correctly cited
❏ The facts presented are accurate

Clarity, style and coherence
❏ The rationale of your approach to the topic will be clear to the reader
❏ What you wrote is what you meant to write
❏ The text is fluent, with appropriate use of signpost words
❏ Any informal language has been removed
❏ The style is academic and appropriate for the task
❏ The content and style of each section is consistent
❏ The tense used in each section is suited to the time frame of your text
❏ The length of the text sections are balanced appropriately

Grammatical correctness
❏ All sentences are complete
❏ All sentences make sense
❏ Paragraphs have been correctly used
❏ Suggestions made by grammar checker have been accepted/rejected
❏ Text has been checked against your own checklist of recurrent errors
❏ Text is consistent in adopting either British or American English

Spelling and punctuation
❏ Any blatant 'typos' have been corrected by reading for meaning
❏ Text has been spellchecked or read through carefully for spelling
❏ A check has been made for spelling of subject-specific and foreign words
❏ Punctuation has been checked, if possible, by reading aloud (p. 170)
❏ Proper names are correctly capitalised
❏ Overlong sentences have been divided

Presentation
❏ If no word-count target is given, the overall length will depend on the amount of time you were given to complete the task. Ask your tutor, if you're uncertain
❏ The text length meets the word-count target – neither too short nor too long
❏ Overall neatness checked
❏ The cover-sheet details and presentation aspects are as required
❏ The bibliography/reference list is correctly formatted according to the recommended style
❏ Page numbers have been included (in position stipulated, if given)
❏ The figures and tables are in appropriate format

Table 16.2 Editing strategies – quick reference. The reviewing/editing/proof-reading process can be done in a single 'sweep'. As you become more experienced, you will become adept at doing this. However, initially, it might help you to focus on each of these three broad aspects in a separate 'sweep' of the text. Note that the first two sections develop aspects considered in Table 16.1. Further discussion of presentational issues is provided in Ch 19.

Content and relevance; clarity, style and coherence
• Read text aloud – your ears will help you to identify errors that your eyes have missed • Revisit the task or question. Check your interpretation against the task as set • Work on a hard copy using editing symbols to correct errors (Table 16.3 p. 176) • Identify that the aims you set out in your introduction have been met • Read objectively and assess whether the text makes sense. Look for inconsistencies in argument • Check that all your facts are correct • Insert additional or overlooked evidence that strengthens the whole • Remove anything that is not relevant or alter the text so that it is clear and unambiguous. Reducing text by 10–25 per cent can improve quality considerably • Critically assess your material to ensure that you have attributed ideas to the sources, that is, check that you have not committed plagiarism • Remodel any expressions that are too informal for academic contexts • Eliminate gendered or discriminatory language
Grammatical correctness, spelling and punctuation
• Check titles and subtitles are appropriate to the style of the work and stand out by using bold or underlining (not both) • Consider whether the different parts link together well – if not, introduce signpost words to guide the reader through the text (pp. 48-9 and p. 122) • Check for fluency in sentence and paragraph structure – remodel as required • Check sentence length – remodel to shorter or longer sentences. Sometimes shorter sentences are more effective than longer ones • Ensure that you have been consistent in spelling conventions, for example, following British English rather than American English spelling or *vice versa* • Spelling errors – use the spellchecker but be prepared to double-check in a standard dictionary if you are in doubt or cannot find a spelling within the spellchecker facility • Check for cumbersome constructions – divide or restructure sentence(s); consider whether active or passive is more suitable. Consider using vocabulary that might convey your point more eloquently • Check for use of 'absolute' terms to ensure that you maintain objectivity

Table 16.2 continued

Presentation
• Check that you have made good use of white space, that is, not crammed the text into too tight a space, and that your text is neat and legible with minimum 1.5 line spacing if no recommendation is made otherwise • If your text is word-processed, check that you have followed standard typing conventions. Follow any 'house style' rules stipulated by your department • Check that you have included a reference list, consistently following a recognised method, and that all citations in the text are matched by an entry in the reference list and vice versa • Ensure all pages are numbered and are stapled or clipped, and, if appropriate, ensure that the cover page is included • Check that your name, matriculation number and course number are included. You may wish to add this information as a footnote that appears on each page • Ensure question number and title are included • Check that labelling of diagrams, charts and other visual material is in sequence and consistently presented • Ensure that supporting material is added in sequence as appendices, footnotes, endnotes or as a glossary as applicable

Technical notes

The word processor has made the reviewing and editing task much easier. Here are some tips for using this software effectively:

- Use the word-count facility to check on length.
- Use the 'View' facility to check page breaks and general layout before you print out.
- Use the facilities within the 'Format' or 'Page layout' menu to control presentational aspects like paragraph spacing, tabs for indents and styles for bulleted and numbered lists.
- Use the spell- and grammar-checkers to guide you, but do not rely on them 100 per cent as they are fallible.
- Sometimes the grammar checker will announce that you have used the passive voice. This is often a standard academic usage and, therefore, is not an error.
- Sometimes staff add comments to students' work using 'Track Changes' on the Microsoft Word software. Depending on the version you are using, feedback information can usually be accepted or rejected by right-clicking on the word or punctuation point that has been marked for alteration.

Table 16.3 **Common proof-reading symbols.** University lecturers and tutors use a variety of symbols on students' assignments to indicate errors, corrections or suggestions. These can apply to punctuation, spelling, presentation or grammar. The symbols provide a kind of 'shorthand' that acts as a code to help you see how you might be able to amend your text so that it reads correctly and fluently. In this table some of the more commonly used correction marks are shown alongside their meanings. The sample text shows how these symbols may be used either in the text or the margin to indicate where a change is recommended.

Correction mark	Meaning	Example
⌐ (np)	(new) paragraph	*Text* · · · · · · · · · · · · *margin*
≢	change CAPITALS to small letters (lower case)	The correction marks that tutors use in students' texts are generally
~~	change into **bold** type	made to help identify where there
≡	change into CAPITALS	have been errors of spelling or ⅄e/⅄g
◠	close up (delete space)	punctuation. They can often (STET)
/ or ⅂ or ⊢⊣	delete	indicate where there is lack of
⅄	insert a word or letter	paragraphing or grammatical
⋎	insert space	accuracy. If you find that work is (np)
.... or (STET)	leave unchanged	returned to you with such
Insert punctuation symbol in a circle Ⓟ	punctuation	marks correction, then it is ⌐⌐ worthwhile spending some time analysing the common errors as ⅂
plag.	plagiarism	well as the comments, because this
⟶	run on (no new paragraph)	will help you to improve the quality of presentation and content
Sp.	spelling	of your work this reviewing can ⊙/≡
⌐⌐	transpose text	have a positive effect on your
?	what do you mean?	assessed mark.
??	text does not seem to make sense	*In the margin, the error symbols are*
✔	good point/correct	*separated by a slash (/) if there is more*
✗	error	*than one per line.*

● The value of reviewing, editing and proof-reading

Although the editing process may seem tedious and more complex than it might have appeared at first, a text revised in this way will be far more likely to receive a favourable reading – and possibly a higher mark – than one that is not reviewed, edited and proofed.

Professional writers – novelists as well as academics – often report that their initial drafts are often much longer than the final version. If you follow their example of writing 'large' and then cutting down the text with intelligent editing, then your text will be crisper. Some of the things that can be easily removed are redundant words ('in order to = 'to') or lengthy expressions ('a lot of' = 'many') which will help to achieve that crispness of expression. At sentence level, you may find that you have written something like:

These changes have caused shortages in almost all commodities in the market that are derived from milk. This means that milk products are in short-supply.

Essentially, these two sentences mean the same and so you could eliminate one of them. Which one you decide to cut might depend on the context; equally, it might depend on your word count. Either way, the resulting, shorter, text will send a clearer message to your reader.

It is the mix of style, content, structure and presentation that will gain you marks, and anything you can do to increase your mark-earning power will be to your advantage. In the longer term, learning how to edit your work properly will help you to develop a skill of critical analysis that will stand you in good stead throughout your career.

The practical tips that follow give you more detailed explanation of the strategies that you could develop to review, edit and proof your work, both for coursework and during exams. These are summarised in the checklist in Table 16.1 on p. 173 and in the quick-reference editing strategies listed in Table 16.2 on pp. 174-5.

 Practical tips for reviewing, editing and proof-reading your work for coursework and examination scripts

Coursework

Make time for checking. When planning the writing of an essay or assignment, ensure that you have allowed adequate time for reviewing and proof-reading. You don't want to spoil all your hard work by skimping on the final stage. Leave some time between finishing the final draft and returning to check the whole text, because you will return to your work with a fresh and possibly more critical eye.

Work from a hard copy. Reading through your work laid out on paper, which is the format in which your marker will probably see it, will help you identify errors and inconsistencies more readily than might be possible on the screen. A paper version is also easier to annotate (although this can also be done using the 'Track Changes' facility on your word processor). A printout also allows you to see the whole work in overview, and focus on the way the text 'flows'. If necessary, spread it out on the desk in front of you.

Follow the 'reading aloud' check. This is a tried and tested technique to ensure that what you have written actually makes sense. Simply read your text aloud to yourself. Your ears will hear the errors that your eyes might miss on a silent reading of the text. This will help you correct grammatical and spelling inconsistencies, as well as punctuation omissions. (Note: for obvious reasons, this method is not suitable for use in exams.)

Map your work to obtain an overview. 'Label' each paragraph with a topic heading and list these in a linear way on a separate paper. This will provide you with a 'snapshot' of your text and will allow you to appraise the order, check against any original plan, and adjust the position of parts as you feel necessary.

Check for relevance. Ensure that you have written and interpreted the question as set and have not 'made up' another title for the task. Whatever you have written will be judged by the terms of the original question, not by one that you have created.

Check for consistency in the elements of your text. For example, ensure that your introduction and conclusion complement and do not contradict each other.

Check for factual accuracy. Ensure that all the facts are correct, for example, in a history essay that the date sequences are consistent, or in a scientific paper that a numerical answer you have reached is realistic. It is very easy to type a date erroneously or make a final slip in the transposition of a number from one area of the page to another and, thus, lose marks.

Stick to your word limits/targets. Remember that too few words can be just as bad as too many. The key point is that your writing must be clear to your reader. Sometimes this means giving a longer explanation; sometimes it means simplifying what you have written. However, at this stage, if you are over the word-count limit, then check for ways in which you can reword the text to eliminate redundant words while maintaining the sense you intended to convey.

Create 'white space'. To help produce a more 'reader-friendly' document that will not deter the marker, try to create 'white space' by:

- leaving space (one 'return' space) between paragraphs;
- justifying only on the left side of the page;
- leaving space around diagrams, tables and other visual material; and
- leaving reasonable spaces between headings, sub-headings and text.

Check that all the 'secretarial' aspects are in place. Neat presentation, punctuation and spelling all help your reader to access the information, ideas and argument of your writing. While this may not gain you marks, it will certainly ensure that you do not lose marks even indirectly by making the marker struggle to 'decode' your work.

Check other visual aspects. Diagrams, tables and figures should be drawn using a ruler, if you cannot create these electronically. Only in some subjects would freehand drawing be acceptable, for example, in the study of Architecture.

Examination scripts

Factor in time to allow you to review your script. When working out how long you can afford to spend on each element of your exam paper, include some time for checking it over. It is probably better to keep this as a chunk of time towards the end of the exam as this will mean that you will have completed the paper in its entirety and it will have given you a break between writing the response and carrying out your review/edit/proof stages.

Be ready to work quickly. Clearly, time is at a premium in an exam and so you need to cover each aspect as speedily as possible. If you have practised reviewing, editing and proof-reading your coursework, you will have developed some skill in doing this. However, remember that you will have to do this by hand.

Appraise the legibility of your handwriting as part of the review process. Working under pressure can mean that handwriting becomes less well-formed and so you need to make sure that words are legible and that, if you have used non-standard 'shorthand' expressions e.g. 'govt' for 'government' that you have made it clear in the text what that abbreviation means.

Annotate our script clearly. As you skim-read your answers you can make adjustments. Sometimes, this will simply mean inserting a mark (⋏ or ^) between words and writing a missing word or phrase in the space above. In other instances, you can insert the ⋏ or ^ and write 'see additional paragraph x at *** (which you can add either on the facing page or at the end of that particular answer.

Look out for repeated errors. Under pressure, students sometimes find that they have consistently made an error, for example, referred to Louis XIV throughout as Louis XVI or written 'Louise' rather than 'Louis'. If this happens to you, then just put an asterisk (*) beside the first occurrence of the error and add a note at the end of your answer or in the margin for example: *consistent error. Please read as 'Louis XIV' throughout*. Note that you will not lose marks for correcting your work in this way.

 And now . . .

16.1 Reflect on past submissions. Look at an essay or assignment that you have already submitted and go through it using the checklist in Table 16.1. Concentrate on two pages and, using a highlighter, mark all flaws, inconsistencies or errors. Look at the overall effect of these errors and reflect on the extent to which this may have lost you marks; then consider how you might allow for more time for the editing/proof-reading phase next time round.

16.2 Practise using the standard proof-reading marks. On the same piece of text, insert the relevant standard proof-reading symbols (Table 16.3) on the text and in the margin. Learning how to use these symbols will help you speed up the proof-reading process.

16.3 Practise condensing a piece of text. This is an acknowledged way of improving your work, though you have to bear in mind any word targets that have been set. Look at your text for irrelevant points, wordy phrases, repetitions and excessive examples; if you can reduce its original length by 10–25 per cent, you will probably find that you have created a much tighter, easier-to-read piece of writing.

Accessing job opportunities

Headlines will always be negative: look beyond them. The market is tough – but there are always vacancies.

Carl Gilleard, Chief Executive, Association of Graduate Recruiters

This chapter looks at how employers get their vacancies into the marketplace, which means we show you where the job opportunities are, and how you can find them. It is important to remember that employers are looking for the right person to fill their job with just as much commitment and concern as you show when you are looking for your brilliant job.

Supply and demand: it takes two

The basic principle of the graduate labour market is that two equally important elements must be in place for the market to work, namely: supply and demand (for an in-depth exploration of the graduate labour market, have a look at Chapter 2). In the graduate labour market you as the jobseeker are the supply, and the employer offering the job is the demand. Clearly, for the job market to function at all, both supply and demand each need to know of the other's existence, which means that you (supply) have to make your presence in the marketplace known, and the employers (demand) equally have to make it known that they have a job that they want to fill.

From Chapter 1 of *Graduate Career Handbook*, 1/e. Judith Done and Rachel Mulvey.
© Pearson Education Limited 2011. All rights reserved.

brilliant definitions

You, the jobseeker, are the **supply side** of the graduate labour market; the employers are the **demand side**.

The employer's perspective

For an employer, taking on a new person is a big deal. It is going to increase their payroll, it is probably going to cost them money just to get their vacancy publicised and, when they do find someone, they are going to have to allocate time (which is a valuable resource) to integrate the new employee into the workplace quickly, so that they can function well and be a valued addition to the organisation. Employers care a great deal about getting the right person for the job. They don't want a huge range of applicants: what they want is to choose from a range of suitable candidates so that they recruit the right one for their job, which is why employers are keen to get their job out there where people can see it. They can use a range of media to do this: print, online and networking (sometimes called word of mouth). Instead of responding to job vacancies that are advertised, you can take the initiative and approach an employer to see if there is a possible vacancy; this is called a speculative application. You can also choose to work for yourself, rather than work for someone else, namely self-employment. So let's look at each of these in turn.

How employers get their jobs out there

Vacancies in print

Newspapers

Print media comprises newspapers, magazines and directories. In some cases, the vacancies advertised will only be a small part of the publication. This is the case with newspapers, for example. The national newspapers (including *The Times*, the *Daily Telegraph*, the *Guardian* and the *Independent*) often group vacancies by sector and publish all those vacancies on the same day each week, e.g. education jobs appear in the *Guardian* on Tuesdays. You need to check with the individual newspaper title to see what cluster of job adverts are published on which day of the week. Newspapers also publish supplements given over exclusively to job vacancies. This can be by sector (engineering or social care) or by level (graduate jobs). As these supplements tend to be occasional rather than regular you'll need to keep an eye out for announcements which appear in the paper itself.

brilliant tip

Check the national quality newspapers to see what kind of job vacancies are advertised on which day of the week.

Regional and local papers

You have plenty of choice when it comes to local and regional papers: over 1,500 titles are listed in the UK. Some publish daily, such as: the *Manchester Evening News*; the *Evening Standard* (London); the *Belfast Telegraph* and the *Herald* (Glasgow). Others come out weekly, ranging from the *Abergavenny Free Press* to the *Whitby Gazette,* and many of them are freely accessible online. These newspapers will include the whole range of jobs on offer in the locality, not just graduate-only jobs. You'll have to comb through all the ads to check for graduate or direct-entry jobs, but this will give you a good overview of the labour market conditions in that area. If you are keen to live in a particular location, this actually could work to your advantage, because it will make you look at non-graduate jobs as well, and tell you about jobs in that area. So you could always apply for that kind of job to get you to the place you want to be and, once there, start looking for the perfect job for you.

brilliant tip

Quality newspapers offer very good student discounts; just go online to get the vouchers. Not only will you get regular access to job ads, you'll also develop a good habit of serious reading.

Vacancy bulletins and directories

Some publications are devoted entirely to advertising vacancies. They are probably published less frequently than newspapers. There are several produced by Graduate Prospects which are aimed specifically at graduates, and free copies should be available at your university careers service. One example is *Real Prospects Directory* – a comprehensive directory of both graduate recruiters and job opportunities written specifically for students in the final year of their degree. It is produced annually in October. The *Finalist* is a magazine with job vacancies, again aimed at final-year students, and published three times a year in October, January and April.

Specialist bulletins and directories

As well as these two general publications, there are also specialist ones such as *Law,* which lists training contracts and law course vacancies for both law and non-law students. It is an annual publication that appears in September.

Postgraduate bulletins and directories

There are several specialist directories for postgraduate opportunities, including the *Postgraduate Directory,* which includes everything you could want to know about postgraduate courses and opportunities. The *Postgraduate Magazine* covers the same ground, but is published three times a year, in autumn, spring and summer. The *MBA Directory* restricts itself to Master in Business Administration programmes; and finally, the *Funding Guide* (published annually in September) is definitely one you'll need if you intend to continue your studies to postgraduate level.

Directory of work experience and internships for non-finalists

No need to feel left out if you're not yet in your final year. There is one annual publication aimed at non-finalists: *Work Experience and Internships,* that comes out in October.

brilliant tip

Your university careers service should have free copies of these directories and vacancy bulletins, or you can access the digital editions online at **www.prospects.ac.uk**.

Vacancies online

Posting job vacancies online is increasingly common. To find them, you simply need to go online and start looking. You'll find plenty of employers advertising direct to online jobsites. Or perhaps their newspaper advert is made accessible online by the newspaper in question. There are also employment agencies that work on behalf of a range of employers, which means that they might be comprehensive (e.g. **www.monster.co.uk**) or specialised by: occupational sector, such as healthcare and medical jobs (e.g. **www.healthcare.jobs.com**); jobs in the financial sector (e.g. **www.roberthalf.co.uk**); by restricted entry (e.g. **www.thegraduate. co.uk**); or by geography such as jobs in Italy (e.g. **www.italialavoro.net**). Certainly, if you are looking for a job outside the UK, online searches are probably the easiest way to access vacancies. Jobcentre online is the official government jobsite (**www.jobcentreonline.com**) and is searchable by region, industry or company. Some big employers may have their own vacancy web pages such as the NHS (**www.jobs.nhs.uk**). Graduate Prospects is the best-known graduate careers website and is pretty comprehensive, but there are other websites that specialise in graduate recruitment, including **www.milkround.com** and **www.gradunet.co.uk**.

brilliant tip

Include new information and communication technologies in your jobsearch. Recruiters make use of any medium that is cost effective, so don't rule any out.

Print vacancies accessible online

The distinction between print and online is increasingly blurred. For example, many newspapers run their advertised vacancies online, and actually make this a selling point when persuading employers to advertise with them. As a jobseeker, this is useful if you forget to check a specific newspaper on a particular day, if you overlooked a vacancy, or if you don't want to buy all the papers every day.

Many of the *Prospects* publications listed earlier in this chapter (see 'Vacancies in print' on p.6) are also available online and are, in some cases, free to download.

Choose a handful of online sites and limit yourself to those for a couple of weeks. You can always change your choice of sites if you're not getting the leads you want from the sites you have chosen; and consider setting up RSS feeds (see below) so that you only get the vacancies you have set parameters for – more on this later in the chapter.

Online vacancies: is more necessarily better?

There is no doubt that by advertising a vacancy online an employer can reach a far greater pool of potential applicants. What is more doubtful is whether the greater pool will necessarily have greater talent. The same goes for you as the jobseeker. By browsing online, you can easily access thousands of job vacancies. In one way, this is great, but you will need to narrow this choice down so you find the kind of job you want, and the kind of job you are a suitable candidate for. Without some kind of filtering mechanism, you could waste a lot of time looking at irrelevant jobs, and you could waste even more time applying for jobs without really thinking. You might even find that you are overwhelmed by the sheer volume of vacancies advertised online and that you become stuck, not knowing how to deal with them all. You do need to have a look at these websites and get a feel for what they offer and how they work. Then you need to make them work for you by being selective.

brilliant timesaver

Actively manage your online jobsearch: set filters and review your website choices regularly. Allocate a specific, limited time for checking vacancies online.

RSS feeds: saving you time

If you find a vacancy website that you like, instead of you continually going back and checking that website for updates, you can set up an RSS feed. There are different interpretations of what RSS stands for, but a widely accepted version is the Really Simple Syndication. The feed is basically a bite-sized summary of what's new on that website. Obviously, this saves you time because you don't have to visit each website individually to see what has been updated.

Setting up the feeds

To set up an RSS feed, you are going to need an RSS reader. This is basically a piece of software that checks web pages for updates. Different RSS readers are available for different platforms, so you will need to choose one that works with your computer. An RSS reader can be: web-based, desktop-based or mobile device-based. A web (or browser)-based RSS lets you catch up with your RSS subscriptions from any computer, so has the great advantage of not tying you to a specific computer.

Subscribing to feeds

Having signed up for a web-based RSS reader, first you will need to find sites that syndicate their content, and then subscribe to the feeds you want. You install your reader, add the URL of the feed that you want, then sit back and let the feed come to you. As vacancy sites really want people to see what they have to offer, many are geared up to make an RSS feed as easy to use as possible. You might like to go to the Graduate Prospects site to get you started (**www.prospects.ac.uk**).

 brilliant timesaver

Install a web-based RSS feeder, subscribe to feeds from online vacancy sites, then let the updates come to you.

Networking or word of mouth

Why network?

You'll hear a lot about networking within the context of jobsearch in particular and business in general. There is no doubt that networking is important and, in some occupational sectors, it is vital. Take, for example, the University of the Arts London (UAL), whose courses include Art, Fashion, Jewellery and many more. UAL reported that, of the students who graduated in 2009 and found jobs, 80 per cent found their employment through existing networks. Let's try to put that figure in context. This applies only to those students who were employed, and many of the UAL graduates will opt for self-employment. Many UAL graduates move into the creative industries, where contacts and networks are very important in gaining and securing work. Nevertheless, this is a very high percentage, and shows to what extent networking can keep the labour market moving.

brilliant example

'During my internship, I was invited to an event with the then Shadow Home Secretary (Chris Grayling). Quivering like a nervous wreck, I shook his hand, and could barely speak . . . I felt so inferior and out of my depth. I plucked up the courage to ask a question . . . but could literally barely speak I was that nervous. Six months on, we visited a local homeless charity. Chris Grayling arrived . . . he recalled my question from six months back. I realised afterwards the huge difference in my demeanour from our previous encounter.'

Kevin, BSc (Hons) Politics.

Networking in principle

In essence, when you network you take a conscious decision to make the most of every new contact you make, and you treat every single encounter as a possible job lead. You aren't asking them directly for a job, you are simply making them aware that you exist, and that you are the kind of person anyone would want to have working with them. So, no matter how unlikely it may seem, or how remote the chances are of getting a job opening from a random encounter, you work on the principle that every lead could be the one that takes you further towards your brilliant career. Unfortunately, there is no set formula that determines how many contacts equal a job lead. You simply have to be on the alert and be ready to present yourself as a possible employee at any time.

 **tip**

When you network, you aren't asking directly for a job, you are simply making people aware that you exist, and are the kind of person anyone would like to work with. Just by introducing yourself you show that you are confident, so – go and say hello!

Networking in practice

Graduate job fairs

You may be invited to network in a formal, organised way: graduate job fairs, for example. A graduate fair brings together graduate recruiters, employment professionals and graduate jobseekers. A fair may be generalist (covering all aspects of graduate employment) or specialist (by region or occupational area). It gives you the chance to meet people, and for people to meet you. It makes sense to treat a job fair as a possible recruitment opportunity, so think about how you want to appear. For example, in thinking about what to wear, you might choose something that is more formal than informal. So, without going all out for the power suit, perhaps wear trousers rather than jeans, shirt rather than tee-shirt, and go for something clean and ironed rather than something grubby and creased. You might also like to think about taking some copies of your CV, just in case the opportunity to give it to an employer arises. You may also want to take note of contact details; a notebook is fine for this, but if you do take notes on your phone, make sure you've turned the sound off and do not be tempted to make personal calls when you're on display.

brilliant tip

Make sure your mobile is switched off when you are at a job fair. Potential employers are interested in you, not your ringtone.

Alumni or invited speaker events

There may be alumni events at your university, to which you as a student, may be invited. Alumni means people who have already graduated from your university. Sometimes the alumni events are social, but sometimes they are set up for students to make contacts. The big advantage of talking to alumni is that you already have something in common: your university! And, although they may not have a job opening right now, they may at some point in the future have a vacancy they need to fill, and they may remember meeting you. It may be hard for you to believe it when you meet them, but they too were once a student, just like you, so take the plunge and introduce yourself. Invited speaker events usually involve representatives of particular job areas. They may be in a position to recruit themselves, they may have their own story to share and to inspire you, or they may offer some useful advice. You'll only know what you can get out of it by going to hear them.

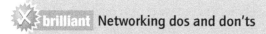 **Networking dos and don'ts**

Do

✔ treat every encounter as a possible lead;

✔ be polite and pleasant to everyone at all times;

✔ be prepared to ask questions as much as answering them;

✔ follow up any leads promptly: send a message or email the next day at the very latest.

Don't

✘ be intimidated: even if it is a disaster the first time, you'll get better with practice;

✘ be casual: don't chew gum, swear or make phone calls;

✘ get disheartened: if you have nothing concrete to show for an hour of networking, at the very least you have made an effort;

✘ monopolise a contact: let other people get access too.

Networking online

The Internet offers unprecedented possibilities of making yourself known to a very wide audience; and these possibilities can work for you or against you. It is possible to find job opportunities and useful leads through your online presence. However, once you have an online presence, it can be readily accessed by your employer or potential employer – who could think the less of you for having seen uncensored comments or images on your page.

You can establish a presence online by: creating a website or a blog; opening a Twitter account; or joining a social network such as Facebook or LinkedIn. You may be asking yourself whether you need to go online to network but, before we address that question, let's run through the online options.

Websites and blogs

Setting up your own web page allows you to showcase who you are and what you can do. In some sectors it is a very good idea to have a web page. The creative industries, for example: if you are looking for a job in design, it is really important that an employer can view your work. This applies as much to a web designer as to a jewellery designer. The web page then functions as a sort of portfolio that can be accessed by anyone at any time.

A blog (the term is a contracted form of web log) is also a type of web page, but with the explicit intention of charting what has been happening. It allows you to update easily, and should really be updated regularly as an out-of-date blog creates a bad impression. Again, a blog can show what you are capable of, and what you have been doing.

brilliant tip

If you have an online presence, keep it up to date. Perhaps not daily but certainly on a regular basis and at least every week.

Forums

A forum may be set up on a website or blog so that the online readers can share responses and ideas on a particular theme. They allow you to express your opinions without necessarily committing to regular input. They also allow you to see what other people are thinking, which might help you to work through a particular issue or challenge. You yourself can use a forum to pose a question and this can be a good way to get into a challenge or problem when you feel really stuck and don't have any clear idea of the way forward. Examples might include: what's a telephone interview like? or, what should I wear to the evening meal at an assessment centre? In this way, you are learning from the collective experience and wisdom of others.

Social networks

Social networks are, at heart, online communities. Just like a real community, you join as a newcomer, make friends and then make friends with your friends' friends. You can then chat, share photos, set up meetings, seek advice and do all the things you would do in real time, but online. There is, however, a clear distinction between different types of social network, what they are used for, and how they are viewed.

Drawing the line between personal and business networks

Broadly speaking, the distinction is between social networking for personal reasons (having fun, gossiping, showing off even) and social networking for professional reasons (getting a job, making business contacts, showing off even). The trick is never to confuse the two. This distinction shows up in the way different social networking sites have developed. Facebook, for example, is definitely for having fun and is therefore a personal space. LinkedIn, on the other hand, is a social network that is clearly aimed at the professional and business side. Keep this distinction clear.

brilliant tip

Facebook is for fun, LinkedIn is for business. Keep personal and professional quite separate.

Looking at your personal pages from the employer perspective

While your friends might find it funny and endearing to hear about you embarrassing yourself at a party, your employer (or potential employer) may take a very different view. There are more and more cases of employers seeing material that their workers have posted and, as a consequence, taking disciplinary action including dismissal; and this is where the material has been posted in a personal capacity. If you already have a social networking page, you might like to go through it and take down anything that would put you in a bad light if seen by an employer. And before you post anything from now on, ask yourself if you would be happy to put the post in your window, where it could be seen by passersby, friends of the family or people who know you but aren't necessarily your friends.

brilliant tip

Review any social network presence you have set up. Ask yourself this: is my online behaviour how I would behave if a potential employer was in the same room?

Twitter

Twitter is also another online social network, but it has the unique selling point of microblogging. As with a blog (or indeed the status aspect of a social network page), people post an update on their page to show what they are doing, what they are thinking, what is happening in their life right now. On Twitter, however, these posts are restricted to a maximum of 140 characters: this makes for microblogs or tweets.

Using Twitter for job opportunities

Twitter can be useful for following people who lead the way in particular industries as you can see what their thinking is and in what direction they, and by extension their work domain, are heading. Twitter can also be a practical source of job vacancies, and employment agencies do post tweets about new vacancies even before the adverts are posted online. Of course, you'll only get a very brief sense of what the vacancy is (because of the restricted length of the tweet) but that might be enough for you to decide whether to follow it up or leave it alone.

Do I really need an online presence?

We know that not all undergraduates are the same; many will be familiar and happy with virtual communities in an online world, others might feel less comfortable, confident or convinced. There is no clear-cut answer about the need to have an online presence. In some industries, it is vital. In others, it is of little consequence. The important thing to know is that you are always in control of what you post. You can choose to have only a professional presence online and you can closely monitor what you post. You could perhaps limit your commitment, by joining a specific forum to add your voice to a particular debate, or using Twitter just to follow a particular person in a field that interests you. It is probably wise to use online networking, even to a limited extent, and for a limited time, because it does show that you are willing to embrace the new and maybe even to come out of your comfort zone.

brilliant tip

If you don't want to commit to a permanent online presence, just contribute to a one-off forum or follow someone on Twitter. Come out of your comfort zone and show you can take on a new challenge.

Speculative applications

Speculative applications (sometimes called applying on spec.) are where you take the initiative and approach an employer to see if there is a possible vacancy, rather than responding to a vacancy once it is advertised. You can of course make speculative applications in a range of media: in person; by email; online; by post. You can waste a lot of time (both yours and also the employer's time) in sending off speculative applications that have no chance of success. And you can feel a lot of rejection if the speculative applications you send out get you nowhere, not even a response. But speculative applications do work, especially in very niche areas. Take a look at our brilliant example, in which Oliver's first job as a junior engineer pays very little, but gives him valuable experience which he uses to secure a better job not once but twice in a row: a brilliant example of leverage in the labour market, as well as speculative applications.

▶brilliant example

'When a new Formula One team was starting up for the following season, I saw an opportunity and speculatively applied for a position. Luckily they saw potential in me, and recognised my experience and qualifications. I spent two-and-a-half years at this Formula One team as a systems engineer on the race team, until they had to withdraw from racing due to financial reasons . . . due to contacts I had gained in the industry, I quickly secured employment with a motorsports electronics company, providing hardware and services to the governing body of motorsport.'

Oliver, ME (Civil), MSc Motorsport Engineering and Management

Focusing your speculative approach

It is important to invest time before you send a speculative application. You'll need to know the market, be clear who are the relevant employers, and have a very good understanding of what their business needs. With a speculative application, you are basically offering your blend of skills and know-how as the solution to a staffing problem the employer hasn't really worked out yet. Online research can really help you here: to look at the individual employer and to put that employer in the overall context of the current market. Networking also plays a strong part, as you identify who to approach, and you approach people who may have some idea of who you are either from a previous encounter or by recommendation.

brilliant example

'I started off looking for a job on the Mediterranean coast because I'd got the chance of accommodation there. So basically I got a load of CVs and went round pretty much every restaurant, because that was where I had most experience . . . it was horrible, really scary because I didn't really know what I was saying (in French). One place phoned back, invited me for an interview, and gave me a job as a runner.'

Hannah, (undergraduate) Economics and Politics with International Studies

Self-employment

You might like to consider creating your own job vacancy by working for yourself. Self-employment is quite common in some sectors, notably the creative industries. However, it can also work in less obvious occupational areas: for example, counselling or computer programming. It will involve a lot of hard work, but it can be very rewarding to shape your own destiny, and to make your first million. You will need to come up with a business idea, and you will need to develop a business plan. Your own university might offer courses in self-employment, or should be able to signpost you to other sources of help. The local jobcentre should be able to point you to sources of advice and often local authorities (the local council) promote and support new businesses. You could perhaps talk to your bank to see what support they can offer: they should be able to give you some idea of what a business plan involves and may even offer access to a business advisor. Networking can really help you here: you can ask successful entrepreneurs how they have achieved their success, and you can ask around for tips and advice from people who have taken this path. You don't even need to do it in person: social networking is perfect for this kind of exploration.

brilliant tip

Make the most of help on offer for a business start-up. This includes help targeted at graduates. Banks can offer useful information, as can jobcentres.

Dimensions: of time, of geography, of chance

The time dimension: watch out for closing dates

A daily newspaper will carry vacancies for which the closing date is likely to be a couple of weeks; in a magazine published less frequently, the vacancies will be around for longer; and in the annual directories, the publication of the directory may happen some months before the closing date. Don't be lulled into a false sense of security here: although there may well be a rolling programme of recruitment, it is nearly always better to apply sooner rather than later.

The geographical dimension: working where *you* want to work

The geographical reach of jobsearch can also vary from local through regional and national to European or global. This applies equally to both sides of the market: you might be looking very widely, and the employer may also be putting a vacancy out into the marketplace at different levels. At the most local level, they can simply put up a notice in the workplace. Typically, this would be in a shop window, just saying something like: VACANCY – ENQUIRE WITHIN. A wider local search would be through local newspapers, the weekly paid or freesheets. Regional search would use daily regional newspapers or local radio. There could even be a regional website advertising, for example, jobs in the North West of England, or a job fair that also covers a regional area. A nationwide approach would use national daily or weekend papers, or websites: these could also be used for global search.

brilliant tip

If you are keen to work in a particular location, try looking at a local paper or vacancy publication in that area. You could even walk around the area and see what kind of employers there are, and then send speculative applications to them.

The chance dimension (sometimes called serendipity)

Sometimes it looks like some people just get lucky: everything comes together and they are in the right place, at the right time, with the right skills for the right job. It can happen like that and, without making any great effort, somebody gets lucky and a job falls into their lap. If you see that happen for someone else, you might be tempted to wait around in the hope that the job fairy will come to your rescue. Or you can start to create your own luck. Because often, much, much more often, things come together after a lot of hard work. Without that hard work, the individual elements would not be ready to come together.

brilliant tip

If you aren't making progress in your jobsearch, try another approach. Think laterally, be resourceful and use the full range of possibilities presented in this chapter.

Creating your own luck

So what can you do to get everything in place? Well, you need to ensure that you have developed the necessary skills and know-how. Chapter 2 'The graduate labour market' takes you through the skills employers are looking for, and Chapter 8 'Work experience; making it purposeful' shows you how to develop your range of desirable skills through purposeful work experience. You also need to ensure that you are ready to respond quickly to a job possibility, by having your CV up to date, perhaps having a completed job application form you can adapt to a new vacancy. Chapter 10 'Making applications: getting past the first post' takes you through all these processes and more. Fundamentally, to get a job you have to be in the job market, and employers have to know that you are in the market for their job. It goes right back to the opening of this chapter: for the market to work, supply (you) and demand (employers) have to know about each other.

⏺ **brilliant** recap

- Look at vacancies from the employer's perspective.

- Use printed media: directories, newspapers, magazines.

- Use online media: online newspapers and websites.

- Look widely to check what's out there, then narrow your search so you aren't wasting your (or the employer's time) with unfocused applications.

- Use timesaving devices: filters, alerts, Twitter, RSS feeds.

- Get networking: job fairs, alumni events, contacts – treat every encounter as a possible step forward towards your job.

- Use social networks, but review your online presence to ensure you present online at all times as a serious contender for a job opening.

- Consider the option of self-employment: take up any help on offer.

- Give the Job Fairy a helping hand by doing everything you can to create your own luck.

What to do next

Check out the demand side of the labour market

If you are thinking about what to do next, you could take one step towards checking out what is in demand in the job market by picking up a quality newspaper (*Guardian, Independent, Daily Telegraph, The Times*) to look at the job vacancies advertised there. Go online, visit a few of the job websites we have included in this chapter. While you're there, try setting up an RSS feed so the jobs adverts come to you.

Make your presence known in the supply side of the labour market

You could take one step towards making your presence (as a jobseeker) known in the job market, by checking if your university is running a job fair – and, if they are, go along to it. Tell people that you are actively seeking work. Think about posting your CV online on one of the job websites. Ideally, you should cover both sides of the job market: checking out the demand side, and making your presence known on the supply side.

Graduate training schemes

This chapter covers one of the better-known options for graduates, and for many graduates it's the option they aspire to. In case you are not quite clear about what's involved, we will start with a definition, before looking at some examples. Finally, we will show you how to be a strong contender, if a graduate training scheme is your preferred option.

What is a graduate training scheme?

 definition

The term **graduate training scheme** is usually applied to graduate entry jobs, with training, in large organisations, both public and private sector – the kind you will meet at graduate recruitment fairs.

Sectoral growth and decline

Graduate training schemes can be found in a whole range of job areas, or sectors. Vacancies are currently on the increase in banking, financial services, insurance, business consulting, construction and accountancy. In other sectors, while there is an overall decline in vacancies, there are still opportunities to be found, for example in retail, investment banking, public sector, law, engineering and IT/telecommunications.

Note that the term graduate training scheme is sometimes used in professions like law, accountancy, teaching and psychology. In this chapter we are looking at more generalist schemes where the subject of your degree may be less important and the training more broadly based.

Direct entry

Many smaller organisations or SMEs (small to medium-sized enterprises) offer the same kind of opportunity for a graduate entrant, but may not label it a graduate training scheme. Remember that in Chapter 2 we defined an SME as an organisation with up to 250 employees. These organisations cover almost 60 per cent of the private sector employment in the UK and this includes graduate-level roles, with training.

On the other hand, be aware that many larger organisations also recruit people, who happen to be graduates, to what are called direct-entry jobs, where a degree is not a requirement. This might give you a route in, if your application for a graduate training scheme has been unsuccessful, and you could still work towards a position similar to someone who has come through the graduate training scheme route.

Three key features

The key defining features of a graduate training scheme are:

- You need a degree.
- You will follow a planned programme which will enable you to sample different work areas and identify your particular strengths and interests.
- You will be employed and therefore paid a salary.

. . . and three myths

- Graduate training schemes usually lead to a job – but not automatically. You may have to apply for internal vacancies, or wait until a suitable role comes up. In some cases, especially in the public sector, graduate training schemes are offered on a fixed-term contract and offer no guarantee of a job.

- You have to go straight into a graduate training scheme as soon as you leave university. Not so – many graduates apply in the year following graduation – or even later than that. Employers are fine with this, as long as you can show some benefit to yourself, and potentially to the employer, deriving from the time since you graduated. Typically, around half of all graduate trainees recruited across the UK will not be straight from university.

- You have to have a first class or upper second class Honours degree. Not so – although some companies have such a requirement, many do not.

Some typical graduate training schemes

These examples come from recently advertised graduate training schemes, and help to illustrate the features they have in common, and where the differences might be. You will see that even this small sample covers a range of occupational areas and includes an SME.

 **examples**

A UK clothing company

- Offers an 18-month scheme involving Design, Development, Marketing and Merchandising.

- Applicants need a degree in Footwear, Fashion, Business or Marketing; work experience in fashion retailing or customer service; and competency in MS Office.

- An interesting additional requirement is that they must have delivered profit in a venture, whether commercial, voluntary or university-based.

A large, national public sector organisation

- A two-year scheme in which graduates choose one of four areas: human resources, finance, infomatics or general management, in each case leading to a professional qualification.

- Before specialising they have a grounding in all four areas. There are several work placements of up to nine months each.

- Applicants need a 2:2 or better in any subject. The organisation states that successful trainees can expect to fast-track their career development.

A large, multinational packaging company

- Recruits finance, business, research and engineering specialists.

- Every graduate trainee takes part in a standard induction programme. This is followed by individually tailored training plans, all of which will include key business and interpersonal skills.

- Finance and engineering trainees follow approved professional training, while business trainees have a series of secondments to different management functions.

- Graduates of all disciplines can apply; the company looks for good interpersonal skills and a genuine interest in a career in the manufacturing industry.

A small to medium-sized enterprise (SME)

- This software and consulting company offers the benefits of a graduate training scheme in a smaller organisation (fewer than 250 employees).

- You would need a 2:1 or better and As and Bs at A level (or the equivalent), good interpersonal skills, an interest in IT and finance and evidence of outstanding academic achievement.

- A five-week induction programme begins a two-year curriculum with in-house and external training to provide a mix of technical, functional and soft skills. There is financial support to gain further qualifications, ranging from foreign languages to financial diplomas and technical accreditations.

Is a graduate training scheme right for you?

Meeting the selection criteria

The harsh reality is that, in order to deal with large numbers of applications, recruiters to graduate training schemes set the bar high in terms of degree classification and sometimes even UCAS points. Sometimes the initial selection is done using computer software. This is highly likely to be the case if you apply online. If you don't meet an essential requirement (for example, you have a 2:2, they want a 2:1) you will be selected out. They may even use UCAS points as a selection tool. And all this will happen well before anyone reads your well-crafted personal statement. So you need to consider if, and how, you can achieve what is being asked for. If you can't, then look for other routes.

brilliant example

A large, multinational business consultancy has an alternative graduate training scheme for people who have fallen short of the academic standards normally required but can demonstrate achievement outside their studies.

In large organisations you need to be prepared for, and willing to commit to, the full range of selection methods. The entire selection process could last a full day or more and may even require an overnight stay. Have a look at Chapter 9 'Dates and deadlines: your timeline for action' for managing all this alongside your study, and Chapter 11 'Succeeding in selection', for more about what might be involved.

A chance to find your strengths and interests

You may know that you would like to work in a large organisation of a particular kind – public sector, logistics, retail, finance – but not yet be clear about a specific direction. Many graduate training schemes offer a programme of rotation through various functions and, while you will be expected to make a contribution in each area you work in, you do have the chance to experience different roles first hand.

Are you flexible?

Large, multi-site organisations will expect you to be prepared to work at different locations. Even if the head office is in your home town, it doesn't mean that you will work there. Make sure you are aware of any requirements to move or work away, and that they fit with your own circumstances.

Can you commit?

A graduate training scheme is long term – think two years minimum, and that's just for the training programme. So, if you plan to work for six months and then travel, it's not for you at this stage. A recruiting organisation wants a return for the cash investment it's making in selection and training – and you will be giving a lot of yourself to get the most from the experience. So be sure that the time is right for you.

How to be a strong contender for a graduate training scheme

Much of what we say elsewhere in this book, about researching the labour market, job opportunities, applications and interviews, applies to graduate training schemes as well as to other options you may be considering, so we will assume that you will dip in to the relevant chapters as you need to. What we will do here is look at the particular demands of graduate training schemes on you, the applicant.

Know the business in context

For every organisation you apply to, you need to know how they generate their revenue, who their competitors are, how they adapt to changes in the market, their strengths, what they are developing, and so on. This knowledge will help you with your application and certainly with your interview. Visit careers fairs, look at websites, talk to anyone who might know anything about the organisations or the sectors they belong to.

Know about recruitment timescales and where to find vacancies

Some graduate training schemes have an annual or twice yearly intake, others a rolling programme. For the first group, being ready to apply at the right time is critical. Sign up for careers fairs, pick up your free copies of graduate directories (a key source for graduate training schemes) from your careers service, use graduate recruitment websites.

It doesn't matter what the business is, there are some fundamental principles: cash flow is king; you've got to make sure there's a bottom line for the profit, and you've got to look at risk. Graduates need to ask where they fit into the critical path within the business process.

Julian Radley, Finance Director, Evotel Holdings

Know about selection methods

We said earlier that graduate training schemes often use the full range of selection methods, in particular assessment centres, so make sure you know what these are, what to expect and how to prepare for them. Read Chapter 11 'Succeeding in selection', for lots more information about this.

Be creative

If you don't meet the academic requirements, is there another way you can gain access? You could look for companies like the brilliant example earlier in this chapter, or you could try a direct approach with a good letter or personal contact at a careers fair. Alternatively you could go for direct entry and aim to progress once you are in the organisation.

Manage your applications

You will almost certainly be applying to more than one graduate training scheme, so keep your applications in order – create a schedule of closing dates and interview dates, make an electronic or paper folder to keep copies of applications, CVs and interview information. Read Chapter 9 'Dates and deadlines' for more about managing your time to hit closing dates and keep your academic work going at the same time.

Seek and make use of feedback

An unsuccessful application can help you to get the next one better. We talk about this in Chapter 10. If you get as far as an interview you should be able to ask the employer for feedback – but do listen to what is said. The employer is telling you how you presented at interview, so try not to defend or justify, because it really doesn't matter – what matters is what the employer saw and heard.

 **brilliant** **timesaver**

Keep track by making a paper or electronic folder for copies of application forms, CVs and interview information.

brilliant **dos and don'ts**

Do

✔ find out about the business and its competitors;

✔ learn about selection methods;

✔ get and use feedback;

✔ look for different routes to where you want to be.

Don't

✘ leave it till the last minute to look for vacancies;

✘ lose track of your applications.

What are the benefits?

We think there are three key benefits of graduate training schemes, and we are not alone. Have a look at the three real-life graduate stories that follow.

In our first example, Paul highlights the benefits of learning to work in a big organisation.

brilliant **example**

'My role as a trainee manager on the graduate training scheme of an international car rental company provides me with valuable training on running a business, working as a manager and working your way up a big organisation. The experience has given me such a big insight into the workings of a big company.'

Paul, BSc (Hons) Sport and Exercise Science

In our next example you can see that a good graduate training scheme will support you in further learning, sometimes leading to specialist qualifications.

brilliant example

'I secured a position with one of the world's biggest banks on their executive management graduate scheme. At university we were introduced to the concept of lifelong learning and with the bank I have the chance to further my studies with qualifications in financial services.'

Phil, BA (Hons) Business Studies

Our final example illustrates the longer-term benefits. Victoria's experience helped her to develop strengths and preferences that enabled her to work out the next stage of her career plan. She is now in her third job after graduating.

brilliant example

'I joined the graduate programme of a consulting company. In two years I learned masses and I still use the tools and skills I gained with them. I use their methods as a mark of what good looks like in my present company. The IT projects I worked on were for a range of blue chip retail companies. However, after two years I wanted to try a move away from IT so I moved to another consultancy for more analysis and strategic projects . . . after another two years I realised that I wanted to work in retail, and within the industry rather than through consultancy. Because of my experience I found the job market very responsive, and I got my present job as a business systems analyst with a multinational retail organisation. I get to travel and work with different cultures, teaching and shaping how countries do business.'

Victoria, MA Geography

 **recap**

Graduate training schemes are great for developing your skills and experience. They help you to refine your career plans, and often include the chance for you to gain a specialist qualification.

What to do next

- Remind yourself of the key features of a graduate training scheme. Could you see yourself as a graduate trainee?

- Think about a job area you might like to work in – marketing, finance, research and development, HR – and see if you can find a suitable graduate training scheme being advertised. Visit websites; useful ones include **www.milkround.com** and **www.prospects.ac.uk**.

- Get hold of a copy of a directory of graduate training schemes from your careers service. Have a browse and look for similarities and differences among different schemes.

- Sign up for the next graduate careers fair in your area. Find out more from your university website or from **www.prospects.ac.uk**.

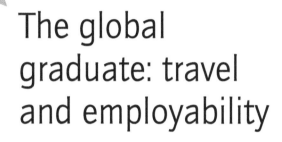

The global graduate: travel and employability

If you are to genuinely understand about the things that really matter, about culture, then language is a barrier unless you have some understanding.

Carl Gilleard, Chief Executive, Association of Graduate Recruiters

You will see from the title of this chapter that we are looking at travel here from an employer's perspective. Employers are increasingly explicit about valuing a jobseeker who has had overseas experience, either through study or professional work. Our brilliant quote here relates to the employer's view of the global graduate being someone who has cultural awareness, and maybe language proficiency, over and above what other graduates offer. The focus here is how your experience abroad works for you in terms of enhancing your employability. This applies even if enhancing your employability was the last thing on your mind when you set off on your travels. This chapter works through why you might want an overseas experience, and how that overseas experience can enhance your employability. We also give an overview of what opportunities there are abroad, and how you would go about getting what is out there. Finally, we go through the practical steps you can take before, during and after your travels.

It doesn't matter why you want to travel

What we are looking at here is travelling and working or studying. These are not mutually exclusive: you can do them at the same time, but you are likely to be driven more by one or the other. So either you want to travel,

From Chapter 5 of *Graduate Career Handbook*, 1/e. Judith Done and Rachel Mulvey.

and working or studying is just a way of satisfying your wanderlust, or you want to work, and are happy to take up employment outside your normal country of residence. You may even find that you enjoy the work as much as you enjoy the location: a brilliant combination.

The reasons people give for travelling are many and varied. Sometimes they can be negative:

> I was unhappy with my situation here; I needed to get away; I wanted to start afresh somewhere.

Sometimes they can be positive:

> I want to experience a different culture; I want to learn a new language; I want to live in the city/country/by the sea/in the mountains.

Sometimes, they can be explicitly about enhancing your professional repertoire:

> If I want to specialise in international economics, it makes sense to get first-hand experience of another economy.

It may just be that you feel like it, or the opportunity came your way.

brilliant tip

It really doesn't matter why you want to travel. There doesn't have to be a rational reason: it is OK to travel just because you feel like it.

It doesn't really matter why you want to travel, and once you are caught up in the practicalities of booking flights, thinking about accommodation and working out what the work options are, thinking about what you do once you come back from your travels might be the very last thing on your mind. However, once you are back on the labour market and find yourself competing with other job seekers who haven't clocked up the air miles, it may matter a lot.

 **tip**

No matter what made you work, study or travel abroad, you are likely to develop (as a result) transferable skills that employers value.

Looking at travel from the employer's perspective

Employers value the transferable skills you will develop abroad

Once you're putting your travels behind you and are applying for work or postgraduate study, it is not about where you went and what you saw: it is how you expanded your professional repertoire and how you can apply what you learned on your travels to your new work situation. It is highly likely that you develop valuable transferable skills through your overseas experience. Chapter 2 takes a detailed look at what transferable skills are, but the most likely skills you will develop as a direct result of your overseas experience are:

- **Self-management**: you will have learnt more about yourself, about how you handle stress and being out of the familiar, or being out of your comfort zone. You may also have had time to think through what is important to you in your life and therefore in your career.

- **Problem solving**: no doubt your overseas experience threw up challenges and problems that you had to solve. Even relatively simple challenges inherent in travel (planning journeys, making connections, getting to the right place at the right time) will make you think through what you are doing and how you are doing it. You may well have found yourself dealing with the unfamiliar and perhaps the unexpected; this in turn demands you find a way through problems.

- **Resilience**: this is the capacity to keep going even when the going gets tough. Living, working, studying and travelling overseas can all be delightful, but can also be challenging. Resilience is how you handle yourself when things seem to be relentlessly challenging. This calls for hope, optimism and being prepared to reframe things mentally.

- **Foreign languages**: frankly, if you come back from an overseas experience with absolutely zero development in your language ability, that's disappointing. Even if you have mastered nothing but very basic language (greetings, thanks, requests) you will have had the valuable experience of realising how limited you are without language. And for many, the overseas experience allows you to develop fluency and understanding of the language in question and, through that, to develop an appreciation of culture and customs.

Employers value subject-specific skills

Our next brilliant example is interesting because Katie already has a job, as a lecturer in animal management at a college of further education. She is travelling in order to enrich her subject knowledge.

▶ brilliant example

'During the summer I plan to travel to Africa to work on an animal conservation project. I am so excited! I look forward to visiting this extraordinary country and working with fellow conservation lovers, caring for wild animals and helping to maintain their environment. I can put my passion into practice and continue to learn in breathtaking surroundings with some of the most magnificent animals.'

Katie, BSc (Hons) Animal Behaviour and Welfare

Employment that demands working abroad

For some people, their career goal is to take up a role that will, by definition, involve working abroad. Examples include teaching English abroad, working for the European Union, or simply working in the profession for which they have been trained, but in another country. A growing number of people are choosing to work in international development, an interest that may start though volunteering and develop into a paid role. Our next brilliant example, Rachel, spent half of the second year of her degree as an English language assistant in Réunion and Madagascar. She returned to Madagascar as a volunteer soon after graduation, working on building and reforestation projects. After a spell back home to earn some money, she returned to Madagascar, and she continues her story.

▶brilliant example

'I led a community health team in a remote region. I did a lot of translating as I was the only French speaker . . . I followed an ecology course as an independent student, being taught by non-government organisation (NGO) professionals . . . on my return to the UK I applied to an international relief and rehabilitation organisation. After a week-long assessment process, I was offered my present post in the Democratic Republic of Congo. I work in French every day, working in medical logistics.'

Rachel, BA (Hons) French and International Development Studies

What opportunities are there abroad?

Erasmus: short-term study abroad as part of your degree

Erasmus is arguably the best-known university exchange programme: over 1 million students have participated in the last 20 years. Under the Erasmus scheme, students spend at least one term studying in a different university in another country. The scheme has operated in at least 28 countries across the European Union (EU) and Switzerland and has recently expanded beyond the EU to other countries all over the world under the Erasmus Mundus scheme.

Erasmus eligibility requirements

In order to participate, you must be: enrolled as a student (undergraduate, postgraduate or doctoral); eligible to participate (which means, broadly speaking, that you should have the right to study in the EU); and your home university (here in the UK) must have a bilateral agreement with the host university (overseas). Your course tutor would know if a bilateral agreement with another university is already in place for the course you are on. Your own department might also have some information, but do look both at departmental and university level for the fullest possible information. Even if nothing is in place for your course, your university might already have a bilateral agreement with another university for other courses, and it could be possible for your subject simply to be added to that bilateral agreement.

So, if you are interested, the best place to start is the international office or possibly the Erasmus office in your own university. They should be able to advise you on what you can study where, and whether you can apply for a grant. Of course, what you make of those opportunities, and how you transfer your learning to your brilliant jobsearch, is very much up to you. Most of what we discuss in this chapter would apply to people taking part in an Erasmus programme: studying abroad gives you a unique opportunity to learn another language, to learn about another culture and to broaden your outlook.

Work experience as part of your degree

Some courses, especially language degrees, include a chance to spend a year working abroad in a role that will complement the academic content of the course, for example as an English language assistant in a school or college. Others may offer a shorter period of time – the kind of experience Joanne talks about.

▶brilliant example

'One of the modules I undertook on my course was called experiential learning. I had the opportunity to work in Romania, delivering drama workshops in communities and schools there. This opened my eyes to all sorts of valuable experiences and taught me so much about education in another country.'

Joanne, BA (Hons) Drama and Theatre Studies

Vacation work while you are a student

Most students need to work in the summer vacation, so why not think about working abroad? There are useful reference books on the subject which you will find in your university careers service or library, and some employers come onto campus to recruit.

brilliant example

'The university careers team were instrumental in helping me secure a vacation job coaching football in the USA for the summer of my first year, something which undoubtedly benefited me and increased my employability.'

Phil, BA (Hons) Business Studies

How to get what's out there

Check if you are allowed to work

You can either secure employment and then travel to your new job – or travel to your destination first, then sort out employment. In some cases, you'll have to get the job first because that's what the law requires. You will find there are restrictions to employment depending on the country of employment and the nationality of the employee, so your normal country of residence is important.

There are, however, many opportunities: European Union (EU) nationals are free to live and work anywhere in the EU; some labour markets allow fixed-term work visas for temporary work, or specialised work that can't readily be filled by a local employee; and some international employers can secure work permits for employees who need them.

brilliant tip

European Union nationals are free to live and work anywhere in the European Union. In addition, temporary work visas are sometimes available for specified workers, either with key skills or in hard-to-fill sectors.

Before taking on employment you will need to check (a) if there are any restrictions and (b) if these restrictions apply to you. This information is readily available by country – though of course it may not be available in English. The best source of reliable information is the Embassy or High Commission of the country you are interested in. There are also compendium books which pull together a number of destination countries. Your university careers service should have these for reference.

Check out job opportunities

Chapter 1 takes you through the process of finding out what jobs are on offer in great detail, and everything in that chapter applies here. Broadly speaking, you need to look at what's on offer in terms of paid work, and you need to let employers know that you are available for work. You can use printed media (newspapers, bulletins and directories) and online media (websites, social networking, RSS feeds). Online is particularly useful for overseas work.

brilliant tip

Make full use of online resources when looking for work abroad. Use websites, including national newspapers which publish job adverts online. Use social networks to find out about working abroad.

You can also look for work on location. If, for example, you are an EU citizen, you can travel anywhere within the EU and then look for a job. You can try the usual labour market channels: local newspapers; employment agencies; speculative applications (i.e. going into an organisation and asking them if they have any vacancies); or word of mouth. It is worth expanding your jobsearch to include some sectors and occupations you wouldn't normally think of; this is particularly useful if the experience of living and working abroad is more important than developing a particular set of job-related competencies.

The problem with looking for a job once you're abroad is that you'll need to stay somewhere, and to fund yourself during your period of jobsearch. This takes money – almost always more than you expect; and it probably takes a fairly good idea of the local job market, and maybe even a bit of luck once you get there to secure the kind of job you want, as shown in our brilliant example.

▶ brilliant example

'I started off looking for a job on the Mediterranean coast, because I'd got the chance of accommodation there. So basically I got a load of CVs and went round to pretty much every restaurant; because that was where I had had most experience, through my Saturday job and work experience at school. It was horrible, really scary, because I didn't really know what I was saying (in French). One place phoned back, invited me for an interview, and gave me a job as a runner.'

Hannah, (Undergraduate) Economics and Politics with International Studies

Check out whether casual work is worth the risks

Beware that you might be offered casual work that is not legitimate. This can be very tempting: often the pay is cash in hand and, at first sight, it does look so much easier to get started working straight away, rather than wade through the hassle of bureaucracy. But working illegally can end up being way more hassle. With no legitimacy and therefore no employment rights or protection, you would be on your own if you had to deal with some of the potential problems of unregulated employment: under payment; accidents at work; bullying; or discrimination.

✦ brilliant tip

Take the bureaucracy of labour laws (work permits) seriously: protect yourself from the potential problems of unregulated work.

What you need to know before you go

The Foreign & Commonwealth Office (FCO) spearheads the 'Know Before You Go' Campaign, which aims to help British nationals to stay safe (and in good health) when abroad. It covers a number of key areas – some of which could save your life:

- get adequate travel insurance;
- check the FCO's country travel advice: this is updated very frequently, to take account of emergency situations, e.g. natural disaster or political unrest;
- research your destination – know the local laws and customs;
- visit your GP as soon you know that you are travelling;
- check your passport is in good condition and valid and you have all necessary visas;
- make copies of important travel documents and/or store them online using a secure data storage site;
- tell someone where you are going and leave emergency contact details with them;
- take enough money and have access to emergency funds.

brilliant tip

Use the Foreign & Commonwealth Office (FCO) website (**www.fco.gov.uk**) for good information and advice about your destination.

Once you're away from home

Enjoying the overseas experience

You might find that the whole experience of working and living away from home is enjoyable from day one: that's brilliant! However, you also might have to put a bit of work into making the experience enjoyable.

Having some language is going to help – and acquiring language once you are there will help even more. Being ready to try new things, eat new food, do things in a new way is also going to help you adjust quickly and fit in. You might also need to make more of an effort to make new friends than you would do at home, just carrying on with your normal social circle. People may well make the first approach to include you in what they are doing, but you'll need to show that you are interested in what's going on and are prepared to fit in. So, try to accept any invitations – even if they turn out to be less than brilliant, you will at least have clocked up one more experience.

 **tip**

Be prepared to put a bit of effort into fitting in: try to pick up some language even if you feel self-conscious. Rather than dismissing an invitation or a suggestion, try to give new things a go.

Surviving the overseas experience

Thanks to social networking sites, you can learn a huge amount, both positive and negative, from other people's experiences. Use them to post questions in advance of your trip, and once you get to your new place. Once there, you can readily tap into the online community, which itself can be a mixture of local people and a more international crew. Your new work mates may also have good advice, which can cover really basic stuff (where to buy food at local supermarkets or markets) to blending in as a local (what are the unwritten rules about dress codes or local etiquette).

Bureaucracy and accessing key documents wherever you are

Once you are away from home, there are a number of really vital documents which, if lost, you would have to replace. Some of these are official: National Insurance documents; passport; visas. Others personal but equally important: insurance policies; tickets; bank details. You can easily create a document that records all the detailed information you would need if the worst were to happen. It will help enormously if you have someone back home who can access the things you need that you have forgotten to bring: your contact lens prescription; your birth certificate; your European Computer Driving Licence certificate. You could also scan these, and other important documents, and save them on an Internet-accessible website account that you can then access from an Internet connection anywhere in the world. Here's Hannah again.

brilliant example

'The bureaucracy (for working abroad) was tedious, but not impossible. Both my employers did what they could to help. If I needed something I didn't have with me, I phoned home and got it faxed out, or went to an Internet café and accessed stuff that way.'

Hannah, (Undergraduate) Economics and Politics with International Studies

Keeping going when the going gets tough

Even if you have really been looking forward to going abroad, you will have difficult times, when you might feel lonely or homesick. You might feel you have made a big mistake and just want to go home. You might feel you are doing everything you possibly can to get work, make friends, join in with people and it's just not getting you where you want to be as fast as you want to get there. This is perfectly normal, and part of any successful transition from one phase of your life to another.

Positive steps to take

Try to keep a sense of perspective: is the setback you're experiencing going to be such a big deal in five days' or in five months' or even in five years' time? When you feel you've had a really rubbish day, just take five minutes on your own and identify three positive things that have happened. These can be quite small steps, for example:

I got off the bus at the right bus stop/I understood my colleague when he asked me to do something.

Positive things can also be outside work, for example:

I smelt the gardenia in blossom/I felt so warm in the heat of the day.

It can help to write these down in a notebook, so that you build up a store of positive experience, which can help to give a sense of perspective when you're feeling down. Try to keep going: put a bad day behind you and, rather than starting the next day convinced things are going to keep going wrong, try to be positive and open about this day going a little bit better.

 **brilliant tip**

Try to put negative experiences and feelings to one side and focus on the positive. Take five minutes, each and every day, to identify three positive experiences, no matter how small they may seem.

Returning

Securing something to come back to: study or work

Update your CV in the light of your experience abroad

Try to capture, on your CV and in your job applications, the ways in which you have expanded your skills and competence. If you have been working, your new skills may well be specific to the work you did, for example:

I learned to speak fluent Spanish; I can cash up a till; I can operate tools and/or machinery and/or programmes.

Have a look at the kind of employability skills all employers want, but also look at anything an employer specifies in a job advert or person specification.

brilliant tip

Rethink your CV in the light of your travelling experience. Think it through from an employer's perspective so you are ready to explain how your travels have added value to you as a prospective employee.

Include soft skills: look at it from the employer's perspective

You may also have developed the so-called soft skills, which are just as sought after by employers. These include:

- communication;
- problem solving;
- self-management; and
- resilience.

It is highly likely that you will have found yourself in situations abroad where you had to be flexible, and perhaps also where you had to keep going when things weren't plain sailing. Teamwork skills, such as persuading/negotiating and respecting others, are undoubtedly skills you had to develop for a good experience abroad. Try to sell your experiences in terms that an employer will buy.

Foreign language ability

Many employers are not satisfied with foreign language fluency in graduates. However, before you claim you can negotiate high-level deals in another language, appraise your language levels. If your newly polished language is restricted to ordering food and drink, you might think about picking up some more commercial language applications as part of your jobsearch.

Get your return destination sorted before you go abroad

Securing a job or place on a postgraduate programme to pick up on your return is exactly the same procedure you followed to get your job abroad – but in reverse. You might be able to get this all sorted before you even go off on your travels, which means you don't have to think about it at all once you're away from home. Or you might decide to apply from abroad before you return. This is certainly worth exploring for postgraduate programmes, as an interview is not always necessary.

How to be interviewed at a distance

Even if you are expected to have an interview, you could explore the possibility of doing the interview at a distance – by Skype, for example. This would mean you would miss out on the chance to visit the campus and to meet other people applying for your programme, so it does have its drawbacks. However, the distance interview does have the major advantage of sparing you the expense of travelling a long way. If you do manage to organise a cyber-interview, treat it exactly as you would a face-to-face meeting: prepare for it thoroughly, and present yourself well. Dress formally, look professional. You can always head for the beach once the Internet interview is over.

brilliant tip

If you need to be interviewed while you are abroad, ask if an online interview is possible, e.g. using Skype. Remember this is still a formal interview, so dress professionally and present yourself well.

Aftermath

brilliant tip

Don't be too shocked if home seems unfamiliar when you first return: you will adjust to the way of life here, just as you did abroad!

Reverse culture shock

Coming home after a spell abroad might seem like the easiest thing in the world, but you need to be aware of reverse culture shock. Quite simply, what has always seemed familiar becomes unfamiliar when you go back to it, having experienced something quite different. You might even feel a bit homesick for your life abroad. This can come as something of a shock and, although it's not something people talk about very much, it is quite common. You can draw on the same techniques as you did when you were away: look for the positive in your experiences, however small, that may at first appear. You will adjust and, in time, things will fall into place again. Just hold on to everything that was good about your experience. Here's a final word from Hannah.

---

brilliant example

'The best thing about working abroad is when you realise that this is your life. You really do have friends here that you care about. You can go out with them and you can really talk to them in French. And it's as real a relationship as if it was in English. It's just very satisfying, and it's what I wanted. Would I recommend working abroad? Yes, definitely, one hundred per cent.'

Hannah, (Undergraduate) Economics and Politics with International Studies

---

brilliant recap

- Working abroad can be both enjoyable and useful.

- Just a few simple steps will help you to be safe and healthy.

- There are opportunities before, during and after your degree course.

- Make sure that you show clearly how your experiences add value to you as a prospective employee, using the language of employability and skills.

What to do next

Have a look at the Erasmus programme (**www.eu-student.eu**) to get an idea of what it does. You could also find out what your university offers under the Erasmus scheme, by talking to your course tutor, or the international or Erasmus office in your university. Use social networks or ask friends who have worked abroad what they made of the experience. Ask employers (at job fairs or alumni events) whether they value overseas experience. Simply think about travelling to enhance your employability, and keep it in mind as a possible option.

Index

dynamics, 121-124

E

editing, 27, 226, 249-255
effort, 19, 78, 249, 270, 305
element, 24, 29, 232, 257
elements, 19, 73, 221, 228, 229, 238, 256, 261
email, 270
Emotional appeal, 105
emotive language, 219
emphasis, 242
empirical, 201
employability, 295
employment, 262, 284, 296
enclosures, 113
end of, 21, 225, 245, 257-258
endnotes, 253
engineering, 263, 283
environment, 298
episode, 138
equation, 214
error-recognition skills, 197
errors, 27, 237-238, 250-252
errors in thinking, 207
essay, 18, 25, 213, 226, 234-235, 239, 250
essays, 19, 211, 223-224, 229, 237, 249
et al., 76, 212
ethics, 216
etiquette, 305
European Union, 231
Evaluation, 76, 211-214, 230
events, 270, 311
evidence, 22, 29, 79, 215-216, 225, 232, 252, 286
examinations, 17
example , 244-245
examples, 76, 213-215, 225, 231, 238, 251, 272, 283, 298
exams, 17-19, 17, 25, 73, 255-256
exchange, 299
exercise, 19, 215, 229, 290
flexibility, 3, 89, 128
expectancy theory, 165-167
expectations, 26, 76, 211-212
experience, 20, 211, 264, 276, 285, 295-298
experiments, 245
expert, 218
explanations, 26, 247
expression, 216, 239, 255
extensions, 35
external examiners, 20
external training, 286

F

face, 309
Facebook, 271-272
Face-to-face communication, 83
factor, 257
factors, 214, 232-233
facts, 73, 211-212, 251-252
fairness, 20
fallacies, 211
family, 80, 273
features, 24, 29, 226, 232, 250, 284-285
feedback, 18, 25-28, 74, 221, 237-238, 253
Feelings, 307
fees, 233
figures, 245, 251
filing system, 81
filters, 266
finance, 285-287
Financial Times, 97
findings, 245
first impressions, 113
flip charts, 121
focus, 19, 217-220, 228, 235, 252, 295
food, 305
food and drink, 308
footnotes, 253
forecasting, 104
formal groups, 138
Formal presentations, 88, 102
formative, 17-18, 25
formative assessment, 17
forms, 17-18, 26, 78, 214, 241, 290
formula, 268
framework, 223, 229
framing, 228
function, 226, 261-262
functions, 271, 286-287
further education, 298

G

gathering information, 73
Gender differences, 184
generalisation, 231
gerunds, 241
globalisation, 46
GLOBE, 140
glossary, 247, 253
goals, 18, 26, 75
government, 245, 265, 299
grades, 20, 26-27, 73
Graduate Prospects, 264-265
grammar, 30, 237-238, 249-251
grammar checkers, 237
grammar errors, 244
greater than, 244
greetings, 298
grounding, 285
Group formation, 163
grouping, 243
groupthink, 143
growth, 283

H

handouts, 74
handwriting, 29, 257
Handy, Charles, 6
hard copy, 252
hardware, 275
harm, 218
Hawthorne effect, 123
headings , 215, 224, 231, 257
headlines, 94, 261
health, 231
highlighting, 238
histograms, 123
Honeywell, 119
hospitality, 199
human resource management, 5, 182
Human skills, 5
humanities, 227

I

identities, 44
identity, 232, 246
impact of, 231, 244
implementation, 195
implication, 28
importance, 28, 76, 212, 224
importance of, 215, 224
improving, 258
income, 233
indents, 253
independent, 75, 262, 299
independent learner, 75
independent study, 188
index, 22, 247
indexing, 170
inference, 244
influence, 24
informal groups, 100, 128
information, 23-24, 28, 73-81, 211-212, 227, 229, 237-238, 253
information technology, 14, 140
initiative, 262
inputs, 128, 202
inspiration, 215
instruction words, 76, 213
instructions, 76-77, 212-213, 234-235
intellectual skills, 5
intelligence, 246
intentions, 227
interests, 274, 284
internal consistency, 174
internships, 264
interpersonal skills, 286
interpretation, 216, 252
interpretation of, 216
Interpretations, 215, 266
interval, 96
interviewing, 14, 45, 155
interviews , 288
introduction, 223-228, 233, 252
isolation, 18

J

jargon, 219, 225
job applications, 14, 34, 307

job enrichment, 122, 167
Job performance, 33
job redesign, 166
job satisfaction, 114, 166
job vacancies, 262-266
judgements, 216
justify, 290

K

keeping notes, 170
key words, 215
Kim, S., 99
knowledge, 75-76, 212, 248, 288, 298
knowledge management, 2
Kolb's learning cycle, 46

L

labour, 261-263, 288, 296
language, 216, 225, 237-239, 251-252
language levels, 308
law, 29, 213-214, 227, 264, 283-284, 301
law reports, 213
layout, 249-250
leaders, 243
leadership style, 121
learning, 17-19, 30, 73-78, 212-213, 248, 255
learning from, 272
learning from experience, 58
learning journals, 46-47
learning logs, 46-47
learning opportunity, 147
learning organisation, 71
learning organisations, 59
learning outcomes, 73-74, 215
learning style, 77
learning styles, 73
lecturers, 17, 27, 254
lectures, 19, 74-75
length, 227, 251-253, 274
less than, 305
library, 74, 216
lifelong learning, 14, 291
limit, 74, 224, 256
limitations, 214
line graphs, 107
line managers, 7
line spacing, 253
LinkedIn, 271-272
list, 29, 74, 251
lists, 217, 227, 242, 253
literacy, 231
location, 263, 296
Lockheed, 120
logic, 28-29, 217-218, 246
loss, 233
Loyalty, 105

M

magazines, 262
main text, 227
management, 75, 275, 285-286, 297-298
management style, 100
management theories, 165
managing, 73-74, 287
managing diversity, 147
market research, 156
marking, 17, 25, 73, 226
marking criteria, 17, 30, 73
marking or assessment criteria, 25
matriculation, 253
matriculation number, 253
Matsushita, 123
matter, 77, 220-221, 247, 268, 289, 295-297
maximum, 273
mean, 25, 213-214, 224, 234, 237, 255, 287, 309
meaning, 211, 239, 251
meaning of, 211
Means, 22, 27, 75-76, 212, 227, 229, 239-240, 249, 261, 299
measurements, 119
mediating, 118
meetings, 272
memory, 79
memos, 100-101, 187
mental models, 35, 163
message, 247, 255, 270
methodologies, 4
methods, 77, 211, 233, 239-240, 287
Microsoft, 226, 253